Big Dream, Little Boat

About the Author

Kevin O'Sullivan is a recently retired Aer Lingus captain, having previously worked there as an aircraft engineer for ten years. Kevin and his wife Angela live with their two adult children in Skerries, County Dublin. This is his first book.

BIG DREAM, LITTLE BOAT

A Kayaker's Journey Around Ireland

Kevin O'Sullivan

The Liffey Press

Published by
The Liffey Press
'Clareville', 307 Clontarf Road
Dublin D03 PO46, Ireland
www.theliffeypress.com

A catalogue record of this book is
available from the British Library.

ISBN 978-1-7397892-9-9

Printed in Poland by L&C Printing Group

CONTENTS

ACKNOLWEDGEMENTS

To complete this adventure I had to draw on the experience and knowledge of some of Ireland's kayaking greats. Mick O'Meara, Jon Hynes, Adrian Harkin and Robin Ruddock all shared a depth of wisdom crucial to making my mission a success. David Walsh's book *Oileain* was an essential guide book that I carried with me and referenced throughout.

The creation of this book presented a second big challenge, one I faced with some trepidation. Never having written one before, I was in unfamiliar territory.

Gary Quinn helped to get me started on this second great journey.

After my first draft was complete, Janet Martin enthusiastically corrected and edited it. Her suggestions, while allowing me to maintain my voice throughout, were greatly appreciated.

David Givens of The Liffey Press then took the text and decided to run with it. He has been a pleasure to work with.

Finally, to my family. Ang, Fionnán and Hannah provided constant support during both of these adventures. They always were, and continue to be, my safe haven.

This book is dedicated to my friend, Mark Murphy,
who was never afraid to embark on a new venture,
who wholeheartedly supported mine, and remained
a touchstone throughout.

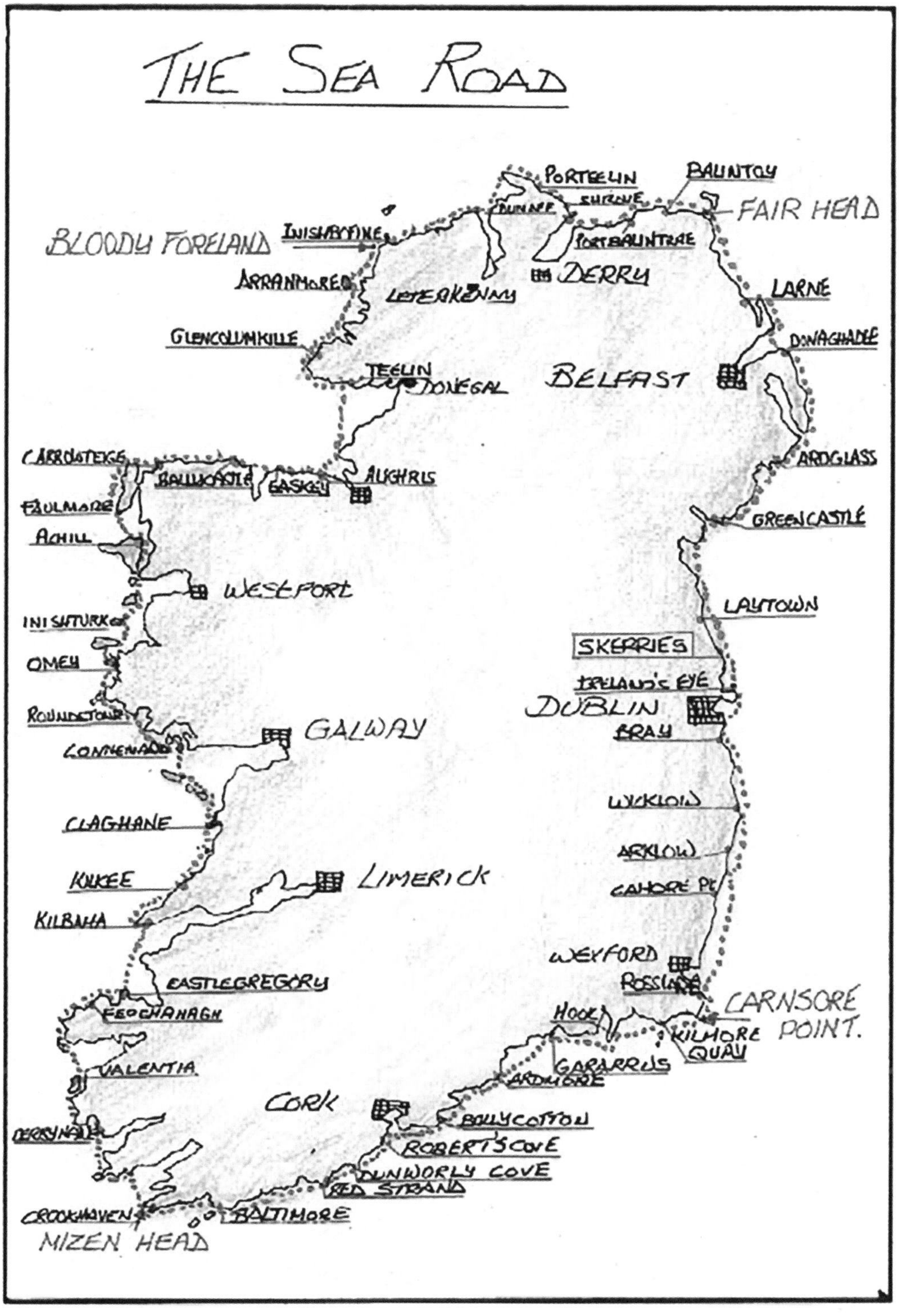

THE SEA ROAD

BLOODY FORELAND

PORTEELIN

SHRUVE

BALLINTOY

FAIR HEAD

INISHAYFINE

DUNREE

PORTBALLINTRAE

ARRANMORED

LETTERKENNY

DERRY

LARNE

GLENCOLUMKILLE

DONAGHADEE

TEELIN

DONEGAL

BELFAST

CARROOTEIGE

BALLYCASTLE

EASKEY

AUGHRIS

ARDGLASS

FAULMORE

ACHILL

GREENCASTLE

INISHTURK

WESTPORT

OMEY

LAYTOWN

ROUNDSTONE

SKERRIES

IRELAND'S EYE

DUBLIN

CONNEMARA

GALWAY

BRAY

WICKLOW

CLAGHANE

ARKLOW

KILKEE

LIMERICK

CAHORE PT

KILBAHA

WEXFORD

ROSSLARE

CARNSORE POINT.

CASTLEGREGORY

FEOCHANAGH

HOOK

KILMORE QUAY

VALENTIA

GARARRUS

ARDMORE

CORK

BALLYCOTTON

DERRYNANE

ROBERT'S COVE

DUNWORLY COVE

RED STRAND

CROOKHAVEN

BALTIMORE

MIZEN HEAD

Introduction

Is This Even Possible?

I bend down, lean forward, and feel the cool stone against my cheek. My eye peeks through the grey slab of limestone standing in front of me. This opening offers a view of two islands, known collectively as Rockabill, six kilometres off the coast from my home town of Skerries. A lighthouse sits on the Rock, the larger of the two, while nearby its unadorned smaller partner, the Bill, remains bare. A light has shone here since 1860, not long after the tragic loss of 350 lives when the clipper ship *RMS Tayleur* dashed onto the rocks off nearby Lambay Island, all for the want of a beacon light to warn of the approaching dangers.

For me though it is 2017, and I am in Ardla Cemetery, on the high ground above Skerries. It is a sun-baked June afternoon. A northeast breeze paints a white ribbon of breaking waves along the coast below. My portal, a circular opening cut through my dear friend's gravestone, is positioned above an inscription. It reads, 'Mark Murphy, 16th Dec 1967 – 6th Feb 2016, A Truly Special Husband, Father, Son, Brother and Friend.' This was all true. Mark was hugely loved and is sorely missed. We worked side by side with Skerries sea scouts for six fulfilling years and had been a great team. At forty-eight years of age, six years my junior, my dear friend had died unexpectedly. With his remains at my feet, his words still exert a powerful reaction in me. He had famously encouraged my upcoming adventure with a simple recommendation, 'just start'. Looking at his grave, minutes away from beginning my great journey, I thank him for his words of wisdom.

My attention shifts slowly from my thoughts to what is going on around me. I notice the wind pushing inland, rising up from the blue sea below rushing through the leaf-filled branches overhead. The fields nearby give off an earthy smell as the summer light paints everything a vibrant version of itself. The silent congregation of headstones speak their own message. They bring a reminder of time's swiftness, each bearing testimony to lives lived, dreams realised, or maybe not. I inhale deeply and feel a new sense of calm. The privilege of being here hits me squarely in the chest. For some reason, I have been granted this wonderful opportunity. I take a final look at Mark's grave, say a goodbye, and turn away. Now I am ready.

I pull the kayak trolley with its lengthy load onto the beach. The tide is high offering me the chance to catch the south-going ebb tide. I am starting out on a twin-track mission over a period of three summers. The first, the obvious one, is to propel my kayak around the island of Ireland using only muscle power. The second, less obvious but equally challenging, is the psychological task of surviving everything thrown at me during the attempt. I stare at the sleek green lines of my kayak. I sit in, snap on my snug spraydeck and settle my feet onto the foot pegs. I instantly become one with my boat. Akin to strapping on my seatbelt, I am now part-human, part-boat, with a five metre long horizontal element encompassing me from the waist down.

A short 22-kilometre spin to Ireland's Eye off Howth will get me going. Memories of Mark constantly whirr about in my brain, keeping the significance of the mission fresh in my mind. I plan to paddle my sea kayak, *Murchú* (Murphy in Irish), in a clockwise direction, completely encompassing the landmass of the island of Ireland, a distance of around 1,750 kilometres.

So, with decades of paddling behind me, a supportive family rooting for me, and the big dream beginning, I will be casting a net around my many memories of living on my island home. Our childhood holidays were always spent somewhere along the coast, and each location will be passed along the way. My interest in various water sports had me visit dozens of beaches, coves, inlets and reefs, all of which will punctuate my travels. In a way I will be revisiting old ground. I anticipate a solo trip full of nostalgia, full of reminiscences and location-jogged memories, coupled with hundreds of miles of new coastline. I am buzzing.

Murchú ready for its 1,750 kilometre adventure

HAVING CLOSELY FOLLOWED THE STORIES of Irish circumnavigations over many years, I always held the dream that some day I would do likewise. Unfortunately, though, my vulnerability to sea sickness seemed to rule out the prospect of me achieving this lofty goal. This unanticipated thorn in my side surfaced fifteen years earlier on a particularly challenging journey when my pal Robert Bolton and I decided to kayak to Scotland from Donaghadee in Northern Ireland. Robert, a doctor working in Belfast's Victoria Hospital, was the adventurous type and happy to come along. It had been in my sights for a while and I was ready after training for months along the coast near Skerries.

With a good weather window, we jumped at the opportunity to leave Donaghadee with our sights on the Scottish coast. With kit well up to spec, we were doubly chuffed to have a handheld first-generation Global Positioning System (GPS) to monitor our progress across the strait. We left the three Copeland Islands astern and headed out into open water. We were buoyant, literally and emotionally, to be venturing deep into the channel and hopefully making good our mission. Three hours in and nearing the midpoint, things begin going slightly awry. My earlier excitement had faded, and a dull malaise took its place. Over the previous hour a creeping unease has put paid to any feelings of harmony. Instead I was experiencing a three part dis-harmony of headache, dizziness and nausea, very unwelcome companions. At first, I refused to accept what was happening, but the trio won through until I finally accepted the inevitable. I was in trouble. The mission was under threat.

I called Robert over. 'Hey Rob. Can you come over? I think I'm gonna throw up.'

My right arm draped across his deck and my face hanging just above the surface, I emptied the contents of my stomach into the sea. As anyone who has suffered seasickness knows, it is a pretty shocking experience, and I ended up shaking with the effort. Thankfully, after a series of excruciating dry retches, I felt a lot better.

Thinking the problem sorted, we resumed progress towards our goal, the small harbour in Portpatrick on the Mull of Galloway. This was the departure point for Scottish settlers bound for Northern Ireland in the early 1600s, and we were tracing the reciprocal route today. I was heartened that things were going swimmingly again. Sadly, my reprieve was short-lived, thanks to the return of the three amigos. All I could do was resume the mental approach. True to form, my efforts were ignored with my full attention now locked into their orbit. Like annoying children pulling at my coat tails, they were not to be disregarded.

Rob watched and I disgorged again, this time on an empty stomach; it had become a series of painful dry wretches. The poor fella witnessed this ugly scene from close quarters, but I was well beyond caring. I could only manage twenty minutes paddling between successive emissions and embarked on a crazy vomiting-paddling-vomiting cycle. The combination of puking and paddling makes for a taxing experience, but fortunately it did not stop me completely. Despite my regular interruptions, Scotland grew before us and after seven-and-a-half hours both our kayaks cleaved into the hard sand of Portpatrick harbour. I told Robert that I appreciated the climactic landing so much that the experience was as good as sex. Luckily for us the following day was mirror calm allowing a problem-free paddle back to Donaghadee. The upshot of the whole endeavour was a great reluctance to plan any future long sea kayak journeys. Ergo, my present mission was far from a foregone conclusion.

So THIS IS WHAT I HAD TO MULL OVER when planning my circumnavigation. Dilemma indeed. Paddling around Ireland was definitely going to be populated with several long open water stretches. Could I hack it, I asked myself. It felt foolhardy, especially since I planned to go solo. Without another boat to lean on, the thoughts of suffering dizziness whilst vomiting, away from the coast, terrified me. I am generally confident in my abilities as a paddler, but this extra challenge made the whole enterprise a rickety prospect. Enter stage right my dearest wife Angela. As a psychologist, and curious about the mental processes that go on inside people's heads, not least her own, she constantly seeks ways they might be optimised for success. She quizzed me about my thoughts, and no, it was not while reclining on the couch.

What were my motivations and what was stopping me? I explained my long held desire to make this dream happen. My experience and fitness should be okay. It was seasickness which stood head and shoulders above all other challenges for this mission. Seeing as my mental battle with that malaise had not been particularly successful, I felt stumped. Angela, ever the lateral thinker, decided to dig further, *quelle surprise*. She plunged further into my mental processes and came up with a new 'angle' on overcoming my *mal de mer*.

'Let us call it an obstacle, rather than a barrier' – a term I had been using for years – 'obstacles can be overcome, barriers cannot.'

'Mmmm,' I remember mouthing, as my dearest continued.

'Research the internet for different methods to tackle seasickness. There must be a solution out there.'

I listened carefully to this, and noticed a small shift in my perspective taking place. Sensing a potential path out of the fugue that was strangling my dream, a stream of possibilities opened up. Finally, I decided to try various brands of travel sickness meds, including the Transderm Scop patch successfully used by air force pilots.

Starting on the East Coast, a generally safer testing ground, allowed for the prospect of experimenting on the first few legs. This was on Ireland's calmer southeastern corner and before the mission proper on the Atlantic. An added plus was that when I reached the ocean off the south coast, these 'test runs' will have eaten into the overall distance. Still, as I mulled over this prospect in the months preceding my departure I was in no way certain it would lead to success. But I was also acutely aware of the old adage that 'fortune favours the brave'.

With a trio of circumnavigators at Skerries RNLI station:
The author, Rob Burgess, Ritchie Diaper and David Simpson

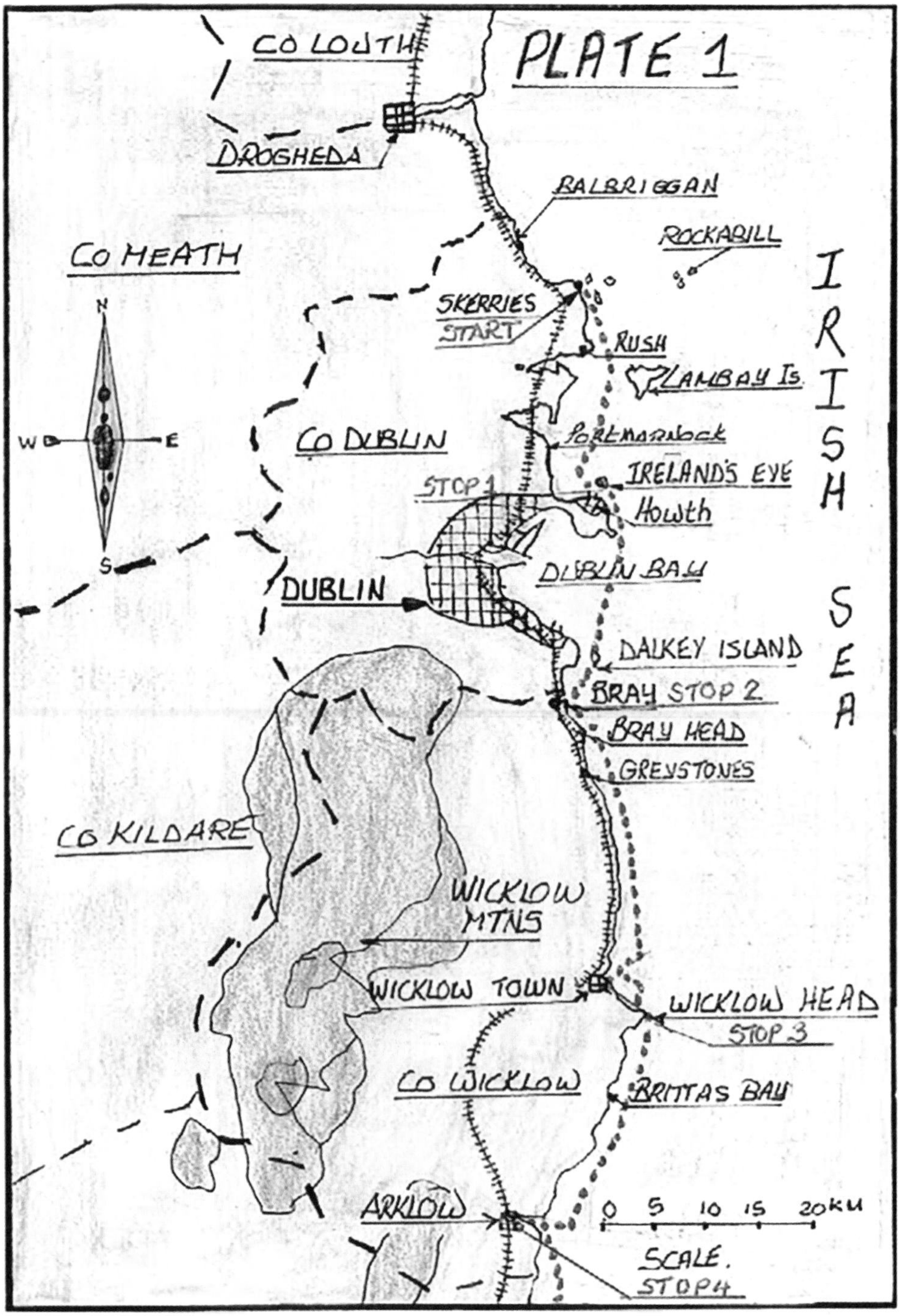

PLATE 1

CO LOUTH

DROGHEDA

CO MEATH

BALBRIGGAN

ROCKABILL

SKERRIES
START

RUSH

LAMBAY IS.

CO DUBLIN

PORTMARNOCK

STOP 1

IRELAND'S EYE
Howth

DUBLIN

DUBLIN BAY

DALKEY ISLAND

BRAY STOP 2

BRAY HEAD

GREYSTONES

CO KILDARE

WICKLOW
MTNS

WICKLOW TOWN

WICKLOW HEAD
STOP 3

CO WICKLOW

BRITTAS BAY

ARKLOW

0   5   10   15   20 KM

SCALE.
STOP 4

I R I S H   S E A

Stage 1

'JUST START'

The pebbles crunch underneath the heavy hull of my fully laden kayak. Slowly, its weight transfers from solid ground to the water. I cross the invisible start line at a snail's pace. A new, long term, intimate relationship with the ocean begins. It feels like a first date and, despite knowing each other for decades, my wish is, literally, not to be ditched. My objective was to simply arrive back at the same spot with the entire coastline of Ireland behind me. The boat trembles, realising its buoyancy. The first transition, though mediocre, is momentous. I look back at Angela and Hannah alongside my friend Magnus and his children and wave. I am brimming with emotion; I am finally away. As Mark had advised, I have 'just started'.

As I said, my initial plan is to hitch a ride south aboard the ebbing tide along with the wave train generated by the light northerly wind pushing down the coast. Thanks to this south going tide, I am on a conveyor belt of currents helping me on my first leg. A perfect set of conditions to start the mission. I punch through small breaking surf and pass by local man Steve Sherwin, out enjoying the waves on his stand-up paddling board. We wave to each other as he surfs back towards the beach and I continue south. He and five pals are planning to paddle their boards from Skerries to Wales, 100 kilometres due east. Now there's another challenge.

It takes me a while to settle into my paddling rhythm. I am surfing downwind, but slightly across the waves in front of the steady breeze. The conditions ask for my undivided attention. Surfing downwind in my Taran sea kayak is challenging as I am still on the learning curve

Getting started

with my new boat. My first time paddling fully laden is going well, however my mind is giddy thanks to the speed. I do my best to focus on the job at hand. The questions that have been swirling around in my head for weeks are now front and centre, all clamouring for attention.

Will my seasickness hit? Will I be fit enough? How will I manage in my new kayak? How will I handle the winds and massive swells? Will my back hold out? What about the flippin' Atlantic? Will I survive the loneliness? Can I stay committed? On and on, out of the fuzz of my agitated mind, these worries surfaced. There are simply too many unanswered questions.

A wave splashes salt spray onto my face, catching me unawares. It is a blessing. My focus returns, thankfully, as the prevailing conditions require it. Keep to the job at hand, Kev. Those qualms will have to wait until later. With Ireland's Eye on the distant horizon I am bearing down on its mighty neighbour, Lambay Island. In a little over an hour I am glissading past the east coast's only inhabited island. Sporting a working farm, a wind turbine, a Norman castle, and an airstrip, it has been in the Bering family for over a hundred years. Bizarrely, since the 1960s it has been home to a colony of now-wild wallabies. Originating from a need to cull Dublin Zoo's expanding population, these lucky

Two aerial photos of Ireland's Eye and Dublin Bay

descendants now enjoy an idyllic lifestyle. Having no predators and free reign across this 600-acre island, they have habituated themselves into kangaroo nirvana. They are accompanied by over 100,000 breeding seabirds during the summer season and a herd of fallow deer also call the island home.

Perched halfway along my evening's paddle, Lambay is a perfect milestone on my first leg. My Taran is clocking up the distance nicely as I capitalise on the southerly flow. I am getting used to my downwind running and more comfortable with my situation. After two hours, I am nearing my first destination, Ireland's Eye off the coastal town of Howth. In the approaching dusk, a subtle change is happening as the swells increase nearer to the island. The ebbing flow from the nearby Baldoyle estuary is pushing directly against the incoming waves, causing them to heighten and break in an unpredictable manner. Because I intend to camp at the Western side of the island, my course is directly through these rougher waters. Slowly, I realise I am facing my first test. Breathe deep, Kev.

The sun disappears behind a cloud and a sombre mood replaces the earlier brightness. I push my knees against the inside of my boat, wedging myself tight. This means I can exert maximum control from a solid base. Like tightening one's bootlaces for surefootedness, this bracing action is well known amongst kayakers. Careering down these waves at speed, my boat tries to deviate from my intended track. Frustratingly, it keeps this new direction a secret until the last moment. My feet push hard on my rudder pedals in a bid to maintain a good track. Basically, angling the toes of my right foot moves the rudder to the right and the opposite is true with the left pedal.

At first, a merry dance starts, but changes are happening quickly transforming the whole ordeal into a battle. Any initial paddling cobwebs are flung off as I am being put to the test. This is not what I expected. The island's Martello tower, only three hundred metres away, looks on mockingly. I want to return its gaze, but cannot. With my goal so close I must resist turning my head to look. My attention is laser focused on the small area around the bow of my boat. Anything outside of this orbit is unimportant. I had chosen the Taran for its speed, which it delivers in abundance, but it also means I am dealing with everything at an accelerated rate. Is there ever a free lunch? Thankfully, I finally sense an easing and a transition to calmer conditions. The turbulence subsides, and my hands instinctively loosen their grip. Having a white knuckle ride so soon in my adventure surprises me.

The 200-year-old Martello Tower stoically observes my arrival onto the gravel beach near its base. Obviously unmoved by my recent struggle, it looks on without providing any solace. The bow of my kayak slices through some small stones. I delay a moment, my boat resting on the shore. I exhale and steady my nerves. I hoist myself out of the sleek kayak and look back over the rough water. Only now does the warm sense of achievement wash over me. Safely on dry land, I allow myself to fully relax. Nearly three hours into my quest to circumnavigate our island home, barely out of sight of the start, my first test is behind me. Little do I know that a second is fast approaching. Before the light fades completely I make a quick scan to find my camping spot for the night.

POSITIONED JUST ONE KILOMETRE OUTSIDE Howth harbour, Ireland's Eye adds a picturesque backdrop to the town. Being near Dublin, it is a popular sea kayaking destination. With vertical cliffs, a sea stack, rocky outcrops and a fine beach, it provides an ideal training ground for up and coming sea paddlers. Populated by day trippers during the summer months, thanks to a ferry service plying the short trip from the nearby harbour, it has a timeless feel. A dramatic sea cave cut into its north facing cliffs is a treat for the passing boater. The picturesque crescent-shaped sandy beach facing back toward the mainland is an east coast gem. I take a few minutes to catch my breath. The unloading of essentials for setting up my camp and a change into dry clothes firmly settles me in.

I love wild camping. Travelling light reminds me of our ancestors, nomadic hunter-gatherers. For me it brings a rare simplicity, a clarity of mind that is often elusive nowadays. Shelter, water, food and exercise are to constitute the main components of my time travelling

First overnight on Ireland's Eye

along our coastline. The 'prey', constantly in my sights, is the 1,750 kilometres of our island's coast. This evening's 22 kilometres is a start. I only have 1,728 more to go.

I now need to light a fire with wood foraged from the beach. Since we are enjoying a warm dry spell I figured there should be plenty lying about. I set off anticipating armfuls for my campfire. My hopes are dashed when I find none. The place is so devoid of flotsam that I am puzzled. I eventually stumble on the probable reason. At this time of year, the age-old tradition of ferrying day trippers over from nearby Howth Harbour is in full swing. These lucky groups, who spend lazy afternoons on the island, must be lighting their campfires along this beach. Every last morsel of firewood has already gone up in smoke. None too pleased, I continue searching, almost in denial. It's not as if I need a campfire, but my vision for this first overnight camp of my trip has one in it.

Eventually I stumble on a big, square structure on the beach. In the fading light I examine it. It turns out to be an old floating pontoon. Clad in hardwood planking, its plastic floating chambers are still attached.

Some of the timbers are broken. This is the fuel I have been searching for. All I need to do is extract it. I attempt to wrestle the fibrous wood apart but the hardwood has great strength and I fail, miserably. I look for a solution to my conundrum. Some large rocks lying about give me an idea. I decide on a wrecking ball approach. I hurl a rock enthusiastically at the platform. Thankfully, it breaks apart and a stash of firewood grows at my feet. I pat myself on the back. A clearer vision of my campfire forms in my mind. Dreams are being realised.

Then I feel a sudden searing pain. I reel from the sudden jolt almost losing my footing. In the increasing darkness I have no idea what is happening, other than my head hurts. My mind works overtime in the fading light. Adrenaline is flooding my veins as I stand riveted to the spot. I am willing myself to figure out what is going on. My attention eventually drifts down to the ground and the puzzle is solved. The rock I had thrown against the wooden platform lies there. My last strike failed to break the wood and instead rebounded into my face striking me above my right eye. Nearly blind due to the near darkness, my hand instinctively goes to the site of the pain and as I draw it away I see a dark spill of my own blood covering my palm.

My thoughts race as I try to process the new scenario. Who would suspect a search for firewood would leave me in this serious situation. My leisurely attitude is sidelined for urgency as I think about my predicament. Alone on an island with a head injury as night approaches is less than ideal. The flickering lights of Howth Village accentuate the darkness. Of course, my mobile phone is safely tucked away back in my tent. I need to get back there for a proper assessment.

'Stay calm, and think logically Kev,' I say out loud.

Focusing on breathing calmly, I must avoid going into shock. Looking at my predicament objectively, I realise a fair dollop of good luck has come my way. The spinning rock has inflicted only a glancing blow above my right eyebrow. Thankfully, not seeing stars and staying conscious improves my mood. I grab the wood I had paid dearly for and scuttle back to base, all the while my hand covering the wound. Crossing the scrubland towards my tent, a huge rat crosses my path. I barely give it a thought but it does add a certain drama to an already eventful evening. I creep into my tent and get out my phone. Using my front camera as a mirror, I inspect the damage. I see blood oozing from the wound above my right eye. I clean it, hoping it is just a graze. I will surely have a shiner in the morning, but I feel any immediate threat is reduced. I am so lucky. I wind a bandage around my head stemming the bleeding. I hold it secure with my cosy woolly hat. I draw my breath again and take stock of my new situation.

Self-administered first aid done, I now realise I am ravenous. The after effects of wood collecting and paddling leave a gaping hole in my stomach. Hot food can wait till morning. I busily sink my teeth into several hastily made cheese sandwiches. I eat at speed. Cocooned in my sleeping bag whilst clutching the soft bread I am thankful for the sustenance and warmth. I am also ready to learn some important lessons for solo paddling. Never depend on getting firewood, and carry my phone everywhere. This particular brand of paddling needs constant vigilance to any potential threat, on land or at sea. I am on the learning curve and will be for hundreds of kilometres. I am happy to stay put and see what the morning brings. I slowly drift off to sleep, surrendering blissfully into the night.

Stage 2

Passing Dublin's Fair City

I stir. Hovering in semi-wakefulness I savour the warmth of my sleeping bag. Keeping my eyes shut, I resist the day's intrusion on my slumber. Finally, I wake to an awareness of heat, in fact, too much heat. The temperature inside my tent is climbing. As the sun hoists itself higher into the sky outside, my indoor microclimate is causing me to sweat. I need to trade my overheating cocoon for some fresh air, pronto. Opening my tent's flap, I squint into the brightness. What greets me is almost intoxicating. A silvery sea glistens like mercury poured from the white sun. My temporary island home and nearby mainland glow in full colour. I love tent openings when the intimacy of wild camping is acutely sensed. As I crawl out I inhale the fresh sea air. Despite the increasing bruise around my eye, I am already confident at the prospect of a wonderful day crossing Dublin Bay towards Bray in County Wicklow.

Finally, I get to fire up my treasure trove of wood, and enjoy a brew to wash down some carb-filled noodles. After an hour and a half, which is how long it takes me to feed, strike camp, don my kit and pack, I strike off. My bandaged eye is hidden under a peaked cap as I laugh at the irony of leaving Ireland's Eye. I look across as Howth slowly comes to life.

Originally *Binn Eadair* in Irish, meaning 'Eader's peak', invaders from overseas renamed it *Hoved* in the eighth century. Meaning 'head' in Norse, the language of the Vikings, the change to Howth happened in the intervening years. These Viking plunderers sailed down the Irish Sea towards France, leaving a trail of looting, destruction and

17

place names in their wake. Ireland's Eye is also a Scandinavian construct, with *Ey* the Old Norse for island, and *Eria* the original female name associated with the place. While on the subject, Skerries drew their attention too. *Sker* means rocks and *eys* is islands, creating a name that accurately describes the location. I am actually following in the wake of our Viking invaders down this watery corridor.

I round the Nose of Howth, and continue below sea cliffs of this moderate headland. The white washed buildings of the Bailey Light shine brilliant in the morning sun. Its sentinel flash blinks a farewell as I pass below. I move into the gaping mouth of Dublin Bay. Often compared to the Bay of Naples, it describes three quarters of a circular arc, with Dublin lining its rim. Halfway along this bay is the country's main port, and the mouth of its river, the Liffey. A city of one and a half million is waking far off to my right as I make a beeline due south towards Dalkey. A decreasing northerly swell helps me as I enjoy the warmth of this perfect day. I smile broadly and feel giddy to be continuing south after the previous night's escapades. I am the luckiest bunny around, I think to myself. With a busy shipping lane to cross I decide that trying to calculate a realistic window is futile. I am going to suck it and see. As ships mostly travel in straight lines, I should be able to move out of their path as needed. As a last resort communicating via my VHF radio is an option. Well, that is my plan, and I am pretty happy with it.

Halfway across, I notice a bright white rectangle far off to my right. I had not seen it earlier and am instantly curious. I continue striking south with the occasional glance to my right. The white rectangle continues to grow until the penny finally drops. I am looking at a large cargo ship's superstructure brightly lit by the dazzling sun to my left. Exiting port, it is beginning its long journey out into the bay and beyond. I reassure myself that I am making good headway, and at more than halfway across in a good situation. I relax, confident the vessel will turn behind me onto the usual northeasterly track out of the bay. Gradually, though, the possibility that we might be on intersecting courses grows. I eye the vessel, red hull and white superstructure, swelling stubbornly along its track. Why is it not turning I ask myself.

Just like a portrait painting whose eyes follow you around a room, this boat remains head on with a bulky stare. When inside one kilometre, I am uncomfortable with the situation. Maybe she is going to take the seldom-used southerly departure route from Dublin. I cast expletives, and decide to sprint away from trouble rather than digging out my VHF radio to hail them.

I reposition myself in the boat as much as I can, bracing myself tightly into its fibreglass shell. I wind up the tempo to a sustainable sprint. I begin counting my strokes in hundreds. One hundred. Two hundred. Three and four. Thinking around five hundred should be enough. The stroke count mounts as steely eyed I keep the ship in my sights. Am I far enough? Is she following me? Am I paddling into her path? All these questions rotate with my paddles, until finally, almost imperceptibly, I start to spot her right flank. Alleluia. This means she is going to pass astern, a combination of her changing course and my sprinting. She deserves the lion's share of the credit as it is now obvious that she is wheeling rapidly onto the usual northern course out of the bay and, more importantly, away from me. Instantly I feel relief, and my stroke rate eases as my inertia continues bringing me south. I mutter to myself, so much for my theories on ship avoidance. Next time I will grab my radio first. Theories are great, but reality is everything.

I AM BEARING DOWN ON DUBLIN'S southside. Colourful houses dot the shoreline. Thanks to the light, the background green and brown of the hills draw them closer. Church spires, trees, avenues and larger buildings, populate the foothills just in from the coast. The scene reminds me more of Cornwall than Dublin. I find it difficult to reconcile it with my previous landside visits as I am now viewing it from a new perspective. My landfall is on Dalkey Island. A tiny cut into the rocks leads to the tiniest slot concealing a small beach inside. The bow crunches into gravel, the second landing on my odyssey. I hoist myself into a welcome stretch, happy that my first open water crossing is complete. I love the myriad challenges popping up for me and am beginning to like being alone at sea, bookended by landings. I lie back on a grassy slope and soak it all up. The warm ground pushes into my back. Amazing, less than twenty-four hours into my mission and already a few stories to tell. My final stop for this instalment will be in Bray harbour in County Wicklow, the second of the seventeen counties to be visited on my journey. It now dawns on me that since leaving yesterday, I still have not touched the mainland. Again, amazing.

Admiring the closeness of the Wicklow hills, I continue south towards Bray. Scouring my new surroundings, I glide into the confines of its small harbour. Kids play on a small strip of sand slowly swelling with the receding tide. I leave my boat and wander off to the Bray Sea Scouts den, a short distance away. The heat of the day radiates off the concrete road. The harbour-side eateries are buzzing with the chatter of lunchtime customers and the clinking of plates stirs my hunger. The world seems happy with itself, or is it just me? Having met no one since leaving yesterday, it is nice to hear voices other than my own. Two welcoming ones are those of Stephen and Fidelma who open their Sea Scout facilities for me. Fidelma, a doctor, is keen to remove my selfie bandage and take a closer look at my injury, while Stephen, her husband, is intent on spiriting my kayak into the boat store under their den. We retire to the kitchen and Fidelma carefully unwinds the salty binding above my eye. My dodgy first aid skills are exposed as my work is examined. I relay how the injury was caused. She immediately stops, fixes her eyes on me, and begins an interrogation.

Being welcomed by Stephen from the Bray Sea Scouts (photo by Fidelma Savage)

'You mean to say you used a rock to break up some wood? Are you not supposed to be a sea scout? Have you not brought your axe with you?'

My pride at reaching Bray is dented as the idiocy of my previous night's transgressions are exposed. Fidelma, seeing her scolding land, begins cleaning and replacing my hasty bandaging efforts. With my dressing professionally redone, and the telling off complete, they change tack by inviting me for a seafood dinner next door to celebrate my achievement. For a second time in hours, I realise I am absolutely ravenous.

LOGISTICS FOR THIS MISSION ARE A CONSTANT concern. By carving the trip up into short routes, rather than doing it as one continuous paddle, I need to book-end each instalment with a commute back home. Braver souls, blessed with more free time than I have, use the conventional method of setting off until it is done. My staggered approach means that the land part of the trip forms another challenge, and one that I look on as part of the adventure. The east coast is set up perfectly for this method, thanks to over 300 kilometres of railway line from Belfast in County Antrim to Rosslare in County Wexford. This provides the perfect conveyor home before returning to continue navigating the Irish Sea.

After eating, Fidelma and Stephen drop me off at the Bray train station. My kayak, in subterranean storage beneath their den, will await my return.

The train whizzes northwards and I look dreamily out over Dublin Bay. Seeing it from here, thoughts drift back to this morning's paddle. I spot the red and green lighthouses guarding Dublin port. They mark the narrow opening at the end of two long narrow piers stretching three kilometres out to sea. Seen from the air, they resemble two spidery pincers tracing an enormous V into the bay. The northernmost of these, known locally as the Bull Wall, is the birthplace of my keen interest in outdoor water sports such as sea swimming.

Leaving Bray Harbour
(photo by Stephen Carville)

Dotted along this wall are numerous bathing shelters, still in use to this day. I am forever grateful to a British Navy Captain for his part in making this facility a reality. In 1800, Captain William Bligh, of *HMS Bounty* fame, was acting as marine surveyor for the British admiralty. Tasked with solving the silting problem at the entrance to Dublin port, his reports suggested the construction of a wall adjoining the sand-bank out in the north side of the bay. It took twenty years to complete, and ever since the scour of the ebbing tide has kept the entrance clear.

A long beach adjoins Bull Wall. At an impressive five kilometres, it easily accommodates hundreds of day-trippers on warm sunny days. During one of my swims I noticed a set of large waves appearing out at sea and careering towards the beach. The inbound car ferry had just passed, and these impressive breakers seemed to be coming from the ship's wake. Having learned how to kayak-surf in the Atlantic rollers, I was keen to see this wave up close. As the east coast is pretty devoid of anything other than wind-blown wave formations, this occurrence warranted further investigation.

The next day, myself and two buddies found ourselves a mile offshore in our kayaks, waiting for the car ferry to appear, madly hoping it was on schedule. Spotting it on the horizon making its way towards port created in us a palpable air of excitement. Eventually, its mighty bulk forged past us like an enormous building cutting through the sea. Echoes of Tom Hanks in *Castaway*, as the huge cargo ship passed him on his rickety raft, came to mind. Preoccupied with the much anticipated wave, it was only then that we were struck by our proximity to the great vessel. It was enormous, and we were frozen to the spot. We heard passengers at the guardrails whistling and shouting down to us. We must have looked like bits of flotsam to them. The ferry passed, leaving us searching for any disturbance in its wake. We noticed a thin line, about fifty metres across, creasing the perfect calm. It resembled a submarine surfacing along the entirety of its length when seen from the side. This was the genesis of a set of huge waves headed our way.

It was only then that we realised what we were dealing with. I shouted a few expletives, turned towards shore, and started paddling to catch a ride home. Rising higher and higher, it caught hold of my kayak and I started to slide down its face. I was on a toboggan run for home. I was completely alive with the thrill of careering down this watery ramp for over a kilometre, eventually coming to rest back at the beach. We regrouped afterwards as though we had uncovered the holy grail, which in many ways we had. Our discovery morphed into a popular kayaking activity for many on sunny summer evenings. Not often do you consult a ferry timetable to go surfing.

Stage 3

ROLLING BY THE RAIL LINE
FROM BRAY TO WICKLOW

Two weeks later, I am southbound again on the train to Bray. My kayaking kit is crammed into my outsize rucksack squatting beside me. My paddles, integral to the whole endeavour, get reverentially treated in their padded bag next to me. Wheeling along under Killiney hill I notice the southeasterly breeze is creating wide shifting patterns on the sea below. It is a little fresher than forecast. Arriving at the station, I spot Stephen outside who ferries me back to the den where we link up with Fidelma. She keenly inspects my eye, which thankfully is almost back to normal. She jokes that she now deems me well enough to continue my travels.

I wheel my sea kayak, *Murchú*, from its bunker and pack it for two days southbound. My wife Angela's surname is Murphy, along with my friend Mark's, and my kayak carries the original Irish version of the name. Translating to 'sea warrior' it is a lofty title I try to live up to. A more apt meaning might be 'sea worrier' at this early stage.

I glide through a colourful flock of moored dinghies and am disgorged from the small harbour mouth. I pass along the ornate promenade, as strollers, oblivious to my quest, enjoy the warm afternoon. Their voices fade away as I move offshore towards the cliffs of nearby Bray Head. From the 1950s to the 1970s, this headland boasted a chairlift to its modest summit where, in 1887, a viewing point was erected for Queen Victoria's jubilee celebrations. Its coastal cliff paths have remained well-worn thoroughfares ever since.

As I near the steep escarpments, the sea conditions start to change. The surface distorts into a varied collection of undulations. I am soaking up this new dynamic when I realise I am being treated to the first taste of 'clapotis' of the trip. This nautical term describes the confused sea state created when different wave patterns collide. Unlike when waves land on beaches or tumble onto rocks, expending most of their energy, when meeting sheer rock faces or cliffs they simply bounce back. Like a snooker ball bouncing off a cushion, they ricochet back out to sea at an angle. These outward-going waves, still carrying most of their energy, interfere with those still incoming creating confusing conditions.

This spiking mass of peaks, troughs and hollows are almost impossible for a kayaker to read and can be a real headache. Depending on how big the swells are, kayaking can become impossible. Today the waves are smaller, but the pattern is still irregular. I sit bolt upright, reacting to every movement of water under the boat. One second I am on a peak, a short-lived watery cone, the next it disappears and I slide into a trough at an angle. Trying to relax, rather than tensing up, is difficult. Twisting and sliding, my new boat reacts differently in these conditions. Most sea kayaks have nice upturned noses and tails that are sympathetic to a wave's shape. The Rockpool Taran I have chosen for this mission is an altogether different iteration.

Designed for speed and not manoeuvrability, and resembling a long green torpedo, its vertical bow slices through the water like a saw blade. It also exhibits almost no rocker. This is the banana shape some sea kayaks have when seen from the side, their upturned ends giving the boat a shallow crescent shape. What this boils down to is a very fast sea boat, but one that does not like confused conditions, and as a matter of fact neither do I. Battling on, I eventually notice a slight change in the sea as we round Bray Head. I catch sight of Greystones which stirs memories of a family holiday back in the 1970s. I distinctly recall the sea being completely calm under a scorching sun the entire time we spent here. It helps me to breathe a semi-sigh of relief.

I continue along the now low-lying coastline, complete with miles of railway track backing onto an unendingly long gravel beach. A train leaves Greystones headed south and gracefully sweeps past me like a horizontal pencil. Because of the straightness of the coast it stays in sight for miles. This is somewhat depressing, as by the time it disappears it is more like a model train in the distance. Also, I am feeling disinterested, a surprise to me since I am supposedly living my dream. The conditions remain lumpy but not too difficult to handle. It must be all that bouncing around under Bray Head that has my head cooked. Wicklow Town is growing almost imperceptibly ahead of me as I put in these hard yards. The sun is descending towards the Wicklow hills to my right and the colours about me are changing. A warm light blankets the land. Suffice to say it contradicts my mood.

Despite the beauty of my surroundings my head feels heavy and my balance is sketchy. I decide to land and take stock. I have taken my Kwells seasickness tablets and am puzzled by my poor state. I go ashore landing near a couple of sea anglers and, uncharacteristically, notice I am in no mood to approach them or engage in conversation. During this break, with less than an hour's paddling to go, I recommit to pushing on. I dally a little while, allow my inner gyros to stabilise, and set off again. I must find a way out of this malaise.

My boat glides into Wicklow's mirror-calm harbour. I stop paddling. My head is spinning and I feel rough. I eventually force myself to paddle to the back of the harbour in search of my base for the night, 7th Wicklow's waterside scouts den where I will be laying down my sore head. I sit on the pier waiting for my host and also for my head to return to normal. When she arrives, I enthusiastically gloss over my sorry state, thankful for her warm welcome and the bag of food she places in my hand. Soon inside, the smell of toast wafting from the kitchen slowly brings me back to myself as I dig into my augmented supplies. Shortly thereafter I am readying myself for a serious night's sleep without dwelling too much on the toll the short paddle took from me.

I WAKE TO A SEA MUCH LESS AGITATED than yesterday. I again take my meds and keep my fingers crossed. In my sights today is a crux point deserving of respect, Wicklow Head. This promontory has shallows dotted about and a confluence of currents and upwellings that can create a challenge even without windblown waves. When river levels in Wicklow are too low for white-water kayakers, they are drawn here to play in the conditions prevailing, especially during spring tides. There are three lighthouses perched above this spot. One is operational, the other two decommissioned. This sad duo had failed to provide a warning light during foggy conditions and were eventually superseded by the remaining one.

Thankfully, I glide past in lake-like conditions, noticing large, bright barnacle-covered rocks just below the surface. Small holiday homes peep out from among the assorted flora lining the coast. Sandy beaches appear below steep slopes and my mood is good. I feel great today. The warm sun to my left is on its journey skyward as the temperature follows suit. Yesterday's malaise is long past and I am relishing being on mission in a much improved state.

Already, I am halfway through County Wicklow, and once beyond Arklow, my next stop, I will be in neighbouring County Wexford, the

Near Arklow

second of three 'W' counties. Waterford will be following suit much later on. Ever the etymologist, these three counties always seem out of step when compared to others. Most Irish counties use an anglicisation of their original Irish names. These three, however, do not follow that trend. Instead they reflect the previously mentioned Viking influence dating back to the eighth century. Wicklow, the county I am soon to leave, originates from *Vykyngelo,* meaning Viking meadow, far removed from its Irish name, *Cill Mhantáin,* or church of the toothless one. I will tell you about the other two later on.

A big plus to paddling along the east coast are the huge stretches of easy beaches for landing. The ache of a bulging bladder need not be endured for long. A simple dash to shore to find a discreet spot and relief is instant. The opportunity to stand up straight, as a substitute to being semi-folded in a kayak, is an added bonus. Mindful of physiological pressures, I give myself targets to reach before considering a stop. I look for interesting coves, inlets or natural harbours that segue off the sea road and come ashore. This stepping-stone principle is working well for me today, and after four hours paddling and a couple more in accumulated stops, Arklow Harbour welcomes me and *Murchú* into its embrace.

This port doubles as the mouth of the Avonmore river and I notice a strong flow is pushing out to sea at the entrance. I scurry close to the bank where the current is weakest, eventually leaving this contra-flow into a more inviting basin. This small square area of water has several private boats moored. I run my boat onto a tiny bit of sand beside a ramp. Arklow sea scouts den is nearby and I stroll over to locate today's hosts. Having forewarned them of my arrival, they greet me warmly and some senior scouts willingly assist moving my kit to their den, not a hundred metres from the water. The promise of my boat being cared for, along with the nearby train station, decides the end point of a pleasant day paddling. My spirits are up.

The bustle at their enormous den resembles an army readying themselves for battle. In a way, that is exactly what they are doing. They are about to go kayaking on the river and are choosing boats and kit from their vast stock of equipment. Instructions are being ex-

Arklow Sea Scout helpers

changed enthusiastically among the group. Standing on a grassy area of about an acre, the outhouses, changing rooms, store rooms and lines of trees constitute a well-used amenity for the youth of the area. The proximity to the river and harbour are ideal for these sea scouts, some of whom I chat with about my quest. I wonder if the germ of an idea will take root in the minds of some of those listening. I retire to the kitchen to face a heaped plate of beans, sausages and toast, the typical scout staple. A big nosh up seems to be standard hospitality with the scout groups I meet. After leaving my kayak in the den, I enjoy being chauffeur driven to the station by Majella Myler, whose husband, Jimmy, is already leading the flotilla of kayaks upstream.

Another northbound train transports me home. Despite the challenges I face, I am making headway, although a day of fairly debilitating sea sickness means I remain unconvinced that I am up for the full circuit. My journey blog, shared to a limited audience via Facebook, is quite coy and I have taken to calling the trip my 'Odyssey'. How non-committal is that? I mentally return to my much-loved mantra, 'Hold on to your vision but deal with what you have in front of you'.

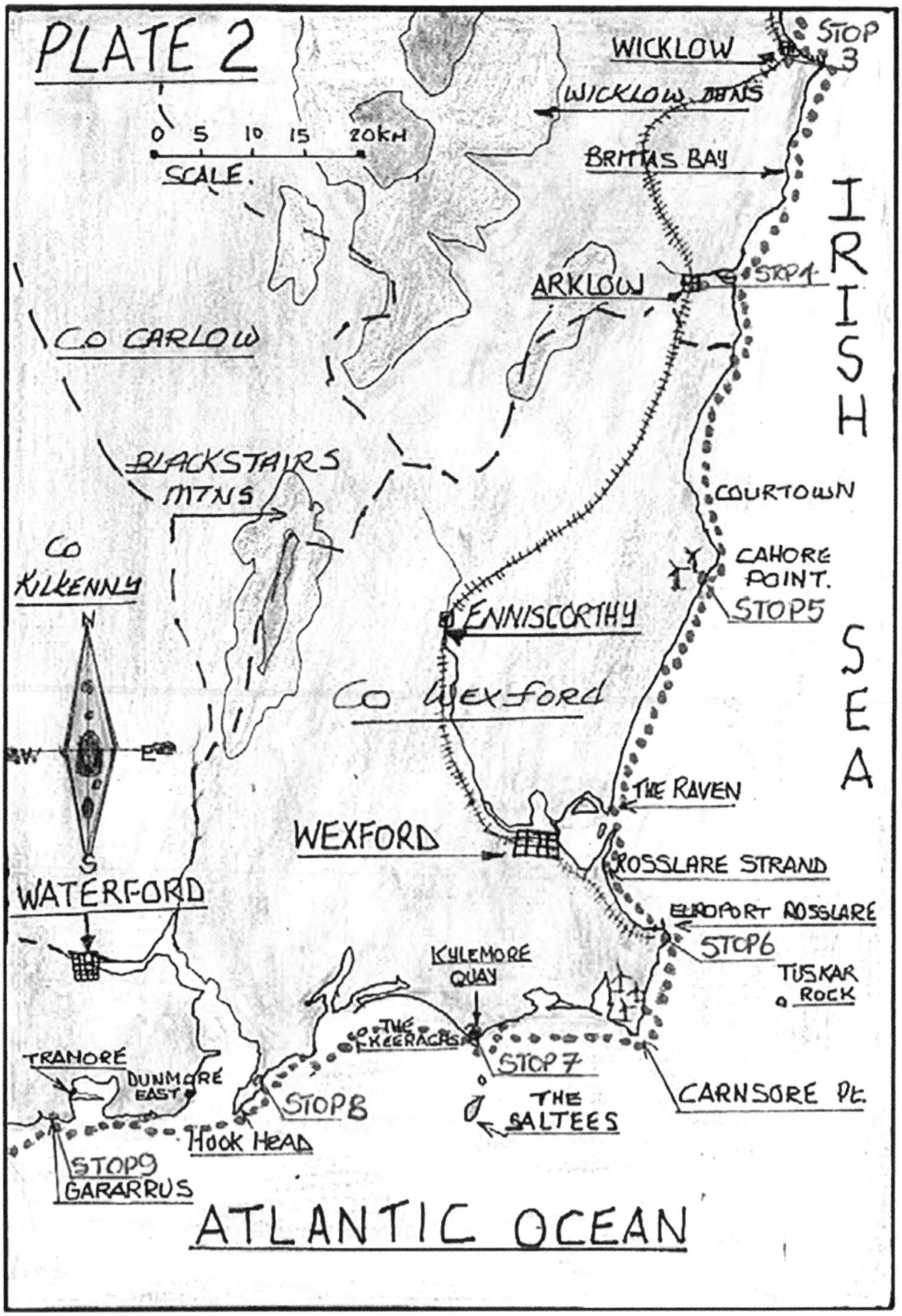

PLATE 2

SCALE.
0 5 10 15 20KM

WICKLOW
WICKLOW DNS
BRITTAS BAY
STOP 3
STOP 1
ARKLOW

IRISH SEA

CO CARLOW

BLACKSTAIRS MTNS

CO KILKENNY

N
W E
S

ENNISCORTHY

CO WEXFORD

COURTOWN

CAHORE POINT.
STOP 5

THE RAVEN

WEXFORD

ROSSLARE STRAND

WATERFORD

EUROPORT ROSSLARE
STOP 6

TUSKAR ROCK

KYLEMORE QUAY

TRAMORE
DUNMORE EAST

THE KEERAGHS
STOP 7

STOP 8

THE SALTEES

CARNSORE PT.

HOOK HEAD

STOP 9
GARARRUS

ATLANTIC OCEAN

Stage 4

ARKLOW'S ACHILLES HEEL

Between work, poor weather and family holidays to Baltimore in West Cork, seven weeks pass before I return to Arklow. The vagueness as to when I might return has to be frustrating for those who offer to store *Murchú*. The conversations I share on this topic are becoming a kind of dance. I cannot really say … it depends on the weather ... it could be this week … it might be next month … I might only have a few days' notice …' and so on. I feel like I am testing them while trying to keep the thread of my journey intact. In fairness, though, this exists mainly in my head. I continue to be fortunate with my hosts.

Another train ride south deposits me in Arklow. Majella meets me and cheerfully ferries me to their den and my kayak. I meet Jimmy again, and we lower *Murchú* from the store room loft while we chat about my trip. He proudly gives me a guided tour of their considerable base. He notices my enthusiasm for their set up, and extends an invitation to our sea scouts to visit. Again, I am bowled over by their generosity in supporting my trip.

I wheel my kayak back to the ramp, pack slowly and set off. The day is grey and an oily calm inside the harbour creates an industrial feel. I pass out to sea and head south again, hitching a ride on another ebb tide emptying the Irish Sea towards the Atlantic. As along the previous stretch, the coastline is low-lying and, coupled with the greyness of the day, banal. The after-effects of an earlier wind has left a choppy sea that rocks the boat as I track parallel to the coast. Dotted along this stretch are scatterings of holiday homes looking out over the pale wet sand. Only a few miles outside Arklow, I seamlessly arrive into Wex-

31

ford, the third county on my trip. This is my second 'W' county, and this one means 'the Inlet of the Mudflats' in old Norse. This all makes sense really, as it describes the characteristics of the approaches to the town of the same name. The Irish name for Wexford is *Loch Garman*, meaning 'Lake of Garman', which leaves the seafarer none the wiser.

I potter along on a grey, choppy sea on what I can only describe as a mediocre day. The average pace of between six and seven kilometres per hour just adds to the humdrum atmosphere. The tide is helping, but the chop slows me down. Slowly I am reeling in small headlands, passing holiday homes, spotting small fishing boats as I continue my way south. About two hours in, I start to feel more tired than I should. My paddle rate has dropped and I start to feel a bit off. I am wondering if it is something I ate, or am I suffering from a cold. I press on. Eventually, I schedule a food stop, aiming for a small cove nestled inside a headland not too far ahead. It reveals itself into a tiny, semi-circular, tree-lined bay, facing north, and flanked by a group of six wooden holiday homes. It reminds me of a scene from an Enid Blyton book, and half expect to see Julian, his three friends and their dog Timothy bathing here. By the time I land, however, I have a heavy heart. My head is throbbing and I feel nauseous. I perch on a dry rock as a small group of elderly ladies arrive to bathe nearby. The place is an idyllic mini amphitheatre, but its quaintness loses its impact due to my ailing mood. I crack open one of my hatches for grub and start to munch on some Cliff Bars and nuts.

As I sit there I realise that reality is screaming at me. It is all very well drawing lines on a chart, planning the route, and jumping at the opportunity, but at the end of the day it is the doing of the deed that matters. The 'doing', unfortunately for me, is becoming 'my undoing'. I need to have a very serious conversation with myself about the wisdom of my mission. This is my second bout of seasickness, and I am not even out of the Irish Sea. I have changed my meds to Sturgeon in the hope of more success. With a long way to go, and the Atlantic seaboard ahead, due attention must be paid to what is happening to me … right here … right now. This is no time to bury my head in the sand, which, ironically, is now at my feet. I feel absolutely terrible. Today's

goal to reach Cahore Point, still hours away, feels like a joke. It is nearly too much for my sore head to handle. I need to break things down.

The coastline here is friendly so I can potter along and see how I get
on. I can come ashore whenever I like, I can even forget about Cahore
and camp wherever I choose. My next dose of seasickness pills is hours
away. I do, however, have many hours of daylight left. The stop has
me feeling marginally better so that goes into the mix. In gathering together these few positive shreds, my predicament's heaviness lessens.
My head feels lighter and my mood lifts. The three women bathers
are chatting away and are now cautiously joined by a young teenager,
possibly a grandson. Ah, that must be Julian, I joke to myself. They are
oblivious to the internal struggle I am experiencing. Their indifference
helps draw me out of myself and I soak up their exuberant chatter.

After a solid three-quarters of an hour break, I ready *Murchú* for
another wetting. As I pack away my gear I spot my first-aid kit. It stops
me. Suffering the odd migraine over the years I have taken some co-
deine with me, just in case. Seeing as a symptom of my seasickness is a
thumping headache, maybe this can help. I am looking for some way
to clamber out of the hole I am in. I decide to pop these pills into my
water bottle, swallow a good slug, and head off.

Four hours later I am closing in on the windmills of Cahore Point.
Almost thirty kilometres on the clock and I am glad to be scanning for
a place to camp. The distance is not massive but my sense of achievement is. My water bottle concoction put an end to my headache and
my day is now ending after a very pleasant potter further down the
coast. I am elated to have a method for tackling this situation should I
have to face it again.

I land and walk the hundred metres to the top of an embankment
that backs on to the beach. A dense scrubby hedge with an occasional
gap funnels walkers out on to the soft sand as they enjoy the evening
glow beside the sea. I walk through one of these green portals and enter
another world. A campsite of caravans, camper vans and tents greet
me as the happy din of delighted holidaymakers hits my ears. Completely hidden from the beach, it stops me dead. Barbecue smoke wafts
by, activating my hunger. Dogs are running around, being chased by

Camping on Cahore Beach

children, and laughter erupts from deck-chaired parents outside their temporary homes. I foresee my stay punctuated by endless explanations as to what I am doing here, coupled with the gargantuan effort in hauling *Murchú* through deep sand. In the end, after enjoying a delicious ice cream bought from the campsite's shop, I decide to head further south and paddle *Murchú* another kilometre.

A peculiar quirk of the tides around these parts is their modest range. The maximum here is one and a half metres, whereas back home in Skerries it is a handsome four and a half. This means the shoreline moves very little, which helps me determine how close to the water I can camp. Tonight's campsite is on the sand only 50 metres from the water's edge. It's deep softness will be wonderful to sleep on, but acts like treacle for dragging my boat across. And needless to say, in the middle of a calm night, the shore break sounds much closer than 50 metres.

The next day works out much better, with little or no malaise. Initially, I make my way south along 26 kilometres of beach towards Raven Point. The early morning fog hides the open sea which gives me a feeling of paddling on a wide river rather than the ocean. A lack

Wexford's eroding coastline

of swell allows me to hug the shore, often so closely that I can share a greeting with a few shoreside strollers. About an hour in, I stop to stretch my legs, settling any minor discomforts that need attention. This sort of thing is easily overlooked, but for me it becomes increasingly important on longer stretches. A badly-fitting bit of kit can become the focus of discomfort and eventually irritation.

At one stage I spot a break in the sand cliff that has flanked me for miles. I decide to use it as an excuse to stop. A tiny river flows out to sea here, no doubt the creator of the gap. I spot a toilet block, which I gladly use, wandering afterwards into the adjoining field. A few small caravans are scattered about with a couple of older guys chatting. I ramble in their direction and ask where I might get some fresh water. Pointing to a nearby tap, one of them informs me, 'fill away lad, there's as much there as you'll ever need'.

Noticing he has electrical power attached to his caravan and seeing as he is the generous type, I sheepishly ask would charging my phone be a possibility.

'Surely,' he chirps, 'bring it here, I'll plug it in for ya.'

He then adds, 'Sure I'll pop the kettle on, you'll have to wait for a bit.'

By the time I am back, a large pot of tea and a plateful of sandwiches sits on a table outside his caravan. We chat away, and thanks to my inability to refuse food, my phone is well charged by the time I leave. I discover Joe lives nearly 70 kilometres away in County Laois, and interestingly, down the road from my sister and husband, whom he knows. He stays here for big chunks of the summer, and as the season is just ending has started packing up to leave.

With a pep in my step I return to *Murchú* and the sea. I can make out Raven Point, its extensive, dark green scar visible from a long way off. There is a large, mature, conifer forest growing there. Angela and I trekked through this forest years ago, pre-children. Walking through those pines one imagines oneself in Canada and not Ireland's sunny south east. I have dreamed so many times about passing this magical spot that when I get here I clamber out of my green machine, run up on to the dunes, and breathe in the whole scene. During my dreams for this mission, seeing this place again was pivotal. Now I inhale this warm, windswept, almost otherworldly scene. An indescribable electricity shoots through my veins. The dying embers felt yesterday

Raven Point

are again burning brightly. Feeling buoyant and childlike, I skip back down to my partner *Murchú* patiently waiting for me. I can see Wexford's 'inlet of the mudflats' ahead and Rosslare Harbour beyond. I take off south again at a ferocious rate of knots.

Wexford harbour lives up to its Norse name. A conglomeration of shallow mudflats, sand bars, channels and low lying islets, it is a minefield for mariners. When heavy weather arrives from the east it is a place to avoid. Today it shimmers in the fresh southerly breeze. The water, a vibrant turquoise, is flanked by areas of white sand. With the north side's dark pines painted onto the sun blushed sky, it looks Caribbean. I navigate between sandbars, avoid dead ends, and strike out into open water. Rosslare Strand is visible on the far side of the bay to the south. For decades a thriving holiday destination, it is my last port of call before Rosslare Europort. This is where I am due to meet up with another friendly scouter, Patrick Quirke of Tuskar Sea Scouts, along with my evening train home. Wexford town lies on the western side of this bay, sadly no longer the bustling seaport it once was. Since the mid-1800s, the volume of seawater entering and exiting the bay has declined due to reclamations of the north and south slobs. The resulting sandbars scattered about are testimony to this short sighted 'land grab', which was originally intended to keep the bay's entrance open. The original Norse moniker could nowadays be amended to, 'Ex-ford'.

I land at Rosslare Strand, a beach scene of swimmers, walkers and picnickers. A barefooted guy walks up and quizzes me about my strange boat. As I answer he licks his quickly melting ice cream. Happy with what he hears, he ambles on and I start tucking into my own treats. I look across to the Europort terminal only a short distance away. This facility, serving both France and Wales, is also where the railway from Dublin ends. An enormous white ferry dwarfs the pier. I relish being where I am. Psychologically I am in a good spot. To be standing with Ireland's south eastern corner only a few kilometres away feels so rewarding. The next foray will put me, and *Murchú*, beyond that corner, and into the Atlantic. I feel ready for that leap now. After a mixed jaunt down the Irish Sea I no longer feel foolhardy. I am cautiously content to recommit.

Rosslare Strand

Patrick and Madeline Quirke treat me royally in Rosslare. I shower, enjoy some grub, and am entertained by this great couple at their dream home perched above the town. Surrounded by small fields, the wild flowers dance in the sea breeze. I hear skylarks and meadow pipits creating their summer music. I feel light, sinking into enthralling conversations about adventures, dreams and sea tales. Patrick, an ex-school teacher, runs a boating business, alongside volunteering for the Royal National Lifeboat Institution, RNLI, as well as the local sea scouts. In me he finds a willing listener. Madeline, active in the community, has tons to share too. As I sit there in their kitchen, with endless food on offer, I feel completely at home. It is difficult to tear myself away, but my departure looms. Generously, on the way to the train Patrick detours along the high road to oversee my next stretch of sea road. I am grateful for the sneak preview of my next instalment. Later, on the train home, I luxuriate in my five days paddling from Skerries and keen to share my own stories with my family.

Stage 5

CARNSORE POINT:
GATEWAY TO THE ATLANTIC

A big project needs to be divided into segments to make it palatable. The analogy of eating an elephant comes to mind. I am consuming this adventure one mouthful at a time. This year, reaching Gararrus Beach near Tramore, County Waterford, is my goal. The reason for this dates back two years to a blustery June afternoon in Skerries.

Pottering away at home I got a phone call from Gary, a kayaking friend, wondering if I could meet legendary paddler Mick O'Meara, who had just landed in Skerries. He was on his attempt to break the Irish circumnavigation record. Years previous Gary had kayaked with Mick along the Copper Coast. He was writing an article for *The Irish Times* and Mick was guiding him along his home stretch. With Gary stuck in work, he asked me to welcome Mick to Skerries. Five minutes later, I am searching the harbourside pubs for Mick. Huddled into a cosy corner of Stoops, he looked like an Everest summiteer wrapped around a steaming bowl of chowder. He recalls that since turning into the Irish Sea at Antrim's Fair Head, he had battled southerly headwinds. Today, crossing directly from Carlingford, it was a nonstop slog. As a seasoned marathon paddler Mick knew how to dig deep. Having won numerous titles, he is one of Ireland's foremost long distance kayakers. I am shocked to see how drained he is. He was 19 days into his mission, and it had taken its toll.

I was impressed, and moved, by Mick's recollections of long days paddling since leaving his home in Waterford. This emotive conversation strikes something deep in me. I made a mental note to myself.

Later, back in our house, we continue our conversation, piling food onto Mick's plate as quickly as it disappears. He notices my interest in circumnavigating. As he had assessed my competency for kayak instructorship years previously, he knows my form. He enthuses that I am well up for the task, locking eyes to make sure I take on board what he is saying. The next day Mick continues his battle with the 'sickening southerly', as he calls it. He makes Ireland's Eye and takes shelter from the winds. Such are the conditions that he becomes completely airborne on the way. At 9.00 pm that evening, he resumes paddling across Dublin Bay to Greystones arriving there at 2.00 am. He lands back home on Gararrus Beach three days later, having set a new 23 day record, which still stands at the time of writing.

My clifftop B&B above Rosslare Harbour affords lofty views over the next stretch of coastline towards Carnsore. Before breakfast I wander outside and look down to the sea below. With little swell, it looks inviting. I will be chasing the sun as it arcs across the sky today. Initially,

Rosslare Harbour

a short spin east, turning south to Ireland's southeastern extremity, and then a ninety degree swing westerly, onto the south coast. At 30 kilometres, it is well within my capacity, even if the forecast southwesterlies kick in. I am not going for heroics on my first date with the Atlantic.

Over breakfast I ask my host if I can leave my car at her place until my return in two days' time. She agrees enthusiastically, prompting my second request, of possibly getting a lift back to the harbour to move all my kit down to sea level. With both replies in the affirmative, an hour later I am pushing off from the small boat harbour at Rosslare. I creep by the main pier and under the bow of an enormous cross-channel ferry. I crazily ponder the reality that this vessel, like me, is just floating on the ocean. With its metal sides disappearing into the depths beside me I glide by feeling quite vulnerable taking on the ocean. Thankfully, I am soon enjoying some pretty low lying coastline as I weave my way along. There is no swell, allowing me to track close to shore, so close that at one stage I paddle between a wading fisherman and the beach. I am not sure who is more surprised but we find time to wave to each other as our worlds briefly intersect. After an hour and a half I pull into Carne pier, the final harbour before the Point. I spot a few men leaving a small fishing boat and make a beeline to ask about rounding the Point. My fear, as I await their answer, is couched in my knowledge learned about the Irish Sea's interplay with the Atlantic.

The Irish Sea behaves like an estuary. With a smaller opening between Antrim and Scotland, and a larger one between where I am and Wales, water sluices in and out with each tidal cycle. As the tide rises in the Irish Sea, it is fed by water coming in from the Atlantic. When the tide is dropping, the water returns back to the ocean. It is almost impossible to visualise the volume of water that moves under the effect of these forces, the double cycle happening twice every 25 hours. As the water funnels through these openings strong currents are created. Kayakers often hitch a ride on these vast watery conveyor belts. These flows can become a big problem, however, when they run into swells coming from the opposite direction. Today the flows are heading southwest, which unfortunately for me is directly into the path of the expected swell.

Carne, County Wexford

One of the fishermen explains that they have come in from the Point because it was too rough. My stomach lurches as I try to digest this unwanted news . He sees the blood drain from my face and decides to add a caveat, that by the time I get there, it will have died off a bit. I am not convinced. I sheepishly declare that I am bound for Kilmore Quay, only now half-believing I will make it. He continues to advise that after rounding the point to stay well offshore as a counter current whips along inshore which I would do my best to avoid. I am a bit downhearted after this exchange but manage to share a few pleasantries before moseying, leaden-footed, back to *Murchú*. I know it is time for more self-talk. Mick had mentioned there would be times like these. When solo, and faced with a challenge, an honest debate must take place. It is a proper ding-dong of pros and cons with everything going into the mix. I mentally project myself forward to the scene using my years of sea kayaking experience.

In my mind's eye I see a maelstrom of cascading waves rushing towards me in a frenzied attack of salty spray. I see myself climbing through the driving spindrift as the salt laden wind stings my eyes. I grasp occasional glimpses of the low lying corner of Ireland whilst cresting over the watery hills. My muscles, worn out by my unwillingness to give up the good fight, pull for all their worth. If unable to handle the conditions I am prepared to make a beeline for shore taking my chances at landing onto the beach or among the rocks. I must now find a way to face my inner demons.

These thoughts are whirling about in my mind as I bear down on the Point. From a distance things look rough but not scarily so. Onwards I paddle, watching my bow slice through the darkening sea. For some reason it feels like an icebreaker as it drives forward. My breathing is hurried as I ready myself for fight or flight. This much used phrase summarises exactly how I am feeling. I am ready for whatever happens, and hoping it is not beyond my capabilities. I press on slowly spotting the giant wind turbines majestically towering out of the most southeastern field in Ireland. Wheeling around in the freshening breeze, they look otherworldly and pull my attention away from what lies in store beneath them.

Ireland's first nuclear power plant was planned for this same field back in the 1970s and I recall visiting the site whilst on a family holi-

The calm before Carnsore

day nearby. There were groups of protesters camped there, who with other less radical objectors of the day were successful in preventing nuclear development, but in the meantime the encampment became a tourist attraction. My abiding memory was seeing an almost naked, long-haired protester stroll by wearing a strategically placed leaf held in place by a leather thong. At first our eyes were on him, but then we swung our worried gaze towards my Mam, a religious and conservative woman. Her comment was priceless: 'That fella' must be freezing,' she quipped. We all erupted, thankful the situation had not upset her.

The fishermen's predictions are fairly accurate and the seas at the corner are rough, but nothing like what I had visualised. I turn *Murchú* through a sweeping 90 degree turn onto a westerly heading. The colour of sea and sky has changed from the earlier blue to the dull grey reflecting the steadily increasing clouds. I catch sight of darker clouds indicating the approaching frontal system out west. Kilmore Quay is 16 kilometres distant and it looks like I will have a headwind all the way. I slowly edge my way past the corner of Ireland as the Irish Sea disgorges into the Atlantic.

My kayak is bouncing over wave after wave keeping my concentration locked and focused. My muscles tighten as I absorb fully the effect of the wind. Further offshore, to my left, I spot a reef of sharp black rocks surrounded by waves and foam. Sheets of white spray are launching themselves into the air with every impact. I am not close enough to hear the noise generated, but the image speaks for itself. I force myself to concentrate as I move further from shore as Carnsore Point recedes behind. I am putting in my first kilometres on the Atlantic, and though buzzed, I am still breathing heavily. I tell myself that the maelstrom is not going to happen today and I talk myself down to a more relaxed state. Still, I am very conscious of my increasing remoteness. To dispel any unhelpful fears I turn my concentration to negotiating the expansive watery obstacle course I am tackling.

An hour past the corner a slight easing of conditions relieves my concern. I consider a stop before my destination which now resembles a toy village on the horizon. Things look far away for a long time when travelling by kayak. I land a few kilometres short of the quay for a break on the beach. I shelter behind a large, solitary boulder, basking in its lee. I munch on some nuts and a deliciously sweet Mars bar. I feel drawn to converse with this large inanimate object as I near my goal for the day. Firstly, I am so thankful for the shelter. It has taken hours to get from Carne to here and I am weary of the headwinds. It feels like I am indoors, such is the effectiveness of my stony friend. I cast my eyes across the sand to the sea, or the ocean, as it has now become. I am thankful for the relative reprieve it has dealt me today. I am on the Atlantic. The Atlantic feckin' ocean is just there, right beside me.

I am just short of St Patrick's bridge, a long thin reef stretching from just east of Kilmore towards the nearest of its two islands. The flows around these parts can create some unwelcome conditions, but luckily for me the tide is low enough that most of the reef is above the water. Now all I have to do is paddle around it. I can see Kilmore ahead but I cannot paddle directly towards it. Instead I have to head out to sea and make a long V-shaped dog-leg to get there. A short while later I glide into the harbour's perfect calm and see the fishing fleet tied to the pier as the lifeboat waits by the marina. The former looks well worn, the latter pristine with its blue hull and orange upper deck.

I land on the slip and grab my VHF radio to let Rosslare coast-guard know I am at my destination. I cannot raise them, so I instead transmit 'blind'. I do this hoping they can at least hear me. It is then I

With RNLI mechanic Brian Kehoe, aka Blondie

spot a fair-haired man hovering close by. He says he has heard my VHF transmissions and has relayed my message to Rosslare. He turns out to be a long-serving RNLI mechanic, Brian Kehoe, or Blondie, who has worked at the station for an incredible 48 years. After explaining my plans he offers the empty RNLI boathouse for my kayak. He is delighted to have a boat back inside the station, albeit a tiny one, and when I mention that I am fundraising for the RNLI and Medecins Sans Frontières he adds, 'sure it's only right so'.

My B&B behind the lifeboat station gives me a hearty welcome. Over piping hot tea and scones, May, the woman of the house, quizzes me about my trip. She recalls visits from previous circumnavigators and the concept of following in the footsteps of others resonates. Thanks to her fondness for the RNLI and in recognition of my fundraising efforts she offers me free accommodation, the sort of instant generosity that moves me. On a blustery September afternoon, I wander down to Kehoes pub by the harbour, ready for a massive plate of fish and chips. I fall into conversation with a couple sitting at the bar. He is a member of the local darts club and throws darts as we chat. To arrive into this cosy pub from the sea is a privilege I sense acutely.

Whilst recalling some of my tales to these regulars, I feel doubly welcome. How often do fishermen thank their lucky stars for being indoors after surviving horrendous weather offshore. I can relate as they quiz me on my exploits. I ask him for a match, claiming very limited darts ability. I swiftly beat him which leads to uproarious laughter from his partner, who claims, falsely, that I am out to hustle him. That idea is soon put to bed when my beginners' luck runs out. I lose the next four games and decide to retire. He generously comments that I would definitely beat him in a kayak race.

The following morning Kilmore's two nearby islands are the backdrop to my breakfast table. Lying within five kilometres, the Saltees resemble sentinels. Meaning 'Salt Islands' in Norse, they are the first substantial islands I have seen since Dalkey. I would dearly love to visit the bigger of the two, but today I am committed to heading west. I promise to return.

Comprising the Great and Little Saltee, the former became privately owned in 1943. Bought by Michael and Anne Neale, their descendants still maintain their house there. Crowning himself Prince Michael the First (Anne becoming its princess), it is unique among Ireland's islands in that it also has its own flag. This black and red pennant has seven stars each representing their children. Six of the stars are white, while a black one sadly represents a death at birth. The island is open to visitors on condition respect be shown to the large seabird colonies that share this island home. Fulfilling a promise to his mother, Michael had a throne erected high on the island. The inscription on it reads.

The Great Saltee with its own flag

This chair is erected in memory of my mother to whom I made a vow when I was ten years old that one day I would own the Saltee Islands and become the First Prince of the Saltees. Henceforth my heirs and successors can only proclaim themselves Prince of these Islands by sitting in this chair fully garbed in the robes and crown of the Islands and take the Oath of Succession – Michael the First.

With sister Mary

My planned return to Rosslare brings my sister Mary to the coast. She is keen to help out, hopefully grabbing a swim in the process. Like my other siblings, she is imbued with a great love of the sea though she lives in Laois, Ireland's only county bordered by counties without a coastline. We drive at a snail's pace out of Kilmore, marvelling at its collection of thatched cottages. Most of these immaculate nineteenth century homesteads are white as snow. The town's reputation as 'thatched cottage capital of Ireland' is appropriate. The trip across these country roads presents a chance to connect with my sister, as we head back to where I left my car yesterday. We detour, intent on taking a dip by Carne Pier. With *Murchú* safely stored further along the coast, I have only to make Mick's place and my mission is accomplished for the year.

Stage 6

ACROSS TRAMORE BAY TO
GARRARUS, WATERFORD

One month later, in mid-November, I am back in Kilmore. Lifeboatman Blondie puts a cup of tea in my hand for a guided tour of the station. Still on its trolley, *Murchú* looks lost in the cavernous boat shed. I am reluctant to leave as I am in such good company, preferring to linger and chat for a while longer. I finally tear myself away. It is reassuring that Blondie is so interested in my plans.

I wheel my gear to the harbour, carrying some trepidation for my imminent departure for the Hook. November is late in the year for heading out into the Atlantic solo. Care is warranted. The forecast is for a fresh northwesterly, an offshore wind, so I am keeping my fingers crossed it does not get too strong. In the meantime I must get some housekeeping done. Standing on the slipway, I turn on my VHF and relay my route to Rosslare Coastguard.

> *'This is Sea kayak Murchú, Echo, India, Uniform, Delta, Eight,*
> *out of Kilmore, bound for Sandeel Bay on the Hook peninsu-*
> *la. ETA c 4 pm. Will call you on arrival.'*

They confirm they received my call and kindly relay the weather forecast which tallies with the one I have. The coastguard service will get to know me well by the time I finally make it around Malin Head in North Donegal, but for now it's great to know that Blondie will also be listening in on my calls. He says he will monitor the radio 'all day'. Some people are amazingly generous.

Approaching Hook Head

I am feeling fit and with no excuses left I snap on my spray deck and put to sea. Out of the harbour's shelter, I turn west, and into the breeze. Soon passing the sadly named Forlorn Point, I begin a two hour paddle to the Keeraghs. These two nondescript islands resemble flattened cowpats. So low lying they remain unseen until I am only a few kilometres distant. They seem so benign and I find it hard to imagine an amazing rescue that took place here over a century ago.

In February 1914, a Norwegian barque, *The Mexico*, was driven onto these reefs in a storm. The Fethard Lifeboat was launched but was dashed onto the same rocks. Nine of its 14 crew perished. The remaining five joined the eight surviving Norwegian sailors miserably clinging to the rocks as the storm continued to rage. The Rosslare Lifeboat was then launched but was unable to come close enough to affect a rescue. Finally, two lifeboat men, Jim Wickham and Bill Duggan, used a small punt to ferry the survivors to safety. They carried out six trips transferring the survivors to the lifeboat. On the second of these sorties they were holed, but quickly plugged the rupture with a loaf of bread wrapped in oilskins. The two heroes of the day were honoured by the RNLI, the King of Norway and the Gaelic Athletic Association. The latter had gold medals struck for their bravery, unique in that organisation as never before, nor since, have GAA gold medals been awarded for an achievement other than on the field of sport.

I continue across Bannow Bay to the Hook. This five kilometre finger stretches across my path ending at the famous lighthouse out of view to my left. For today, I will be happy to land on its eastern side after a modest 23 kilometres paddling. I will be passing the famous

Landing on Sandeel Bay

Hook Lighthouse soon, on my last trip this year. Now, entering the peninsula's shelter, I notice conditions calm considerably.

To find a place to exit the water near my B&B, I turned to Google Earth. This amazing satellite imaging app reveals all sorts of nooks and crannies useful to the sea kayaker. I come across Sandeel Bay, complete with its tiny beach, access road and small slipway. I surmised I could easily land, wheel my kayak up the ramp, and continue the 1,500 metres to my accommodation.

I beach *Murchú* on the flat sand of Sandeel Bay and discover that my careful planning holds a hidden flaw. There is an embankment of rocks piled high between the small beach and the slip. Well-worn and rounded, some as big as medicine balls, it was not visible on the satellite shots. I stare at the unusual obstacle in disbelief. I need to examine this situation carefully. The last time I got involved with a rock I came away with a head wound. I could easily sprain an ankle here. I need to come up with a plan.

I decide to unpack all the kit from the boat and, piece by piece, carry it over the boulders to the slipway. Then, manoeuvring the emptied *Murchú* across the mound, I lift its tail moving it in a giant arc and place it back down. I then move to the nose and do the same. Akin to repositioning a large pole one end at a time, I manage to walk my kayak to the slipway without ever lifting it completely. After twenty minutes I

51

am well chuffed to have the obstacle astern, and begin wheeling my trusty steed along the back roads of the Hook to my accommodation.

My bed for the night is 1,500 metres away, so I am happy to get moving after all the time spent delicately dealing with the rock challenge. With a November evening approaching I am starting to feel the chill. There is a half hour walk ahead of me, according to my Google Earth measurements. Although I am on dry land, I am buoyant. Five hundred metres in and I come to the junction which should allow me to track directly towards my destination. I look in disbelief as a set of gates are locked to each other blocking the way. Despite the satellite showing a public road, only a laneway across farmland exists. I end up diverting and clocking my longest trolley commute of two and a half kilometres.

A retired English couple is kindly reopening their B&B to accommodate me. I am their last guest of the season. As they swing their car into their driveway, minutes after my arrival, they bombard me with questions. My answers seem to plunge them into a state of bewilderment, and I find myself almost apologising. The first question is where is my car. When they learn it is in Kilmore Quay, they are visibly puzzled and ask how I got here. When I tell them I kayaked across to Sandeel Bay, they continue the interrogation. In their final attempt to piece together my arrival at their door, they ask how I got from Sandeel Bay to their house. I sheepishly point to my trolley, something they seem unwilling or unable to believe, reminding me that it is almost two miles away.

My host is a retired London bobby and his wife, an ex-teacher, both keen to sell up and move back to the UK. They want to be near their children, but unfortunately are having trouble finding a buyer. It is a strange experience not being able to connect more closely with these folk. I normally manage to find some common ground, but today I feel we are on different planets. I opt to remain civil which is never a bad option. He kindly drops me to the local Templar Inn, where I feast on a seafood dinner, choosing afterwards to experience the Hook by night. I amble home under a black canopy pierced by what seems to me an endless number of stars. Out to the west a constellation of orange light reveals Dunmore East. A more distant Tramore group is visible too.

Hook Head B&B

I love these moments. I am enjoying the privilege of just being here, and that muscle and will power have gotten me this far. The successful completion of this project is not a foregone conclusion, and I am only too aware that I am stretching myself to attempt it. This mission has become a type of reckoning. It feels like my life's learning is on trial. Despite my fears and misgivings, so far it is going pretty well. As I saunter home, I am owning my achievement and allowing my self-belief to grow. No one else is here, I am totally alone under the night sky, but I am involved in the critical job of bolstering my own essence. By the time I make it back to my B&B, I know I am giving myself every chance of making this dream a reality.

Over breakfast the next morning I ask about leaving my kayak there for the week, which I had mentioned when booking. Unfortunately, as his shed measures only 16 feet, he says it would be impossible. I tell him it does not need to be under cover; in fact, behind his hedge would be grand. As I deposit *Murchú* among the shrubbery his astonishment is rekindled by my nonchalance. He suggests my boat must not be worth much and when he learns it cost over €3,000 my fate is sealed. He realises they have been host to a real basket case. I am completely beyond saving.

A WEEK LATER, I AM DRIVING SOUTH on the N11 and hear the ice warning on the radio. It is dark and cold, and thanks to an early start I am hoping to be afloat by 9:30 am. This is driven by the reduced daylight which makes today's mission a shoe-horning operation. Needs must. I drive into the B&B and am heartened by the sight of *Murchú*. It always lifts my spirits. Like seeing a familiar face, I hoist it on the roof rack and begin tying on, ready for the short trip to Sandeel Bay. I decide not to wake my previous weekend's hosts and load up as quietly as possible. As I do this I begin to have a sense of someone nearby. Turning around to investigate, I jump. My host has silently walked up on me and is now standing directly behind me. Not saying a word he silently observes the operation.

'Crikey,' I exclaim.

'I never heard you arrive.'

I reckon he must have made the perfect bobby, soundlessly sidling into a situation purely to observe. Anyway, he is visibly relieved that my kayak has lasted the week, and wishes me well for my journey. He promises to observe my progress across Waterford harbour later that morning. I make a promise to call him when I arrive, and finally put an end to his worrying about me, a slightly deranged transient winter visitor.

Winter is a tricky time to find reasonable weather for longer sea trips. This is particularly true for the Atlantic seaboard. With depressions tracking in from the ocean, less daylight and cold temperatures, windows of opportunity narrow considerably. Sometimes these windows are bolted shut. Depressions carry with them lots of baggage. High winds, heavy rain and big waves, essential ingredients for creating amazing sights along our coasts every year but far from ideal for the journeying kayaker. Storms do their dirty work far out at sea, whipping up great undulations onto the ocean's surface, which then travel unfettered until they reach the shallower waters along our shores. Storms often change direction, leaving their progeny alone to head towards the coast. Ocean waves, travelling at a paltry ten miles every hour, take roughly four days to cover about 1,000 miles, so a storm could be over by the time its waves reach land. This characteristic often explains the mysterious arrival of big swells on perfectly calm days, the days surfers dream of.

Hoisted by my goal to reach Mick's local beach at Gararrus before year's end, the weather forecasts have been examined closely by us both. He suggests the smallest window between two weather systems presents a gap I can use. Huge swells have been battering this coast for days but a small reprieve is expected. He also warns me not to dally. Forecasts, although sequentially accurate, often follow their own time-line. Anyway, there is a gap between two transatlantic depressions and I am going to try to squeeze into it.

I arrive at Sandeel Bay under a bright blue sky. I am readying myself for a reversal of last week's boulder crossing episode, but that is not the case today. The tide is high, and the embankment of boulders and the beach itself are almost completely underwater. In fact almost everything is. Small swells tumble across sharp rocks poking through the surface. There appears to be no suitable area to launch from. Fully loaded, my boat is too heavy to lift alone so I am forced to find a spot to position it, ferry all my kit across, pack it fully, and go. Normally, this is done from a slipway or a beach, but today neither option is available. I need to find a way.

With the tiny cove almost full of water, it is not apparent where I can carry out these tasks. Future circumnavigators take note: at this stage I am getting used to expecting the unexpected. One part of me smiles, while another part winces. After several minutes examining my predicament I spot something by the cliff. There is the smallest patch of sand there, occasionally washed over by a shallow spill of foam. Like eyeing prey, I give it my undivided attention for several minutes, and whilst not ideal, it presents a chance. I jump into action and, fortunately, twenty minutes later I am afloat, thankfully still pretty much on schedule.

Quitting last week's paddle on the sheltered eastern side of the Hook now becomes ideal. Benign conditions allow me to settle back into a rhythm after a week-long break. I head south along the Hook peninsula in order to circumvent it. Along the way the blue sea is edged by a ribbon of dark rocks. Behind these, tan coloured earthen embankments rise to field level as light zephyrs intermittently spoil the sea's slickness. After a half hour I pull into the small harbour at Slade and am immediately immersed into the shadow cast by its large castle. Of Anglo-Norman origin, it was built in the late 1400s by the Laffin family, one of the original settlers after the invasion of 1169. A recent restoration makes it an unexpected gem on my travels. I briefly explore it while munching on a few biscuits.

I push out of Slade, tickled to have visited a place that shares its name with a band I loved during my teens. Passing the Hook Light is another major milestone on my long paddle. Seeing it for the first time from the sea I admire its prime location as a marker beacon. It was built at the request of Strongbow's son-in-law, William Marshall, then earl of Pembroke, who had established a port at New Ross, 30 kilometres upriver. He wanted to guarantee safe passage for arriving ships. The squat, black and white tower stands four stories high and has walls four metres thick. Thanks to these dimensions it has withstood the test of time since its construction in the 1200s, though tradition states that fires were lit here since the fifth century by local monks. It claims to be the oldest operational lighthouse in the world, and is referred to in guide books as the Granddaddy of all Lighthouses.

With my attention magnetically drawn to this mediaeval marvel, I notice my perspective changing. This naturally occurs as I pass by various features along the coast, causing a lateral or sideways change. Now, however, my perspective is being changed along the vertical axis. I am being elevated and dropped several metres, fairground style, by the remnants of a large swell sweeping under me. This disturbance was nowhere to be seen until rounding the headland and even now is hard to pinpoint as the surface remains completely slick in the calm air. The swells end their journey by slamming into the nearby rocky coastline. The walloping thuds as they spill themselves onto the shore contradicts the brilliant sunshine and windless conditions. I admit to being a bit wary of the whole affair and glance to my left to spot any larger ones heading my way.

I round the Hook and strike off across the wide mouth of Waterford harbour towards the cliff shore opposite. Just inside the estuary sits the quaint fishing village of Dunmore East, which sadly is not part of today's plans. I am heading out into open water to reunite with the opposite shore, its base whitened with breaking waves. My plan is to stop roughly halfway along these cliffs at Rathmoylan Cove to feed and have a stretch. Mick's voice resonates in my head as his local knowledge starts to come to life with the passing coastline. As I near the cove I notice some sentinel reefs banging away outside the entrance. They are not unexpected so I manoeuvre well clear. My initial concern is short-lived as I manoeuvre around a protruding flat slab of rock to a side entrance of sorts leading to a narrow perfectly sheltered red sandy beach. As I hoist myself from sitting and step onto the flat ochre sand,

Big swells passing the Hook

I realise it is my first footfall in County Waterford, as well as leaving Leinster for a new province, Munster.

Fed, watered and stretched, I continue under Brownstown Head at the eastern extremity of Tramore Bay which I am about to cross. Easily mistaken for Hook Head, sailing ships sometimes turned here believing they were entering Waterford Harbour. In the early 1800s when a convoy of three ships were wrecked with the loss of over 500 lives, Trinity House, the UK's administrative centre for lighthouses, decided to build two towers on this headland to avoid confusion. On the next headland west, marking the opposite side of the bay, they built another three. As I crossed Tramore Bay within sight of these five structures, I pondered the terrified eyes that would have peered at these previously unmarked headlands during stormy weather wondering how they had missed Waterford Harbour.

I cross the bay and notice the forecasted offshore winds are freshening. Because *Murchú* is designed for speed it sports a knife-like bow. This feature, though narrow, has a large surface area not unlike the blunt end of a butter knife. She cuts through the water in much the same way. With the wind now blowing across my bows I am being nudged off course and use my rudder to keep the three towers directly ahead. Today is my first experience of an offshore breeze (one that blows out to sea) in my new craft, so I observe closely how she behaves. The wind is not too strong, around ten knots, so I have no worries. Should it double in strength things would become interesting. Without needing to look over my left shoulder, I know the next stop could be Cornwall or France.

These might seem like fanciful musings, but when faced with hours at sea, alone, an element that must be handled is what is going on upstairs. Thoughts arrive, unbidden, into my mind, demand attention, and then pass. Of course, my brain is primarily focused on the job at hand, but along the way there is room for unfettered neural activity. Long-distance kayaking comprises hours and hours clocking up the kilometres. For me, once I had settled into my metronomic rhythm, addressing my own thoughts and having a full internal discussion about them becomes a necessity. The irony of the situation is that once I am any distance offshore I cannot really go anywhere else. Many personal issues can be reflected on whilst offshore – one of them being whether I should in fact 'be offshore' – but as a solo paddler, stopping out at sea is not really an option. I am out here, alone, and simply must deal with whatever thoughts arrive.

Safely across Tramore Bay I pass under three white towers standing at the cliff edge. The iron Metal Man figure stands on top of the central pillar. This is a cast iron statue of a British sailor pointing out to sea warning ships of the hazards hereabouts. Clad in a blue jacket and white pants, he is continuing the job he was tasked with two hundred years earlier. His garb, lovingly painted to this day, shows him in the then typical British sailors outfit. Being here, under these structures, I am near Mick's home patch. What presents ahead is a maze of rocky spikes, islets and broken coastline which would be a serious challenge in a decent swell. Luckily for me, these are continuing to drop. On the other hand, the wind seems to be funnelling strangely between gaps higher up in the cliffs. Slamming down into the sea with unexpected gusts, it almost catches me off guard, especially since my grip is looser now after crossing the bay. Thinking I was home and dry with only 500 metres to go I instantly berate myself. Just like a car journey, it is not over until you are safely in your driveway. I keep *Murchú* heading west until I weather this small event, finally landing onto Garrarus Beach amid great relief.

So, at 2.15 pm on 24 November, I bring my first year's instalment of my circumnavigation to a successful conclusion. Despite having to drag my laden trolley through the deep fluffy sand towards the slip I notice I am beaming. I take a moment and look further west at the next stretch along the Copper Coast. It whets my appetite nicely, but that is for another year. The steep road out has my legs working overtime, a most pleasing experience after nearly five hours stuffed into my boat. A middle aged couple is walking towards me and I notice they are discussing the sight I present before them. Grinning widely, he comments: 'Sure, you're going the wrong way, the sea is behind you'. We erupt into peals of laughter, each going our separate way.

I EVENTUALLY END UP AT MICK'S PLACE, via a short stop at one of his friends who lives nearer the beach. I am there just long enough to partake in one of my favourite post-paddling pastimes, eating fresh sambos whilst downing hot tea. Mick arrives and he is abuzz, us chatting like long lost friends. Despite talking only yesterday, I feel more than a day has passed since. We drive to his house and he reveals how delighted he is that I am off the ocean. The next depression is a stinker and is charging in. Today's window was narrow. Knowing Mick is enough for me to register the truth in what he says. I make a mental note.

I meet Una, his wife, and their three children and more food is offered which I unapologetically hoover up and chat for as long as I can. Sadly, time calls, and I need to head to Sandeel Bay where my car is waiting. We transplant our conversation to his car as we begin the commute. This entails a quaint ferry crossing from Passage East to Ballyhack. This is where Waterford harbour morphs into a 500 metre wide tidal river. The water is black as it heads towards the

End of Year One at Garrarus Beach, County Waterford

ocean. Dark branches dangle into the inky flow and the steep fields on either side wrap around us. This flooded valley soon narrows and continues inland, flanked by steep slopes of green. I imagine the joy of mariners, having made it safely around the Hook, being suddenly immersed into this lush countryside bound for the inland ports of New Ross or Waterford.

Driving home on the M11 later that evening, with ice warnings broadcast for a second day, I breathe a huge sigh of relief to have reached my goal for 2017. 'Just start', was what Mark had said to me not long before he died last year. As a result of heeding his advice, I am a happy man driving home, mission accomplished for year one. The spring will roll around soon enough, and in the meantime I am just going to enjoy my achievements to date. I turn up the volume on 'Shine On You Crazy Diamond' from Pink Floyd's greatest hits, glide over the M11's smooth blackness sipping hot coffee and am struck by a powerful realisation. I am absolutely content.

With legendary Mick O'Meara and his daughter Eimear-Rose

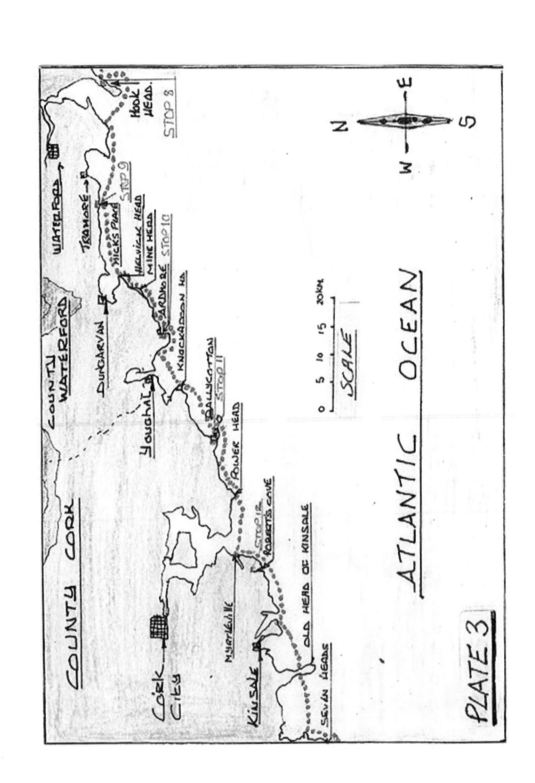

PLATE 3

Stage 7

SERIOUS BUSINESS, ROUND TWO

It is April 2018, three months after my Mam passed away. She had been succumbing to dementia for years and we reluctantly moved her into Beechwood nursing home near Carlow. To say she blossomed there is an understatement. She loved singing and praying, and having a laugh, all enjoyed in abundance in her new home. Our reluctance to move her turned out to be unfounded. Although somewhat incapacitated, she thankfully never failed to recognize us, greeting us with unbridled excitement each time we visited. It was a privilege for me, and my brother Michael, to hold her hands as she breathed her last. Thankfully, she suffered little, having contracted an illness only days before. Her warm, gentle nature will be sorely missed.

When I eventually return to Mick's place that April, Mam is embedded in my heart. Similar to the impact of Mark's death at the start of my trip, I find myself buoyed by the privilege of being alive and continuing my coastal odyssey. After Mick's kind offer of a bed for the night I am only a stone's throw from my put-in. I am treated like family for breakfast as his three kids lap up the novelty of a guest on a school day. I down my Sturgeon tablets, and after the scholars depart Una ferries me to the beach and shortly thereafter I am afloat again.

It is a delicious feeling, and thanks to various pep talks over the winter I aim to tackle bigger chunks from now on, with longer distances and more consecutive days on the water. I have three days paddling ahead of me, which should put me deep into County Cork. I am excited to apply another county decal onto *Murchú's* foredeck. Wicklow, Wexford and Waterford are in need of a new companion. Today's goal is Ardmore, where Ronan O'Connor's promise of accommodation in his outdoor adventure centre awaits. This is my last stop in Waterford and, at 43 kilometres, will be my first time exceeding a Marathon distance. It will also be my longest daily paddle to date.

The landmass of southwest Ireland has mountains and headlands oriented in an east-west direction. The long, half submerged finger-like peninsulas of Cork and Kerry are perfect examples of this. My west bound journey on the southern seaboard is punctuated by headlands hooked back against my track, leaving sheltered, east-facing bays. When seen on the map they resemble barbs on a hook. Helvick, Ardmore, Knockadoon and Ballycotton are amazingly similar geographically, which no doubt caused confusion amongst early mariners.

After a four month winter break, *Murchú* and I are back on the sea road. Winds are light and the coastline is friendly. To me this means I have places to land should I need to. The weather is benign, a gift I have patiently waited for. The first stretch of coast I am passing is the Copper Coast. Ireland's first UNESCO Global Geopark, this 25 kilometres long, coastal park reflects the copper mining that took place here in the 1800s and the unique geological importance of the area, to quote its website. Whatever its history, it has character in spades.

I have been lucky enough to have had an aerial view of this stretch of coastline while flying into and out of Cork airport. From sea level the steep coastline leans back from the ocean looking less ominous than the vertical escarpments of our western seaboard. With the height of the cliff edge never going much above 100 feet it is not so overpowering and its appearance pleases my eye. The nearby rocks, blackened by the sea, morph into limestone grey above the reach of the tide. Stacked above these and marching up the cliff, is a sun blushed tan that continues to the flat top where a fringe of green grass appears. The whole scene resembles a stout rock-cake.

Great sea arches reveal the unending process of sea erosion greedily eating away at softer pieces of land. It patiently bores into solid rock creating spectacular openings. Birds avail of this unspoilt and irregular real estate. The angelic kittiwake settles here while the pied colours of the guillemot populate the tiniest of ledges. Scatterings of gulls like a collection of white rags hang about menacingly, ready to pounce on any morsel that may be on offer. My neck is strained admiring the wonders of this cupric coastline, so much so that I almost forget I am sitting in a kayak on my marathon mission until my course shunts me offshore and my focus returns.

One of the challenges of sea kayaking is the combination of long distances and slow pace. With modern sea kayaks travelling a paltry five to nine kilometres per hour, patience is called for. While involved in this mode of travel, just above a fast walking pace, one's attitude to time must change. To properly adjust I need to suspend my eagerness to get the job done quickly, relax into the moment by moment experience, and take in the sights. Distractions in the form of coastal features or nearby islands prevent me from checking my watch too much. What luck today to have the Copper Coast to accompany me for the first few hours of my resumed odyssey.

My progress along this coastline has me generally heading just south of west, dropping slowly down the latitudes. Baltimore in West Cork is my next big turn, where I will be swinging north along our western seaboard. I am making a beeline for Helvick Head, lying 25 kilometres southwest. This way-stop is further than many of my previous daily distances. I am setting a good marker for myself. The sea is concrete grey and the water murky. Herring gulls, scavengers of the seas, are careering about, curious about this passerby. Cradled by the ocean, I am elated to be moving so early in the year. Last season's accumulated efforts, while heartening, fell way short on what I plan for this year. With 250 kilometres of the overall 1,750 kilometres covered, I have to triple both this and next year's instalments to make my deadline. I have given myself 1,000 days to complete the mission, which means I have to make serious inroads up the west coast this year.

I land at a swimmers' cove beside the entrance to Helvick Bay. With four hours paddling done my arms ache pleasantly and my stomach demands a feed. The throb of a dull headache distracts me as I retrieve a bag of snacks from my boat. The rock-lined opening resembles a naturally occurring squash court which faces east, providing shelter from most weather. With a tiny islet within 50 metres, it is a popular snorkelling spot, in no small part due to the caves, hollows and openings that perforate the rocks here. Helvick is another Norse moniker, meaning holy, or safe, bay. Yet again, I am thrown into visualising those Nordic seafarers. I clamber over flat stones and sit at the back of the dark cove hoping the pulsing in my skull will subside. I look back over the coastline just travelled and am chuffed at the distance already covered.

The next stretch, around Mine Head, will be more of a challenge. With no get-out on offer, I am committed to 17 kilometres of continuous paddling, come what may. Kayaking at the base of vertical hundred foot cliffs throughout, I will have to stay well focused. I am not one of those sea kayakers who can spend endless hours at sea, allowing them to cover greater distances if needed. I need to stop at regular intervals; like a first generation electric car, I am in need of constant recharging. Any long stretches, like this one, require careful planning and a strong mind. Unfortunately, the latter is suffering from the continued throbbing in my head. I know a challenge awaits me as I strike off cautiously, hoping for the best.

Mine Head has a squat lighthouse marking a 90 degree corner in the coastline. Striking south out of Helvick I approach the sentinel, ready to turn west again. Thanks to the thinning cloud, the sea sports a silvery coat and an air of cautious optimism pervades. The headland, earlier blocking the view ahead, now uncovers a grand vista and an air of expectancy fills me. What unfolds is a picture postcard array of jutting cliff edges standing stoutly against the ocean. Like the bows of a fleet of outsize ships the folds in the cliff stretch off into the hazy distance. The first half of my day was a dawdle compared to this. Mine Head has been sheltering me from these ocean delights.

I move along the rugged coastline admiring the swell's interaction with the cliffs. My head seems heavier with each passing hour so I welcome the distraction. It's a different day out here and the sea is dancing energetically. The surface of the ocean is electric, like a living creature trying to shake off an unwelcome guest. Maybe that is what I am, a rodeo rider at a fairground bucking bronco ride. Neptune has his hand on the controls and all I can do is react to his every move. The place is abuzz with movement as sea-birds cavort above. Slow progress eats into my optimism as I concentrate on tightening my grip to avoid any sloppiness. I plod on, my knife-like bow cleaving through the moving water. Mimicking a rock fragment, my horizontal fibreglass shard stretches out in front of me. This oscillating wedge of green has been my view since day one, and now it begins a wild dance in front of me. Like a three metre beak, its every rise and fall remains in my orbit as we cut our way through the ocean.

Taking a break in Helvick

Resembling the metronomic arm of an oil rig, it is hypnotising. Occasionally I am glued to its rhythmic bounding and find it difficult to tear myself away. Akin to the terrifying feeling of almost nodding off whilst driving, I know I must resist these temptations. My heavy mind is compromised and it is becoming harder to concentrate. Though the waves are not big, the sea is confused and the boat's movement giddy. Worryingly, the confusion is seeping into me too. Rebounded waves are spoiling any regular pattern to the swells so the whole business is becoming demanding. Knowing these conditions may continue for many kilometres, I force myself to stay focused. My mouth is dry and occasional flicks of sea water sting my eyes.

I finally admit to myself that I am descending into a difficult place. My old nemesis – seasickness – has reared its ugly head. Not even halfway through this stretch, I find myself in a vast area of clapotis. As previously mentioned, this occurs off steep cliffs when a swell is running and reflected waves interact in a haphazard fashion. It is one of the most difficult conditions to negotiate by kayak. It robs the opportunity to settle into any rhythm because there is no pattern or shape to what is happening. Hollows, troughs, spikes and tumbling areas of water surround the boat as if the sea is having an epileptic fit. Feeling nauseous here is far from ideal, and such is my limited perspective I cannot see how far it extends. I am being unceremoniously evicted from my comfort zone. Where can I go? I have only six of the 17 kilometres to Ardmore done, with cliffs to my right and the vast ocean to my left. I am out of options. My years of stubbornness need to be drawn on to win this fight. It dawns on me that this is a make-or-break day. What a way to start my year's paddling.

I have taken my seasickness tablets, gulped down some Solpadene, and still find myself between a rock and a hard place. Bit by bit, my resolve is being undermined. My gnawing uneasiness creeping into every fibre has me wanting to curl into the foetal position, pull the covers over my head and disappear. It is bonkers to be thinking like this, but out here on the edge, unexpected thoughts can arise. I dangerously ponder failure with some unfettered self-talk.

'Crikey, Kev, stay with the game, don't drift away.'

'Stay focused.'

'I know you weren't expecting this, but it's real.'

'What happens if I capsize?'

'Will my roll work now that I'm a bit dizzy?'

'What happens if I end up out of my kayak?'

'I've no exit at the base of these cliffs, and the open sea isn't much better.'

'Will the coast guard receive my distress call?'

'Will these cliffs block my VHF signal?'

I know what I have to do but it is becoming increasingly difficult to do it. I hear the voice of my instructor, Benny, whispering in my brain, 'Break it down, break it down.' It is a new thought, so I grant it attention. It is telling me I should be aiming at smaller goals. I focus almost a half kilometre ahead to a black shard of rock spiking through the surface, surrounded with a necklace of foam. Perhaps this offers me an opportunity. Watching the spume flying into the air as it stands stubbornly against the incoming waves, my whole world is now consumed with reaching it. A scattering of smaller shards protrude nearby. It is no wonder a lighthouse stands high overhead to warn of these dangers. I start to create a mental map of my surroundings, planning a course through this nasty rock garden. I formulate a plan to reach this witch's hat and take it from there. I continue to nudge along at a snail's pace. My head drops as this new task is overtaken under the unrelenting snowball effect of my malady. I find myself locking eyes on *Murchú's* green deck instead of the ocean. The debilitating force is powerful and wrestles me with its grip. I am banging my very sore head against an invisible brick wall. It is hurting. My body begins to shake, I begin shivering, as my mind and body plead with me to stop what I am doing.

Going around in mental circles I am struck by the loneliness of my experience. The cliff looks more menacing than when I first saw it, and the black daggers sticking out of the water resemble weapons of war. Strangely, a new element arrives on the scene, at first almost imperceptibly. It comes as soundwaves pulse in my eardrums. It starts to seep into my sore brain. It starts to affect the thoughts of my tortured mind, and if nothing else, it is a welcome distraction. It keeps coming. I begin to respond positively. On and on it chirps away, like a familiar bird singing a song of comfort outside the window of my mind. Unbelievably, my mood lifts slightly. My burden lessens, as the edge is taken off my dulled existence. These sounds are ambrosia for my bruised mind. I soak them up greedily.

The sounds that are helping me come from a source I never anticipated. The vibrations now oscillating my eardrums have origins very close. What has started to give me some reprieve is, miraculously, my own voice. With nowhere else to turn, words of encouragement are tumbling out of my mouth and filling the air around me. I have brought an extra element to my dilemma. So beneath these cliffs, in this cursed clapotis, suffering seasickness, and with an incredible desire just to run away, I am rising to full volume. As my own number one fan, I am encouraging myself to persevere, and as I let go, my egotistical exclamations run riot. The only potential listeners are the seabirds, who are oblivious, and maybe some cliff-top walkers who would barely make out my cries. I care not. I am going to roar myself through this test. I feel an amazing bond with myself. A Mobius strip of self-love swirls through me and offers just enough purchase that reaching that bloody spike seems possible.

It works. I eventually reach the spike and am heartened. But this is only a transient event and not the finish line. I need another waymark. A slice of cliff will act as my next goal, an unusual bulge in the rocks, another, then it is a turn in the coastline, then a reef, and on and on. This stepping-stone approach inches me along the jagged shoreline. I am clawing my way west as my quest continues. I am hanging by a thread. I continue, doggedly. Almost imperceptibly at first, I spot a beach. A beach translates as a place to land. Jesus, a beach will do just nicely. It is still a long way off and three kilometres short of Ardmore, but it is solid ground where I can settle for a bit. So keen am I to land that on approach I am caught by a wave and unceremoniously dumped onto the hard sand. It is not pretty, but I am long past caring. I scramble dizzily onto my feet pulling my boat clear of the impact zone. *Terra firma* for me is akin to jumping into a warm bed. It is intoxicating. I sit on a log unable or unwilling to get anything from my boat. I am shaking after the experience. I cannot fully reflect on things yet. That will all happen later after I have reached tonight's base. For now, I am luxuriating on solid ground and it is delightful.

After a welcome half hour break, reluctantly, I put to sea again, breaking through the nasty line of surf and turn for home. After an accumulated 43 kilometres of paddling, I land at Ardmore. I am like a limping, Second World War bomber pilot after a tough sortie. I am sore, tired and, most of all, concerned. My host, Ronan, clad in his shorts despite it being a chilly April evening, strides across the beach to help me with my kit. I gladly let him install me into his beachside centre for the night. We strike up a conversation as I struggle to mask my unease after my day on the ocean. I am raw, psychologically and physically, and, unbelievably, close to tears. Being alone at sea is a challenge, but right now being with anyone else is equally demanding. I need to get dry, grub up and seriously consider my predicament, alone. Thankfully, Ronan has a pressing engagement and, wishing me luck, departs.

Later, when fed and watered, I settle with a cuppa in the chilly centre to write my short blog on Facebook. Surrounded by pictures and posters of great exploits, I reflect on my own still thrumming through my bones. Several of my friends post comments which provide a welcome boost to my dented morale. Today's blog withholds the exact details of my struggle in case it invites too much concern. I share the achievement of my first marathon distance bagged on my odyssey, and a brief mention of the challenge under the cliffs. If I honestly describe what the day involved I fear it would add another obstacle to overcome. Naysayers can have a very debilitating influence on a risky endeavour and I am not for giving anyone a handle in that regard. My mission, a long held dream, is becoming the focal point of a commitment the likes of which I have never experienced before. After so many successful days since Skerries, today has caught me off guard. Perhaps it was my four month lay-off, and the subsequent loss of my sea legs, or maybe the first four hour segment without a shore break? Who knows? I am left puzzling over this while pulling my sleeping bag tight to keep out the chilly April night. To the sound of breaking waves nearby, I settle into a broken and fitful sleep.

Stage 8

TACKLING DEMONS:
ARDMORE TO ROBERT'S COVE

At this point you may wonder what kind of masochistic madness this is, and to a certain extent it is a fair question. My response to this is simple, though not necessarily easy to relate to. Any great endeavour worth attempting brings with it myriad challenges. Akin to entering battle where the enemy may attack on any front, it is a real test of character. To succeed, each setback must be overcome. I am fortunate, thus far, to have scraped by, albeit in a compromised state. Seasickness has been the *bête noire* of the trip, and I would do almost anything to swap it for something else. Give me fatigue, bigger seas, or aches and pains and I would find a way through. But fate has hand-picked this particular stumbling block for me to negotiate. No amount of denial will change it. I consign yesterday's low point as an aberration, and am setting out this morning with a pep in my step. It is indeed a new day.

I wander up to the local grocers as the town stirs. A few locals ahead of me are happily sharing gossip with the check-out assistant. Dark trees above the town sway in a light morning breeze as cackling jackdaws and rooks mill around in loose formations. Who knows the lives I am intersecting with. I am a happy voyeur, struck by the gentle pace of things. I am soaking up the contact after my previous evening spent mostly alone. Even though I made it to the pub, it was a sleepy affair. Mid-week in April is far from the high season.

After a high carb breakfast of noodles and sambos I ready myself for the short stroll across the road to the beach. I am cocooned into a drysuit again today, essentially a waterproof full-body affair, ideal for winter kayaking. Resembling a loose fitting space suit with tight neck and wrist seals plus waterproof socks, it allows me to wear dry clothes underneath. If the seals hold, I will re-emerge dry when I reach Ballycotton. Unfortunately, whilst enthusiastically pulling the zip across my shoulders, it jams. It will neither open nor close and, despite my Houdini-like efforts, I am trapped. The day's schedule, which has been worked out carefully, is now under threat so I feel a sense of urgency.

I scan the empty street outside. The many closed doors taunt me. I must find some help. I spot two older women clutching shopping bags and ambling, full of chatter, towards the grocers. They are my quarry. I make a beeline for them, quickly explaining my predicament, and wondering would they be so kind to zip me up. Immediately their eyes light up, both launching into peals of laughter. Their infectious chuckling washes over me and I am swept along with their merriment. After much tugging and grunting, I am properly zipped and sealed for the day. With their mission accomplished, these two ladies continue up the street not knowing the positive effect they have had on me. I grip the toggle on my kayak's bow and wheel it across the empty road to the beach. We are a team again, *Murchú* and me. The distinct odour of seaweed and salt blows from the beach into my nostrils. A few gulls are scattered about the beach. Like me, they must be wondering what delights are in store for them today.

Ardmore is situated where a long beach meets a jutting headland at 90 degrees, essentially the town being tucked into a corner. I sit *Murchú* on the beach, hop in, and thanks to being on schedule, wait. The tide is rising so I allow myself the small luxury of letting it decide when to float me. This feels decadent, but I indulge myself. The white noise from the small breaking waves spills towards me. I passionately put out the wish that today will be a better day. Generally, I do this a lot, but today I am seriously invested in it happening. At only 30 kilometres, and with more get-outs on offer, I am optimistic.

Eventually, in fits and starts, *Murchú* begins to lift off the sand, and finally I am away. I paddle parallel to this rocky strip of land staring up at the undulating ribbon of houses above, imagining the great vista they command. The famous cliff house hotel peers down, its angular square face framed by trees.

It was in these waters that I successfully qualified as a sea kayak instructor. Over a full weekend of assessments, my ability to perform and teach various strokes, rescues and manoeuvres were put under the microscope by two highly experienced examiners. As a natural show off, this suited my personality and skill level perfectly. Part of the evaluation had some local volunteers gather for us to instruct. I remember thinking how odd it must have been for these individuals being taught how to kayak whilst *their instructors* were under test. After developing a great rapport from the get-go, I specifically remember having a great laugh with them. It was the only time I have laughed, appropriately, during an exam. One of the examiners back then was Mick O'Meara. Recalling the memory of that weekend's success bolsters me further. The day is only beginning and my positivity is getting a welcome boost.

I punch through the surf breaking along the headland. A few of the bigger waves sting as they smack into my face. The salty water drips from my cap as I spot familiar landmarks as memories come back in a flash. A domed piece of rock the size of a small truck jogs various images in my mind. The sky is broken and the glinting sun throws silver onto the moving ocean. I round the headland and spot the rusting remains of the *Samson*, a crane barge shipwrecked here in 1987. Like an ochre brown electricity pylon, its top half angled away from the vertical, it is jammed tight to the base of the cliffs. She was under tow from Liverpool for Malta when gales hit her off Wales, and despite several attempts to reattach the line it was finally abandoned to its fate. She remains trapped here, decaying slowly every year, a waymark along this much visited coastline. As I pass her remains, I am reminded of the power of the ocean.

Leaving the *Samson* astern I continue to a remote beach for a stop-off. Little over an hour has elapsed and a clean swell is running which allows me to catch a wave directly ashore. No getting caught off-guard like last evening. The seawater is a vivid green and uncannily clear. The waves seem brighter today and I wonder with the positive mood I am enjoying if my eyes are influencing the messages to my brain. I land into a tired rural scene which contradicts my mood. An unkempt bungalow is surrounded by rusting farm machinery. A few fibreglass boats in various states of disrepair lie scattered about. Broken barbed wire fences take away any beauty that might salvage this place. I try to make sense of what I see. Some plastic toys strewn about suggest that maybe a young family grew up here. I visualise them running down the slope to play in the summer sea then hurrying home for a hearty supper afterwards. Their shrieking voices play in my mind as they splash in and out of the chilly waters.

I scan the sweep of this semicircular bay towards Knockadoon head, and the port of Youghal far off to my right. I am considering making a 10 kilometre beeline across the bight, depositing me nicely into County Cork for the first time. The northeast wind, now at my back, is goading me to do it. It will be a classic downwinder, I reckon. *Murchú* is specifically designed for these conditions and I am thinking it is a good opportunity to let it rip. I feed, settle myself, and strike off on a diametrical track. The helpful wavelets push my seven kilometres an hour up to a dizzying ten. I always enjoyed the adrenalin buzz of high speed kayaking, usually on whitewater rapids or careering down surf waves, but now, running before this fresh breeze is urgent and addictive. I am grinning from ear to ear.

Initially the waves are small, growing in size as I leave the shelter of the beach heading into the centre of the bay. I am thrumming forward with less effort and more speed. As I approach halfway I notice a strange shape ahead. It seems like a squat building with a flagpole attached. I am puzzled and with hurried glances, interrogate my deck mounted chart for any sign of a small island or lighthouse. Save a couple of port-entry marks, my path should be clear. I continue my supercharged run across, hoping the mystery object will explain itself. The waves on either side tumble along with me as I match their speed. Surprisingly a plume of smoke erupts up ahead. It comes from the earlier spotted structure and dirties the scene. As I puzzle over this, it shifts slightly. Until now only a small section was visible, but now the black foredeck of a small freighter appears. Originally nose into wind it was partially hidden by the waves. I have been fooled. Seen from this low in the water objects compress and distort, especially in any type of swell. I lock eyes on this revelation, now sputtering into life as it makes its way towards port. Whilst none too menacing, it nonetheless adds a nice sideshow to my high speed dash. When close enough *CEG Galaxy* is revealed in white lettering on its hull.

By the time I crunch into the stony beach at Knockadoon I am in a high state of elation. What a difference a day makes? Knockadoon Head, translating to the hill of the fort, is a quiet backwater. The tiny jetty and beach under the green headland fit together perfectly, no doubt offering the essential ingredients for a summer afternoon escape. I notice an incongruous black and white structure close by which transpires to be a religious centre. Looking sadly neglected, it reflects the treatment of many unfortunates who found themselves looking to these Irish institutions for solace. I turn my attention away from the religious centre to look out over the bay just crossed. Such was my concentration during the traverse that I never looked back, so viewing it from this new perspective allows me to fully appreciate where I now find myself, a further 10 kilometres into my quest, halfway to Ballycotton. Now that I have booked myself into the Schooner Tavern B&B, an enormous carrot dangles in front of me. I salivate as I imagine downing a large plate of fish and chips there. After my chilly night back in Ardmore, it will be pure luxury.

I arrive in Ballycotton three hours later and begin dragging my kayak up a steep slipway which disappears into a cluster of trees and looks to have been built far enough from the harbour for more local use. After 30 metres it morphs into a gravel roadway flanked by a terrace of four white cottages stepped into the incline. Like steps of stairs and with doors opening onto the track, I am enchanted. One of them opens, producing a short stocky guy. He is greeted by an 18 foot green torpedo pausing outside his door. He gently asks me to explain what is going on, whilst intermittently sucking on a stout cigar in well worn, stubby fingers. On hearing of my mission, and that I am bound for The Schooner, he suggests parking *Murchú* beside his house rather than dragging it any further up the hill. I relax instantly, as dragging *Murchú*, fully-loaded up this incline has my pulse rocketing. His instant offer makes a big impression on me, and on my mood. This guy's caring nature bubbles forth. His name is Huey, and his intervention proves invaluable, as my stomach is a little sore from mild nausea that has grown over the last half hour of my paddle. His warm and friendly manner touches me, as I notice a pattern of goodwill from strangers that is becoming a theme on my trip. For some reason, passing Huey's door today felt like he had been expecting me. Already, I have an ally, and that is before I reach my accommodation.

The Schooner, basic and clean, is everything I need. The manager gives me an enormous family room which by the time I am heading downstairs resembles the inside of a laundry. Every available hook, door and curtain rail has bits of my drying kit draped over it. Having the added bonus of wholesome pub grub downstairs in the vast but inviting lounge, I decide to stay put. I install myself in a cosy corner, order fish and chips and start my blog and review tomorrow's mission. The wall mounted television flashes out the news, post work pints are being downed at the bar, and cooking smells hit me from steaming plates en route to patrons. I am pinching myself that I am in Ballycotton. Yesterday evening's Ardmore reflections had me seriously looking at the wisdom of continuing. But somehow, after a night's rest and some self-talk, I convinced myself to go for it today. Thankfully, I was mostly okay with only an echo of yesterday's unease over the last few kilometres. Having read various quotes about commitment and perseverance, the deep power of these words hits me now. This venture is a fairly big ordeal no matter what way one looks at it, but add to it the debilitating effect of seasickness and it borders on the impossible, even stu-

Huey, an unexpected helper

pid. So far, having suffered seriously from it twice, I am in no mood to continue if this becomes the order of the day. I am not into self-flagellation, and do not want to start now. For now, stubbornness is winning, and I find myself happily ensconced in the corner of this pub. I think it is definitely time for another plateful of chips.

Later, I get a message from Karl, a friend from Skerries. He is working at the nearby Whitegate oil refinery and hopes to pop over in the morning after his night shift to see me off. This is a nice unexpected boost for me and with 75 kilometres covered in two days, including the misery of Mine Head, I am happy to meet up. Tomorrow will be my third and final day of this stretch and will see me cross the entrance to Cork Harbour and begin my journey along the West Cork coastline.

Karl arrives just as I am returning to The Schooner after packing my kayak. We sit and chat over a morning coffee, as I make a mental note to pay another visit to the men's room before I leave. A full bladder at sea is an unnecessary burden. Karl was also friends with Mark, so we share a sense of loss at his absence. His optimism, despite coming off a night shift, gives me a boost before I depart. With his contract

Karl Macken, a friend from Skerries

work taking him away for big chunks of time he relishes any chance to meet up. I am struck again by the real affect others have on my mission. Not only was my previous evening's journal cathartic, it also attracted many positive responses like shots into my arm.

The sweet smell of cigar smoke descends the slipway, and turning I see Huey slowly ambling down. My choice to land near his door has dovetailed perfectly with his seemingly unhurried lifestyle. He breaks into conversation with Karl, his Zen-like demeanour causing a smile to crease my face. The two men sharing a moment together constitutes my farewell party as I embark on my third consecutive day afloat. I sit into *Murchú*, wave happily to them, and launch towards Ballycotton's harbour perched at the southern tip of the headland. The rising land is covered with a tiered array of handsomely sized houses which observe me squarely. Just offshore, two dome-shaped islands of green and black mimic the look of the mainland.

I pass the pier, marking both the end of the town and the land, swinging almost 180 degrees from east to west as I head towards the mouth of Cork harbour. It is a good 10 kilometres before I can land for my customary stretch. When I come ashore I sink my teeth into a peanut butter Cliff bar. These things are my mini-meals and do well to keep my motor functioning. I roll its dense mass in my mouth and enjoy the simple pleasure of replenishing my tank.

The next headland visible is Power Head which blocks my view into one of Europe's best natural harbours. The irony of approaching Power Head is that my own source of energy appears to be dwindling again. The sea is lumpy, and its sickly grey-green undulations pull at my mood. The sun has refused to appear and the leaden sky has dropped to touch the land. Hauntingly, peeping over the cliff edge a

Leaving Ballycotton
(photo by Karl Macken)

small building stands. It is sepia-coloured adding a palpable heaviness to the scene. Save my green foredeck, the world is becoming monochrome. An uncertainty enters my mind and my eyes feel strangely loose in my skull. Unexpectedly overheating, I splash some water on my face, which is refreshing but leaves a residual taste of salt which is mildly sickening.

Today, I am more familiar with what is happening to me, so any denial is short-lived as I am once again consigned to my fate. It is strange that my thoughts, up until now a free flowing stream of consciousness, instantly switch to a higher gear. I examine the scenario, far less daunting than previous ones, to see how I can best tackle it. I have two options. The first lies beyond the gaping mouth of Cork harbour where a safe landing sits five kilometres distant. The second is directly abeam at a much closer two kilometres and a small gravel beach. I choose the former knowing I can dig in for the hour it might take to make my first footfall in West Cork. Roches Point lighthouse observes my slow progress across its path as I paddle out into the port's shipping lanes. The narrow mouth disgorges a flotilla of fishing craft reminding me of the city that lies within. A tiny red boat is moving so erratically it is unsettling to watch. Three guys are crammed aboard enthusiastically swinging their rods in an attempt to hook some dinner.

As I cross the central shipping lane the brightest thing I have seen all day appears. A searing white guide beam is shining out through the sound. Resembling the visual landing systems in use by aircraft, it confirms my position over the deepest section of the channel. This brilliant guide is cleverly constructed in that it is flanked by a red and a green beam. If, while following this white beam into port, it changes to red or green it tells the ship's captain they are off course. If it changes to red they are too far left, whereas for green their course has brought them too far right. As long as they alter course back to the central white beam, a safe passage is guaranteed. Mostly superseded by Global Positioning System satellite navigation, it still provides a useful belt and braces for mariners.

The channel I am above is a handsome 15 metres deep and is the first of two I am about to cross. They are separated in the middle of the harbour mouth by a shallow ridge named Harbour Rock which large traffic must avoid. This area is a magnet for fish, and as a consequence, the local fishermen are out hunting them. Not least among these marine creatures are conger eels, with specimens weighing up to 13 kilos being hooked here. Sharp toothed and energetic, these silver-scaled creatures, sometimes nearing two metres in length, lodge themselves into narrow openings ready to launch explosive attacks on their prey. Thanks to the huge volumes of water moving in and out of the harbour their food is delivered right to their waiting mouths. They have inflicted serious wounds on divers and fishermen alike, so are afforded great respect. Along with many species of fish beneath my boat there are also acres of kelp and bladderwrack swaying in the currents emptying and filling Cork's Harbour twice every day. Essentially, I am kayaking across Ireland's greatest plughole now draining the biggest enclosed basin on the island.

The scene here would fit perfectly into the midlands of Ireland. It is as though the gentle countryside has been inundated by the sea. The land now falls down to the shore which is lined with houses scattered about. A small string of terraced dwellings appears from behind the lighthouse flanking the low coast road serving the sentinel. Further in the distance, the rim of Cork Harbour is lined with a mostly grey-green ribbon of varying height with fields, houses and small stands of trees painted on. It feels rural and busy and a distinct peaty odour hits me as I near the shore.

The sea feels like treacle, thanks to the emptying flow pouring through the port's entrance which makes the going tougher. Amber coloured leaves flow past as the increasingly black water adds to the day's gloom. A boggy stream close by is spewing the recent rains back into a darkening sea. I land into the tree lined cove at Myrtleville and step out of *Murchú* to take my first steps in West Cork. Named after nearby Myrtle House, it conjures up a happy image which contradicts my state of mind. A canopy of leaf-laden branches lean over the cove's southern flank as high gardens and rooftops do likewise to the north. The village wraps itself around this cove adding a feeling of homeliness. I sink down onto a low wall and replenish myself. For a third day

Landing in Myrtleville

I am feeling ropey and have to dig deep to motivate myself to take to sea towards Roberts Cove only an hour paddling away. I am sick of feeling sick and have to postpone my navel gazing to just get on with the job.

I land into the idyllic Robert's Cove, a finger of ocean which has forced its way inland through a breach in the low cliff. A marine *cul-de-sac,* it is lined by a low sea wall and a string of colourful houses and pubs on its western flank, peering curiously into its green waters. I slice the flat calm like a knife through butter, gliding towards the beach flattened wet by the ebbing tide. The rising terrain on both sides gives a feel of being in an arena with green grass replacing terraces. A bullet-like stonechat flies across the inlet above my boat. This small land bird, easily mistaken for a robin thanks to its russet breast, hangs out on coastal paths but rarely flies over the sea. It adds a certain charm to my arrival. I have travelled into another world, akin to an inland lake. Off to my left, the sea wall hides the road which passes by small colourful stone buildings, including a pub and an inn, which is what gives the cove its character. On sunny summer evenings, patrons from these establishments spill onto the road, enjoying drinks *al fresco* in this little slice of paradise. With *Murchú* finally settled on the wet sand, I

Robert's Cove

remain seated. My three-day mission is complete and I am enjoying a few moments of gratitude.

THE PROCESS OF GETTING MY KAYAK ready for transfer to my brother-in-law Ciaran's house takes a while. When complete, I decide to wander over to the pub to wait. Luckily, I arrive just as the proprietor is opening. With terracotta-coloured walls and dimly lit, it is instantly cosy. Whilst preparing for business she engages me in conversation with her strong Cork accent, including the high inflection at the end of each sentence. I tell her of my mission and the inevitable questions begin to fly. How far do you paddle each day? Are you worried on your own out there? What about bad weather? A local couple joins us minutes later and begin making the same inquiries, and out of politeness I relay the same answers. I catch the eye of the blond-haired proprietor who is now smiling to herself. After a short while the warmness of our exchanges brings me back to myself. Despite being a teetotaller, I love pubs, especially small local ones. Being an ad hoc meeting place where the most unlikely people can meet up and have a heart-warming chat leaves these establishments head and shoulders above all others. When Ciaran finally shows up, I am somewhat reluctant to leave the cosy sanctuary. When I do, the brightness outside hurts my eyes, bringing me back to reality in a flash.

Following lunch at Ciaran's, we shuttle across south Cork to Waterford to Mick's place. Keen as ever to learn about my adventures, Mick hangs on my every word. On hearing about my recurring seasickness, concern spreads across his face. He cannot hide his reaction and quizzes me forensically. I am acutely aware of his facial gestures and body language. Mick, having inspired me to make this journey, has become my guru and is committed to pushing me to complete my mission. Like a boxer being briefed between rounds, I am soaking up his advice. He nearly chides me for being seasick, suggesting that expedition sea kayaking and this malady do not make good bedfellows. Who is he telling, I think to myself, as I struggle to stay upbeat about the whole mad affair. Inside, I am dying and feel as though my quest to circumvent our island home is a ridiculous construct. I want to be celebrating today, not ruminating over headaches, dizziness and generally feeling ill. Ironically, it is me who ends up reassuring Mick that everything will work out, while not having much faith that it will. I honestly have no idea how my days will pan out when I get back to *Murchú*.

Gliding home on the smooth black ribbon of the M11, I sink deeply into the seat's plushness. The magical sounds of Future Islands and Pink Floyd resonate through the car's warm interior. It displaces recent worries from my mind, unearthing the positive result of my efforts in getting *Murchú* to West Cork. Part of me rejoices, while another part trembles. My body has a pleasant ache from three days of solid paddling and I allow myself the privilege of owning my achievements. I am heading home once again to fully absorb my situation. I reach forward and turn up the volume to Pink Floyd's intro to 'Wish You Were Here'. Life is good.

Stage 9

INTO THE BELLY OF THE WHALE:
PASSING KINSALE

The tentative plan for my next three days paddling is to depart Robert's Cove, wheel around the southwest corner of Ireland and start climbing the western seaboard to Crookhaven. A mix of excitement and apprehension tug at my brain thanks to my previous three days' paddling. The beach in Robert's Cove, washed flat by the receding tide, resembles a brown, 100 metre wide, pool table. Ciaran leaves me alone as I pack my gear which disappears inside various compartments in the boat. His generous gesture allows me ample time to stay clear-headed as I move all my kit in relays across the sand to my hungry craft, which happily ingests everything.

My kayak, cleverly designed with a variety of waterproof compartments, allows ample space for expedition supplies. Each is separated by a solid fibreglass bulkhead, creating several flotation chambers. With five in all, I occupy the largest, sealed in by a snug-fitting spray deck while the others use rubber waterproof hatches of varying sizes. The tiniest one, located in the foredeck, is within arm's length and can be opened from the cockpit while afloat. Like a small limpet mine attached inside my boat, it sits between my knees and is accessed from above through a small rubber lid just in front of me. In here I store my glasses, some snacks, a spare compass and any other small bits and pieces I might need *en route*. A large lidded one at the rear houses bulky items such as my bag of dry clothes, cooking equipment and three days' food supply. It also houses a boat repair kit. A long narrow compartment in front of me contains my tent, sleeping bag, extra

85

water supplies and some spare kayaking kit. Immediately behind me in a medium sized day hatch are my day's food supplies, electrical equipment, books and a substantial first aid kit. By the time I have everything packed most of the internal spaces are completely full adding a handsome 20 kilo payload to my craft.

Loading the kit into these compartments is similar to operating a commercial aircraft. As a self-contained unit operating offshore, everything has to be where it can be accessed when needed. As soon as I am afloat, my range of movement is only an arm's length, or less when conditions are rough. As well as below deck, some of my kit is stored on top. On my foredeck I keep a spare set of paddles. These are split paddles, and snap together into the conventional double ended system I use. Also, I have a gimballed compass, a laminated chart, a speedometer and a hand-operated water pump in case a swamped cockpit needs emptying. An inflatable paddle float, resembling a small yellow pillow, is tucked under the lines on my foredeck. This can be strapped over a paddle blade for stability if I am unfortunate enough to be pitched overboard and need to manage re-entry. This is the least worst way of attempting this delicate manoeuvre and would only be attempted if a lot of other things have gone seriously wrong. I mentally avoid visualising this doomsday scenario being visited on me. My back deck is less busy, with my trolley and a helmet, the latter in case a rough landing onto a rocky shore becomes necessary.

The equipment I choose to carry on my person also needs careful attention. Should I become separated from my boat at sea I need to be able to call for help and initiate a rescue as soon as possible. I also need to survive immersion in the ocean. Obviously I wear a personal flotation device which boasts many pockets for carrying important equipment. A large bladder pack allows me instant access to fresh water supply via its supply tube. In the front pocket sits my VHF radio, an Emergency Position Indicating Radio Beacon or EPIRB, flares and a whistle. I carry some meds too, plus some feed bars. Oftentimes these have their wrappers removed to assist with hasty feeds, especially if it is forecast to be rough when access to my glove compartment would be impossible. My mobile phone is in a waterproof pouch and hangs around my neck. Finally, my own state of dress is considered carefully, cognisant of the air and water temperatures, the weather forecast, the time of year and expected duration of the day's activities. Obviously, careful planning is key on a trip such as this one.

I tentatively paddle out of Robert's Cove like a car nosing out onto a highway. Outside, the vast sea awaits as I thread my way through a narrow opening. I am anxious to see what the day will hold. The sea moves, but not erratically. Drops run down the paddle shaft and under my loose fitting wrist seals chilling my arms. My body temperature rises as I develop into a rhythm. Every dent, every cleft, every angle of this undulating rocky coast is new to me. I ponder on what series of cataclysmic events ended up producing such an unfinished job of our coastline. On a day such as today it seems unbelievable that water could eat its way into these cliffs. Absorbing energy from the wind, these two great elemental forces coalesce into a conveyor belt of pulsing swells which run headlong into our coastline. The sea, in an attempt to consume more rock, is endlessly battering against the coast's

Murky Oysterhaven

reluctance to give way. Another, hidden, force is brewing. It will create a large dent in my life over the next few days.

I am a cheeky minnow scratching my way west on the vast ocean. Directly ahead, two building-sized blocks of black rock stand stoutly above the grey sea. This is my first glimpse of the Sovereign Rocks. Known locally as The Sovereigns, they initially appear as one. A hidden slot separating them only becomes visible at close quarters. They mark the portal into the tiny inlet of Oysterhaven, just east of the major port of Kinsale, conveniently removing any confusion with the latter. In need of an early break and mindful of my continuing battle against seasickness, I turn into Oysterhaven seeking a spot to land. A light drizzle is blanketing everything as I notice a flat-stone beach. It appears like an old roman road flanked by sloping rock walls and entices me as I run my kayak aground. Brought along originally for sun protection, my broad-brimmed hat now serves as a makeshift umbrella as the sky's drizzle falls lightly onto everything. I gather my provisions from

Hat becomes an umbrella

the boat and explore the back of the cove finding a small copse of trees where a small stream empties onto the flagstones. I perch on a sodden tuft of grass happy to be sealed into my drysuit. I begin contemplating my next move which features a portal to the Wild Atlantic Way. I will be travelling, not around, but through the Old head of Kinsale.

An echo of Mick's voice in my head reminds me that passing the Old Head will put me and *Murchú* into more serious territory. How appropriate that a real portal marks this transition. Halfway along this elongated headland, narrow portal caves have breached the headland. By transiting the headland this way, I will be experiencing a unique phenomenon, while conveniently avoiding any potentially nasty conditions at the end of the promontory. This is all new ground for me. Having previously quizzed local paddler and circumnavigator Jon Hynes, I am searching for a set of flags marking the entrance to the Old Head Golf Links flying atop the cliff. Conveniently located directly below them is the most favourable of five tunnels recommended for passage. I will soon be entering into a strange underground world.

I steer *Murchú* toward the rising bulk of this bluff blocking my path. The sea is solid green, the sky leaden grey. A fine mist hangs magically in the air. As I cover the last few kilometres, conditions calm considerably. I am searching for an opening in the cliff face, but nothing presents. The cloud, sagging heavily all morning, now erases the top of the cliff. Thankfully, the flags remain visible offering guidance along the imposing rock face. I feel like Harry Potter, who in order to catch the Hogwarts Express had to run headlong into a brick wall. For him, it magically opened at the last second. I paddle forward, keen to solve my own riddle of the caves. I replay Jon's guiding words and continue forward along the steep escarpment.

An eerie quiet settles as the wind, unable to make the steep descent, returns to sea level away from the cliff. I continue, my heart thumping with anticipation. I need to find the correct tunnel to pass through, and avoid the rogues that could cause me problems. I berate myself for not paying more attention to the default route of rounding the head itself, should I fail to negotiate my subterranean option. It all seemed so easy, listening to Jon, reading the accounts, looking at the

Peering through the Old Head of Kinsale

photographs and even watching the odd video. Now, with the entrance eluding me, I am getting agitated. Hugging the cliff, I search for a sign to ease my concern. Sections of black appear only to reveal themselves as false leads created by water stains leaking from above. I creep along, eyes fixed on bare rock waiting for it to magically open in front of me. Finally, discerning a deeper blackness, my hopes rise. I sidle along and slowly a dark tunnel is revealed. My heart lifts.

My eyes search for a light inside, but see nothing. Maybe this is one of the unsuitable passages of the quintet. I paddle on, staring at the rockface, noticing how the sedimentary layers lean around 20 degrees off the vertical. This, I think, might explain how the headland has been breached. A few weaker laminations could allow the sea to eat its way through, much like removing the lower half of a few cards from a standing deck and not allowing the others to close the gap. To my great relief the next blackness reveals a small white orb deep inside. This, however, is well above sea level and immediately reminds me of the light box in Newgrange's passage tomb, another unsuitable path. This process continues until I amass five openings, two of which thankfully have distant lights at sea level. I return to the pair, comparing each with the descriptions in my head. I choose one and hope I have made the right decision. It seems crazy, but only now do I begin to grasp how dark this is going to be. The tunnel itself narrows in all aspects towards its midpoint, like an elongated cone, and opens up at the far side in a similar fashion. I grapple with my camera and manage to get a shot of the entrance, its speck of light drawing me in. I take a few breaths, adjust myself in the boat, and enter the dark chamber.

I am Jonah, voluntarily journeying into the belly of the whale. I look around and see rock everywhere, save a narrow vein of water supporting me. The swell is compressing, lifting me up and letting me back down, creating the illusion that the roof and walls are shrinking in on me. Dark shards of rock hang like knives waiting to plunge into the deep below. A musty odour hangs inside this Gothic cathedral carved out of near vertical strata. This is solo potholing by kayak and is well outside my comfort zone. The swells within are acting strangely in concert with the tunnel, creating a breathing rock-lung type rhythm. Inhaling and exhaling with each rise and fall, I am adjusting to this mesmerising experience.

I continue at a snail's pace, acutely aware of everything. Noises echo around me, magnified in the constriction. The amplified sounds of water pouring from rock ledges catches me by surprise. Despite being on the Atlantic Ocean, the insanity of being underground is messing with my head. I am all too aware what a momentous event this is for me and I am working overtime to process it. I can already taste a ramping up of my journey as I transit under the spine of this elongated headland. I am near halfway, its narrowest point, and begin meeting the swells arriving from the far end. They complement those from behind me such that I am now rising and falling more than expected. Thankfully, the high arched ceiling has remained well clear, but the sensation is disconcerting. I am a passenger at the neck of an outsize horizontal hourglass, with water in place of sand sloshing between the chambers.

I spot a disturbance in the distance outside the exit. Waves are creating a disordered sea, and I am impatient to see what awaits me. I cautiously steer my green needle westward to the cave's gaping mouth. Suddenly disgorged from underground, my eyes hurt in the brightness. All about, the sea is shivering into small spikes as waves rebound off islets, reefs and cliffs. The calmness at the entrance is now eclipsed by the energy of the exit, as a new arena is revealed. Feeling like a time-traveller entering a new day complete with a new set of conditions, I head out on my sea road. To my right stretches a three kilometre cliffline towards Garrylucas Beach. The domed, grassy headland above leans to seaward abruptly stopping at the precipice. With no chance to stop for a breather, I swing my focus across open water to Seven Heads, which at 10 kilometres distant is the next major protrusion in this heavily indented coast. Seven Heads accurately describes this drawn-out, rangy piece of coastline. I am headed towards its eastern flank across a wide sea. The further I move away from the Old Head the calmer the conditions become, allowing me to sink gently into a pleasant rhythm. The sea is pea green, and despite remaining overcast, the day brightens.

Seven Heads, Cork

In a flash, a loose group of shearwaters appear around the boat. These mostly pelagic birds are normally seen far from shore, and are a welcome reward for today's remote paddling. Intermittently flapping and gliding, their highly efficient wings allow them long, high-speed, wheeling glides low over the water. Being the intruder in their kingdom, I see them fearlessly fly close, displaying a mastery of flight that amazes me. One daring individual comes so near I make out its pea-sized black eye watching me. In the split second of observing each other, I sense a connection. It sends a shiver through me. I realise how lucky I am to have this intimate moment with another creature, far offshore and alone. While remoteness can sometimes stoke a fear inside me, it also brings unexpected offerings. Today's visiting shearwater flock are rewarding my endeavours, thanks to their curiosity and their beautifully efficient flight displays.

I continue westwards across the broad bay, my paddles endlessly dipping in and out of the ocean. The day and its wildlife are all resonating to a similar tune. At times I forget that I am paddling, such is the constancy of the cycle. Lean forward, dip the blade, pull and rotate my torso, withdraw the blade and offer the opposite blade a chance to do likewise. This revolving motion goes on and on and on, for hours and hours, adjusting to any change in the sea, as I propel myself and *Murchú* along an invisible line threading its way around our island home. Next up, a line of bunty puffins, abysmally inefficient flyers, gasp past me, their wings ablur. Also called sea parrots, their large, colourful bills are showing their best today, a brilliant orange, indicating their readiness for the breeding season. Like me, they are heading for the opposite shore. Devoid of curiosity, they do not pay me a second glance. Birds and man on a mission.

Further on I spot one of my favourite seabirds, the delicate storm petrel. These tiny, black birds, the size of a house martin and sharing the same white rump patch, spend most of their lives at sea, battling gales and huge waves. I see four while crossing and two cocky ones flew small slow orbits about me. Their curiosity offers a chance to inspect them at close range. Feeding on surface fish and scraps, their highly tuned sense of smell directs them to their quarry. As they pass close by, they occasionally semi-hover to get a closer look. I begin to wonder who is on show today, me or our avian cousins.

I land at Seven Heads through a tight elongated gulley, much like a crocodile's mouth canted at ninety degrees. The almost vertical sedimentary rocks in these parts make for jagged indents into the land. I steer *Murchú* into the rocky scabbard and tie her off, lest she drift away on the tide. The clouds part and a blue sky begins peeking through. I treat myself to a long lunch. Banana sandwiches, chocolate raisins, peanut protein bars accompanied by fresh water. What could be better than downing some serious calories and resting after a good workout?

I find a natural rock cleft, insert myself and relax. I sense my body sink into this receptacle as I absorb the sea, sky and space about me.

Later, I lose count as I round Seven Heads to eventually land further west at the sheltered and strangely named, Dunworley Cove. I exit the water and climb away from a wide sandy area up a recently grooved access ramp. Cut through solid rock it allows me to wheel *Murchú* high above the beach to a fenced-off picnic area. I hear the sound of excited children rising up from the beach below and turn to see a large fin slicing through the shallow waters just vacated. A lone basking shark is causing a stir as it carves lazy circles just 50 metres away. I wonder if it was tailing me. These harmless plankton-eating creatures swim slowly along the surface filtering krill from tons of water. The abundance of wildlife west of the Old Head of Kinsale continues to keep me in its grip.

I am noticing the further west I travel the more dramatic the coastline. As I bear down on my second corner, near Baltimore, I am acutely aware of pulling *Murchú* every inch of the way. I look at my green companion sitting on its trolley, patiently waiting for its next instal-

My campsite at Dunworley Cove

Chilly dawn, Dunworley Cove

ment. I swell in appreciation for all we have done together thus far. My bond with my boat is real, and the more we share the sea road the more it becomes a part of me. Coupled with this comes another realisation, something that has been absent today. Seasickness. A huge grin refuses to leave my face as I pitch my tent on a flat area of grass fifty feet above the beach. I have clocked up a handsome 44 kilometres, a couple further than a marathon, and am well pleased. Now all I have left to do is find the nearest pub.

According to Mr Google it lies three kilometres away in the small village of Butlerstown. After setting up camp and downing some hot food I head off on foot along winding country roads. As I ramble, the noisy chattering of rooks in treetops is joined by the alarm call of a blackbird close by. I pass overgrown ruins, homes long vacated, and occasional farmyards, where the pungent smell of manure hangs in the air. Traffic is light, and nearing the village a car stops to offer me a lift which I gladly accept. A mother and her young son greet me, enquiring as to what I am doing. On explaining my quest, she smiles broadly, informing me that she is a member of the West Cork Sea Kayakers group. She is fascinated by my adventure and keen to learn more, so much so that she offers me a lift back to my tent when returning home later that evening. You could never make this stuff up, I think to myself, as I push open the door into another world, O'Neills pub.

A serious bit of time travelling takes place inside. It feels like I have walked into someone's parlour from the 1970s, with old wallpaper and framed pictures hanging on the walls. Comprising a single room, is the epitome of the original Irish public house. The proprietor, a local woman in her seventies, shuffles out from an opening behind the bar. She tells me it has remained unchanged for decades, and without wifi or television it allows for more conversation and banter. I perch myself at the bar and in exchange for the local lore I share tales from my adventure. As it is early on a Tuesday evening I am her only customer so she graciously stays to chat, disappearing occasionally through the doorway. Elevated on the high stool, I can see above the frosted glass that makes up the lower half of the front window. Across the street, wide open fields are splayed like an enormous green quilt leading away to the wide expanse of the Seven Heads.

At moments like these, I feel at home, settled within myself, devoid of any struggle. I make a mental note of the sense of contentment I am experiencing. Is that what we all are searching for? How often it eludes us. As I sit overlooking fields, from the warmth of this pub from another era, I am completely content knowing that I have 'stopped to smell the roses'. I do not want to miss the opportunity of fully inhabiting my adventure. I do not want to be always projecting myself ahead to the next headland, or bay, or stopover, or morning, or whatever is on my intended path. Instead, I am allowing myself to enjoy this once in a lifetime experience completely. So sitting at O'Neills bar, chatting with the landlady after my great day paddling, I am quenching a thirst both for conversation and refreshment. My promised lift back to base duly arrives, and shortly thereafter I am sliding into my sleeping bag. I post my blog and then enjoy some light reading before lights out. *Oileain: A Guide to the Irish Islands* is my publication of choice.

Stage 10

TWO LOSSES IN SHORT ORDER

In the morning I awake to a cold blue dome hanging overhead. A chilly east wind is scurrying across the bay as the rising sun begins evaporating the dew lying about. Firing up my stove for a brew helps adjust to the chilly reality outside my tent and sleeping bag. I am a butterfly emerging from a chrysalis, stretching my limbs into the new day.

Soon I am underway on what will be an unforgettable day of my journey. I closely follow the irregular coastline where splotches of yellow gorse are splashed onto green fields leaning towards the sea. The sun is brightening into a vibrant acrylic painting. The sea is peppered with mini-whitecaps as I glide along on the warming wind. I head out across another bay, leaving Inchydoney Beach behind and embarking on another 10 kilometre crossing. Clonakilty Bay stretches from Seven Heads to Galley Head, and just shy of the latter is Red Strand, positioned at the back of the modest Dirk Bay, cut into the end of the promontory. At 15 kilometres into my day's paddling, it is where I am planning my first break, afterwards pressing on towards Baltimore.

The sea is alive with wildlife again today and I count myself lucky to spot a pomarine skua close to the boat. Much like a black iteration of a gull, these predators chase other birds, forcing them to drop their catch. Incredibly agile, their tenacity in pursuit is a sight to witness, rivalling World War Two aerial dogfights. Eventually tiring of the chase, the harried bird drops its prey and the skua picks up the spoils. I have only witnessed this twice and both times it was a white herring gull being chased by the much darker skua. Similar in size and shape, it appeared as though the gull was being pursued by its own shadow. I

97

make a mental note to relay this particular sighting to my Dad, who instilled in me and still shares an interest in wild birds.

I wheel around the jagged opening to Dirk Bay and catch sight of an off-white ribbon of sand at the back of the cove. A slow swell gently surges over some grey limestone platforms painting them a glistening black. I paddle over large turquoise shapes below the boat. These are submerged areas of sand stretching far out into the bay. Onshore I notice terracotta stones strewn around the place reflecting the beach's name, Red Strand. It has been a good 15 kilometre crossing and I am in need of some food and a good stretch, not to mention my recurring physiological requirements that must be addressed.

Beneath an earthen embankment and out of the now-burning sun, I plonk myself onto a large log and add a post to my blog. My band of followers react almost instantly providing me with a welcome boost. While happily enjoying another high-energy peanut bar, my phone rings. Brother-in-law Ciaran is nearby and wants to grab a photo of me during my way-stop. Twenty minutes later, I amble over to the sand-covered road behind the seawall and watch him pull up in his car. I am in high spirits, and begin thanking him for coming out to meet me. He smiles, but not as broadly as I expect.

'I'm not here to take your photo, Kev.'

'Ohhhkay,' I reply, unsure where this is going.

'It's your Dad… He's taken a turn.'

'Is he dead?' I blurt.

'No, no', he reassures me. 'He's been taken to Kilkenny hospital. Angela is driving from Dublin to collect you.'

It stops me in my tracks. We lock eyes. He apologises. I feel for him having to bring this sad news to me. With Dad's heart already seriously compromised, I fear the worst. I feel for my sister Mary and her husband David. They have been minding our parents for three years and have weathered all sorts of storms, culminating in our Mam's death only four months ago. Now this is another blow.

Kit and kayak are loaded in a blur and we drive to Carrigaline in Cork where Angela is waiting. In Kilkenny hospital we join my three siblings in a family room awaiting the doctor. Dad has suffered a massive heart attack while in the car with Mary, a qualified nurse, essentially dying in her arms. When the ambulance arrived they were able to revive him, but only managing to regain a very weak pulse. Now, being kept alive by life support, the doctor tells us that due to the scale of the attack, and his advanced age of 88, along with a poor medical history, the hope for any type of recovery is almost nil. Given a chance to discuss things among ourselves, we decide to let nature take its course. We four, and Angela, are all with him as he slowly drifts away. Afterwards, Mary jokes that 'he'd be laughing now, because he managed to die twice on me'.

What followed is a week of to-ing and fro-ing between Carlow and Dublin. His wake and funeral mass is in Carlow, and then his removal and burial in the family plot in Glasnevin. Friends and relatives appear and disappear throughout that time, it all going by in a flurry. I mostly remember feeling a great wave of support as we lurched through the whole ordeal.

Dad had a great intellect, so despite leaving school in his mid-teens during the Second World War his education continued by reading voraciously. His great interest over his final decade was tomato-growing on which he had become an authority. Ironically, his final words to Mary were about repotting this year's crop. While we shared many interests, we also had very different opinions on things, slowly revealed over the years.

Seeing as I was offered the privilege of eulogising Dad, I paid him every respect I could from the altar realising how similar we were in so many ways. This can be a tough lesson to learn. How often are we like those who irk us in some way? Needless to say, I am forever indebted to him, not least for his interest in watersports and wildlife, which has led me to attempting this circumnavigation.

As the lid of his coffin was about to close, I slipped a red stone into the pocket of his jacket. On it I had written a note wishing him well on his journey. I had picked it up on Red Strand so this turning point would forever be associated with this beautiful place. He would never learn of the pomarine skua I spotted that day. Perhaps it was carrying a message to say that something was changing in my world.

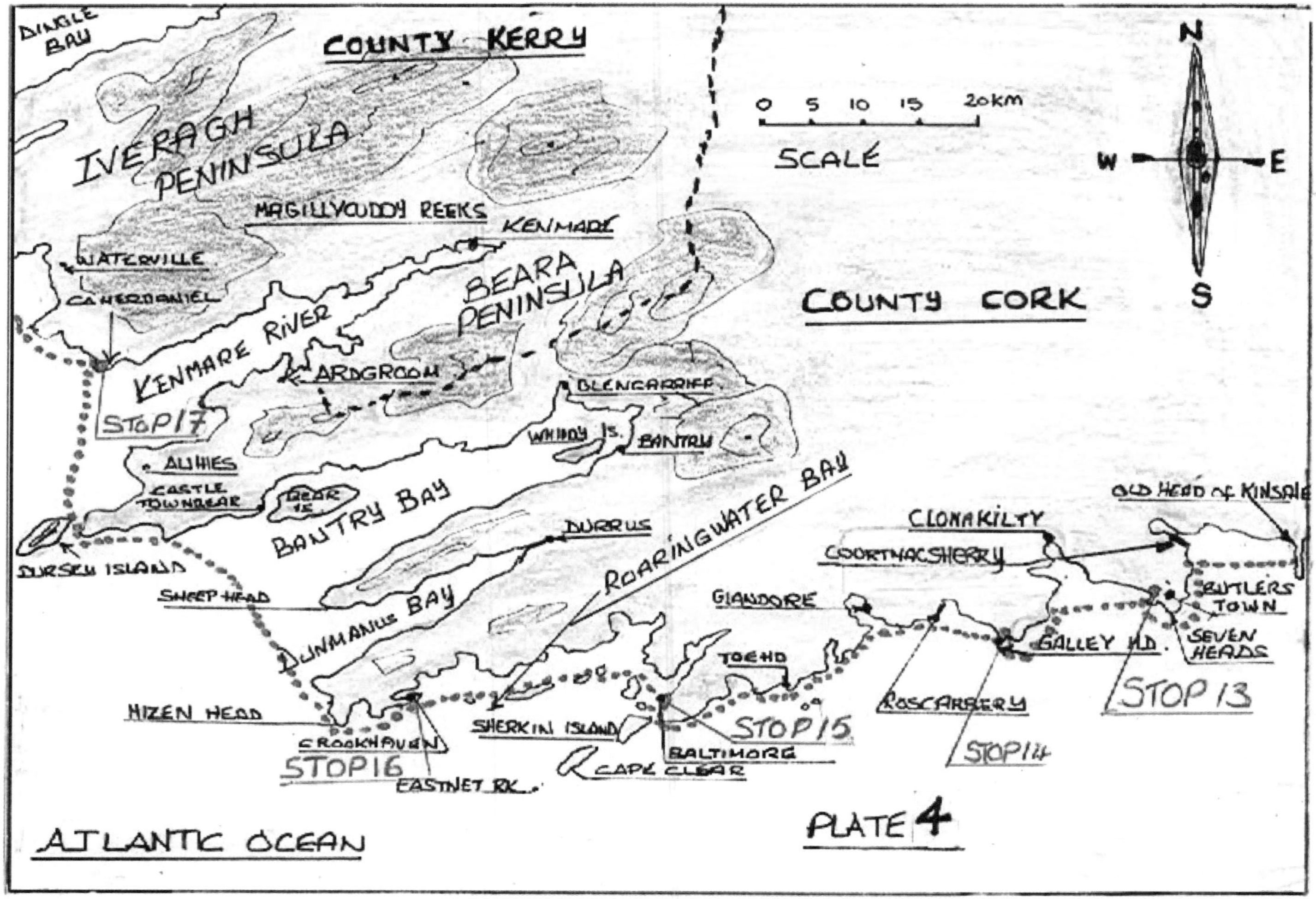

COUNTY KERRY

COUNTY CORK

ATLANTIC OCEAN

PLATE 4

SCALE

0   5   10   15   20km

N   E   W   S

DINGLE BAY

IVERAGH PENINSULA

MACGILLYCUDDY REEKS

WATERVILLE
CAHERDANIEL

KENMARE RIVER

BEARA PENINSULA

KENMARE

GLENGARRIFF

ARDGROOM

ALLIHIES
CASTLE TOWNBERE

BERE IS.

DURSEY ISLAND

STOP 17

WHIDDY IS.

BANTRY

BANTRY BAY

DUNMANUS BAY

SHEEP HEAD

DURRUS

R CARRIGNAWATER BAY

MIZEN HEAD

CROOKHAVEN

STOP 16

FASTNET RK.

SHERKIN ISLAND

CAPE CLEAR

BALTIMORE

STOP 15

TOE HD

GLANDORE

ROSCARBERY

STOP 14

COORTMACSHERRY

CLONAKILTY

GALLEY HD.

STOP 13

BUTLERS TOWN

SEVEN HEADS

OLD HEAD of KINSALE

Stage 11

THE BALTIMORE BEACON
AND UNEXPECTED COMPANY

The unoccupied wooden holiday home hides behind its privet hedge enclosure. On its small front lawn, a heavy mist releases tiny droplets onto my tent pitched in the deep grass. Nearby, the glow of an indoor light shines from a house. It shows how much the brightness has disappeared from the day. I am squatting at Red Strand, to resume my trip in the morning. The thick grass makes for the softest mattress, allowing me a comfortable reflection on the surreal experience of the past seven days. In the space of four months, both my parents have passed, and despite being in their eighties, the loss has been more than expected. I am happy to be on my own again, and as the soft sound of the sea wafts by the tent I settle into my first peaceful slumber in a week.

Brilliant in white, the Galley Head lightkeepers' houses mimic a layer of icing on a 100 foot high cake, complete with its outsize candle, the lighthouse itself. Built on the site of an old Norman stronghold called Dun Deidi, it looks east towards Red Strand and west to Long Strand and Glandore. Nowadays, the cottages are available for rent and according to an ex-navy friend who stays there regularly, it is as close to being at sea without leaving the land.

Another iconic light is put astern and I am chuffed to be heading west again. The low mist refuses to disappear and intermittently blots out the far shore. Two dorsal fins punctuate the surface. I take an educated guess at harbour porpoises, due to their shyness and small size.

I stop at Rabbit Island. A small, uninhabited chunk of land a couple hundred metres from the mainland. Sadly, there are no rabbits to be

Red Strand by Galley Head

seen. Its mirror-like channel reflects sky and land. I bisect it silently, my green blade slowly nudging onto the gravel beach. Situated below the ruins of an old cottage, the scene is one of complete calm. Without a breath of wind the gnarly blackthorn has tiny insects orbiting about it. I climb up through wild and overgrown vegetation to look back at *Murchú's* sleek lines in contrast to the crumbling ruins and the clumpy land. I see impressions of lazy beds, places where potatoes were grown, and I wonder did this island steer clear of the deadly blight during the Famine. Many offshore islands did, but due to its proximity to the mainland, I fear this one may have succumbed.

Soon I am back aboard *Murchú* continuing ever westwards. The grey-blue waters are agitated as I cut across small recesses indented into the shoreline. Bee-lining is one of the great advantages of travelling by sea, and with the next headland being Toe Head, my last south coast promontory, I am on another straight line segment. As I approach this proud buttress of rock, I am looking forward to where I will swing *Murchú's* compass from west to north. Soon, I will be at the southwestern most extremity of my trip, and with the elongated peninsulas of Cork and Kerry pushing out into the Atlantic like digits on an enormous hand, I will have some big open crossings to consider.

Bulging swells swallow a large rock ledge jutting out from shore. Seconds later it reappears, rising from the frothing foam. My mind

Toe Head

wanders, imagining it as a stone whale breaching. Toe Head is getting closer, and strange shards of rock appear on the horizon. I later learn they are called The Stags, large tooth-shaped rocks lying only two kilometres offshore. They mark the site where the supertanker *Kowloon Bridge* sank in 1986, causing Ireland's worst oil spill.

Unceasingly, *Murchú* and I keep tracking westwards. I am chuffed to see the odd black guillemot in its dark summer plumage whirring past. These black beauties are my favourite seabird, bizarrely morphing to near white during the non-breeding season. For me, they push the ever popular puffin into a close second place. With bold white patches on both sides of each wing, and a pair of bright red feet, they keep their distance. Their haughty appearance in flight, head up and tail down, belies their timidity. Interestingly, when landing they splay their webbed feet to create more surface area permitting slower flight, essential when landing on the narrowest of ledges. This characteristic is mimicked by aircraft manufacturers who attach flaps to the rear of an aeroplane's wing.

Up ahead, I notice a disturbance off the headland, something is in the water that I cannot explain. Moving in an erratic, slow fashion, it is too distant for a good sighting. I paddle onwards and spot another disturbance, this time catching sight of a bulky black triangle moving along the surface. In another hundred metres I see five black triangles criss-crossing directly ahead. Basking sharks. Some tidal flows are bulging over submerged rocks which must be bringing nutrients towards the surface that this group is gorging on. They are big, measuring between seven and eight metres, longer than my kayak. With only the mighty whale shark outsizing them, they are the planet's second largest fish. Being directly ahead and on my track, I elect to run the gauntlet. I know this sounds crazy, since they are plankton-feeding leviathans posing no threat, but my heartbeat involuntarily rises at their proximity. Other than the odd porpoise, I have not seen many large creatures whilst afloat. The previous encounter was from the land when a lone one tracked by Dunworley Cove after I landed. This is different.

Automatically, my knees and feet push against the boat. My posture tenses. The hair on the back of my neck stands on end as I approach these enormous fish. A frisson pulses through me. If I were in a group, banter would cut through the stark reality, or should that be shark reality, of being in the company of these great creatures. I paddle into their orbit. Faint bubbling sounds from flaccid fins touch my ears. I am soon surrounded by these grazers of the sea. Underneath the surface, I catch glimpses of their outsize gapes, sifting barrel-loads of ocean. Despite knowing their diet consists of tiny zooplankton, my mind dreams up images of me and my sword-shaped craft being consumed by one. Clearly my imagination could be the ruin of me.

Part of me is loving the experience, while a saner part of my brain hopes it passes quickly. I must be careful not to accidentally bump into one of these guys in case they react abruptly. They are slowly circulating in an area the size of two tennis courts. Appearing and disappearing like wombats at a fairground, my head is swinging left and right watching them intently. A tail fin passes, then a submerged mouth, then a dorsal fin, another tail, now two almost collide. With me in the middle, it feels like being in the bumpers at a fairground, but I am not really into the game. I just keep paddling, watching, adjusting course, moving, until finally I dare to think that up ahead is an area free of slicing fins. I keep watching, just in case a rogue follows me, until at last I allow myself to breathe normally and the tension slowly subsides. Wow, what an experience.

I continue on my way, buoyed up by the unexpected occurrence as my heartbeat slowly returns to normal. Already capitalising on my safe passage, I am reminiscing about what just happened. My thoughts swing to my Dad and how he would have been fascinated by my recollections. I am again saddened at being so recently denied the opportunity of telling him about this one. He opened my eyes to the wonders of the natural world and I will be forever thankful.

My final stop before my southwest turning point at Baltimore is Gokane Point. I paddle into a rocky slot cut into this headland. All along this coastline, the sedimentary rock lies almost vertically. At the back of the slot, some huge grey rock slabs are strewn untidily about as if thrown by a petulant giant. I park my kayak and negotiate the slippery rocks to take a breather. I tie my kayak to a shard just in case it decides to stray off without its pilot.

Next, the Kedge rocks appear. In the distance these vertical rock sheets rise out of the sea to form an interesting family of islets. The largest one, topped with a grassy crown, appears like a mother island. Positioned just 500 metres from shore, local sheep farmers used to graze their small flocks there back in the day. All this lies off an impressive stretch of coastline, where the steep ground climbs away from the sea towards the sky like a steep rooftop. When alongside, my landside horizon is an impressive 60 degrees overhead, a portend of what lies in store for my journey up our most battered, and cliff-strewn, western seaboard.

I push past the Kedge, eagerly searching the cliffs for my gateway. Marked by the iconic Baltimore beacon, a white conical pillar perched 35 metres above sea level, this is the gateway into Baltimore harbour and beyond. The disconnected coastline continues for another 18 kilometres along the southern flanks of both Sherkin and Cape Clear islands, ending finally at the remote Fastnet rock, the southwesternmost part of Ireland. This opening is the first opportunity for smaller boats to begin tracking up our western seaboard. Approaching this sentinel from below, I am enjoying a new perspective compared to previous visits to the area when I took the well-trodden path to stand beside the white beacon to share its magnificent sea views. Built by the British in

1798 in response to the failed Irish rebellion, it was part of the country-wide effort to improve navigation along our coasts. It earned the title 'Lot's Wife' from the locals.

As a last goodbye to the south coast a basking shark's fin swirls around the boat as I slowly enter the passage. I smile, knowing that my earlier shark experience has been absorbed so I am not completely freaked out. Learn, grow and move on. Once inside, the water transforms to a turquoise mirror. I have the promise of a bed for the night so I reduce my speed to a crawl.

The town of Baltimore is spread across the sloping hillside all the way down to its busy harbour. Hundreds of nearby islanders use it to access the mainland. With ferries plying their trade between Sherkin, Hare and Cape Clear islands throughout the day it is a busy place, especially in high season. The orange and white Cape Clear boat passes with its complement of passengers enthusiastically leaning over the rails. My snail pace allows me to enjoy this hive of maritime activity going on all around me. Small fishing boats head out to the ocean as colourful dinghies nudge across the bay in the lightest of breezes. After being alone for most of the day all this bustle gives me with a warm feeling that helps soothe my recent bereavement. The magic that is Baltimore has me under its spell. I already feel at home.

Baltimore Harbour, Force Zero

THE HISTORY OF BALTIMORE IS FASCINATING. An English colony was planted here in the early 1600s with lands leased from the local O'Driscoll clan. Piracy, then a thriving occupation in these parts, was rampant along the coast. In 1631, Barbary pirates from North Africa sacked the town, taking most of the residents back to Algeria as slaves. Two elderly men who were initially taken were released further down the coast. The area stayed depopulated for generations with the remaining population moving east, and inland, to Skibbereen. Some of those enslaved worked as labourers or servants in royal houses. Some were fortunate enough to earn freedom, thanks to accumulating some funds from the small wage they were entitled to. Some of these women were rumoured to have married into royalty, but this is speculation, adding a great dollop of colour to stories that stem from the raid. On the flip and less rosy side, there were others who sadly ended their days working as galley slaves. My host here is a descendant of the original O'Driscoll clan, who enjoys a bit of sailing and less of the piracy, which Tony happily reminds me is lurking just below the surface.

It is baking hot as I heave my fully laden kayak onto its trolley. The house, overlooking the natural harbour, is a steep climb from sea level. These gradients, rarely noticed in a car, take on a new meaning when hauling 50 kilos of kit uphill. It is like being in an oven whilst trying to complete some ridiculous strongman challenge. I stop four times as my heart rate maxes out. Maybe it is the emotional drain of the previous seven days mixing with my day on the water, but finally, when I elevate all my kit to my lodgings, I am beat.

Tony has entrusted me with his place for the evening, so I chill, grab a shower and pop down to partake of the best fish and chips imaginable. I munch heartily, perched above the harbour, observing the sea traffic coming and going. This has to be one of my favourite places to eat al fresco. The hustle and bustle from three eateries spills out onto an open space, and combines with the uninterrupted view over the harbour. As a backdrop is the sea, distant mountains and nearby offshore islands, adding up to a wonderful scene.

Magical Baltimore

bour. As a backdrop is the sea, distant mountains and nearby offshore islands, adding up to a wonderful scene.

Time to ponder alone. Despite being amongst holidaymakers, tourists and locals, I am happy to be on my own this evening. The intensity of the previous week has distracted me from fully absorbing Dad's passing. Last year, as I rounded Ireland's southeast corner, both my parents were alive. Now, as I round this southwestern extremity, they are both gone. I am 'on the top shelf,' as an elderly aunt of mine jokingly refers to her own status. Life, trickling along at its own imperceptible pace, day in, day out, suddenly shifts. A rupture occurs, and part of the world is gone. The logical part of my brain knows it is inevitable, but my emotional side is still catching up. With both my parents well into their eighties it has not been a complete surprise, but the gap now left behind is completely unfamiliar.

I look out over the myriad colours of this vibrant coastal town, across the panorama of green fields, blue sea and sky, while in my mind an image of my folks appears. Just as the surrounding landscape provides a backdrop to this town, they have provided one for my own existence. Blessed to have them for so long, I almost feel wrong in mourning their passing, but I must. After finishing my post-meal drink, I head back along the coast road towards my lodgings. They are

Stage 12

NEGOTIATING MIZEN HEAD

The early morning descent to sea level converts yesterday's hard work to a welcome kinetic benefit. What a thrill to have gravity assist my early departure. The remnants of a disused slip allow me access to the small local cove. I paddle through a liquorice-all-sorts of craft tethered to their mooring buoys and out towards the belly of this natural haven. Moorings always captivate me. From the elegant cruising yachts furthest from shore, to the tiniest open boats nearby, they are a manifestation of the dreams of their owners. A white open fibreglass job with pale blue gunwales looks nicely cared for as I brush close by, while a few serious looking yachts look capable of crossing the Atlantic.

The morning is calm, or *windstille*, as the ever accurate Germans call it. I am threading my way out of Baltimore's enclosed waters, between islands, out into Roaringwater Bay. The sea is an iridescent silver, stretched taut like a vast foil sheet. Normally, I spot some disturbance but not today, no aberration breaks its uniformity. Swinging my eyes to each quarter, all I see is a sleeping ocean. Roaringwater Bay is the opposite of its name. Perfection is the word which best describes the place. Today I am reflecting on my Dad. No more sharings will happen between us. None of these adventures will pass his ears, and any recounting will have to find other listeners, or readers. In many ways writing this book is a way of addressing his absence in my life. As I skim across the perfect ocean today I am bursting with thanks, am aware of the great privilege of being alive and pursuing my dream.

I am heading towards the first unbroken promontory in the south-west, Mizen Head peninsula. Unlike the Baltimore finger, which has been eroded into a southwest pointing archipelago, this one is intact and an obstacle that must be circumvented. My destination is Crookha-ven, a cosy hamlet tucked into a rare east-facing bay short of the Miz-en. The end point of this portion of my trip is determined by a contact who will provide storage for my kayak there.

Most of the islands in this bay are low lying and easily accessed, with signs of habitation in abundance. Actors Jeremy Irons and Sinead Cusack live in Kilcoe Castle, a Norman keep dating from the 1600s and perched on Mannin Beg tucked into its eastern extremities. After 400 years of ruin, it has been transformed into a home. In order to make it liveable the five foot thick walls had to be 'harled', a Scottish term for plastering. Deciding to introduce iron sulphate into the mix the exteri-or turned a bright pink which provoked some criticism. It became re-ferred to as a giant phallus, but over time the locals accepted their new landmark, commenting that in rain or shine the place always looks to be reflecting a golden sunset.

When seen on a map, Roaringwater Bay looks like a large, rectangular-shaped bay containing two lines of islands stretching towards the horizon. While navigating along the three Calf islands, imaginatively named East, Middle and West, I decide to make my customary stop. With zero wind, a white hot sun overhead, and me dressed for the morning chill, I am overheating. Compounded by downing lots of water to ward off dehydration, some relief is called for. I have promised myself not to pee whilst in my boat, unless in a doomsday situation, which thankfully this is not. Nonetheless, I am uncomfortable. I find a secluded spot behind a gorse bush to pee, wondering from whom am I hiding? With the nearest habitation over four kilometres away on the mainland, I laugh to myself, mid-pee, more relaxed than when I started. Oh, the simple pleasures of my world. Unbeknown to me at the time, further up the west coast I will come much closer to crossing that line, but that is for another chapter.

Nestled in its slender east-facing bay, Crookhaven is the last har-bour guaranteeing shelter before Castletownbere, some 30 kilometres

Roaringwater Bay

further north. Comprising a collection of dwellings huddled around its small harbour, two pubs and, bizarrely, a jewellers shop, it exudes quaintness. The finger of land on which it rests is precariously connected to the mainland by a 100 metre wide spit of sand, essentially its umbilical road. Crookhaven is almost an island and it feels like it too thanks to the elongated u-shaped access road that skirts the shore of the inlet.

Due to its remoteness and tiny population, I had no contacts in the area to ask about storing my kayak so turned to fellow circumnavigator Jon Hynes from Kinsale Outdoor Education Centre for help. He had a contact in Jorg Uschkamp, the aforementioned jeweller, who along with his wife Mary run a successful business in this remotest of places. Only managing to speak to them by phone beforehand, an arrangement to store my kayak had been made, but unfortunately, with the passing of my Dad and arriving a week late, they are going to be away. My disappointment is short-lived as they have a plan B. My kayak will be stored in a pier-side shed of a friend of theirs, who will meet me on arrival. And to top that, they are entrusting me with the use of their car to get to Goleen to catch my bus to Cork. I am elated.

111

The prospect of having to arrange all this after landing would have been a nightmare, so having it sorted is a treat.

After driving to Goleen, I am to park outside O'Meara's bar, pop the keys into the envelope provided and hand them in at the bar. They will collect the car on their return. Wow, these guys are really pulling out all the stops for me. This is particularly impressive as they had never laid eyes on me before. I afterwards discover that Jon himself had originally 'cold called' them as he was passing through and they had been equally supportive. Once again, the unstinting generous support offered me along the way is a feature of my trip that will always stay with me.

I RETURN TO CROOKHAVEN AFTER TWO BUSY weeks of ferrying holidaymakers all over Europe as a pilot for Aer Lingus and it is time for my own break. The evening is balmy, more akin to the continent than our island. My mind is preoccupied as I mentally rehearse the plan for the

Landing on Crookhaven

next stretch ahead. Conditions have remained completely calm thanks to a stubborn high pressure over western Europe. The campsite's grass is parched and the musty smell of heat hangs in the evening air. I have been delivered here by my ever supportive brother-in-law Ciaran and his daughter Juliette, with whom I share a delicious seafood meal before going our separate ways. To be honest, I feel uneasy the whole evening, despite finally meeting my two hosts Jorg and Mary outside their jewellery shop. What is constantly on my mind is the prospect of having to round the Mizen in the morning. It has been bearing down on me like a dark cloud these last two weeks, and I know that by this time tomorrow all will be revealed one way or another.

By virtue of the ruggedness of this headland, the most southwesterly in Ireland, I will have to clock up almost 30 kilometres before I can make landfall. Most of this stretch is far out to sea with few escape options, so the previous two weeks have been filled with vivid imaginings of how this passage might go. Fear of the unknown is a terrible thing, and when coupled to a lifetime of kayaking and a vivid

With Crookhaven roadies, Ciaran, Elisa and Juliette

imagination, the end result can be terrifying. I have to remind myself that each and every day I launch into the ocean it is up to me alone to decide whether to continue with my trip.

I sleep soundly, and am up and underway below a baking sun by 9.00 am. I round Brow Head and catch my first glimpse of the Mizen as it peeps out in the distance. It feels like a blind date. There you are, you beauty. This sleeping dragon needs a low pressure system to wake it from its slumber. I am lucky today. It is a soporific day for the beast. Although I still have 25 kilometres before landing, I will not be falling at the first hurdle. I have rounded another great landmark on my journey. The Mizen has been paired with Malin Head up North as the opposite extremities of our island home. Just under 600 kilometres by road it is 750 by my watery route. It is too far away to fathom right now, but it drifts into my thoughts nonetheless.

The Mizen Light, accessed via a white suspension bridge spanning a huge cut, is clearly visible like a stubby white candle nestled high

Camping out in Crookhaven

on the headland. Scattered about lies a jumble of enormous sections of angular rock that have calved off the cliffs. To my untrained eye, the Mizen Head resembles a geological car crash. It is as if some great beast lost its temper and threw lumps of strata about the place leaving an untidy mess. Thinking about the forces needed to create such a scene sends shivers down my spine. The swells that arrive here after their transatlantic journey must be staggering to wreak such havoc. Thankfully, my arrival at this spot has coincided with minimal disturbance. It lifts me up and down less than a metre and leaks in and out of the jumbled mess to my right. I am grateful that my Mizen Head fears were unfounded.

After the Mizen, the lesser known Sheep Head reveals its slightly smaller snout to my right as I strike out across the open water. I am headed towards the next finger of the southwest, the Beara Peninsula. This is a commiting stretch, since the rock finger ending at Sheep Head offers no place to land should I need to run for cover. The crossing to Beara is a 23 kilometre leap, three times the span of Dublin Bay. It is time to put in the big yards, thankfully on a very peaceful ocean. With a high sun as company I pierce the perfect meniscus with my bow, my blades rotating continuously like the cranks of a bicycle. The calmness offers an opportunity to fine tune my strokes as I go. The perfect long distance paddling stroke uses the torso, rather than just arms, to gain maximum propulsion through the water. These are the building blocks on which my whole trip is built, so any small improvements to my technique is welcome. With about 500 paddle strokes per kilometre, by the time I am back home in Skerries I will have accumulated just shy of 900,000, nearly a million rotations. Wow.

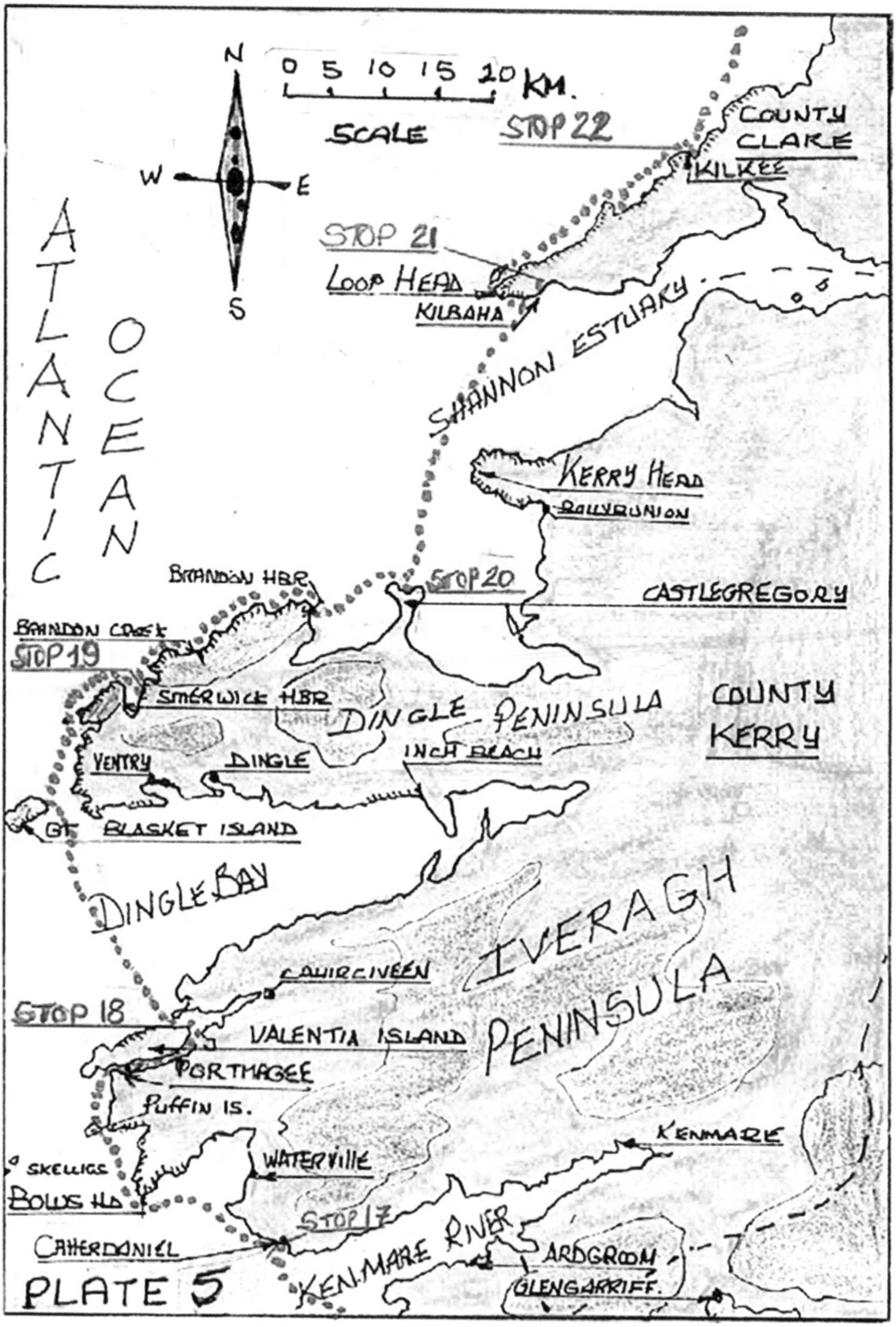

Map showing the Atlantic Ocean coast with the Dingle Peninsula and Iveragh Peninsula in County Kerry and County Clare.

Labels on map:

N, W, E, S

0 5 10 15 20 KM. SCALE

STOP 22

COUNTY CLARE

KILKEE

STOP 21

LOOP HEAD

KILBAHA

SHANNON ESTUARY

KERRY HEAD

BALLYBUNION

BRANDON HBR.

STOP 20

CASTLEGREGORY

BRANDON CREEK STOP 19

SMERWICK HBR.

DINGLE PENINSULA

COUNTY KERRY

VENTRY DINGLE INCH BEACH

GT. BLASKET ISLAND

DINGLE BAY

CAHIRCIVEEN

IVERAGH PENINSULA

STOP 18

VALENTIA ISLAND

PORTMAGEE

PUFFIN IS.

KENMARE

SKELLIGS

WATERVILLE

BOLUS HD.

STOP 17

CAHERDANIEL

KENMARE RIVER

ARDGROOM

GLENGARRIFF.

PLATE 5

ATLANTIC OCEAN

Stage 13

FROM CORK TO KERRY,
BYPASSING THE SKELLIG ISLANDS

I pull in past Black Ball Head to a narrow cove called Lower Reen, the first stop on what is shaping up to be a big day. I am more than happy to have 30 kilometres behind me without even a sniff of seasickness. The day's magnificence reflects my buoyant mood. The meteorological gods have spared me a difficult passage across this big stretch, and I am grateful. All previously imagined scenarios, thankfully, never materialised. I walk back on the flaggy shore and deposit myself on a carefully chosen rock to ponder. A collection of houses are scattered about and two old fibreglass boats have been pulled up onto the grass. The agreeable rock I am sitting on transfers the sun's heat back into me.

I relish these stops completely. Getting around this island is an accumulation of mini-conquests, nothing more, nothing less. While it demands all types of skills and experience, the most important part seems to be the self-talk I engage in beforehand. After paying due attention to the risks versus my capabilities, a commitment to do it is called upon. Once the metaphorical leap is taken, surprisingly, the task is already half done. The second half is where I make the dream real, stroke by stroke. So landing after today's early first passage, I psychologically exhale and enjoy another goal achieved. A great phrase I came across recently seemed to sum it up nicely. 'You can only join the dots when looking back.'

I leave Lower Reen and begin flanking the southern escarpments of the Beara. I am now navigating along the next giant finger of Ireland's southwestern corner. The sloping cliffs are blanched bone dry and are

117

Lower Reen, County Cork

baking under a high sun. I can sense their warmth, and visualise myself luxuriating against their base in splendid isolation. I ponder that my last 200 kilometres of paddling have all been off County Cork, with Kerry's Iveragh peninsula patiently waiting for my arrival, hopefully later today.

I am slowly making my way along some lowish coastline towards Dursey Island. This barely inhabited island is unique in Ireland in that it boasts a cable car. Opened in 1969 by Taoiseach and Corkman Jack Lynch, it continues to be a huge draw for tourists to the area. Angela and I had the pleasure of experiencing it first-hand many years ago. Suspended from cables 50 metres above sea level, a box-shaped cabin transports small groups of up to six people across to the island in ten minutes. I remember gazing down mid-channel at the sea far below questioning the wisdom of boarding such a thing. Perhaps in the Alps on a skiing holiday it would make sense, but in such a remote place it just did not seem right. Still, we spent an afternoon exploring the island and gladly returned to the mainland courtesy of the same contraption. As I make my way towards the island it is not lost on me that this service was initiated because the currents in the narrow channel below made boat journeys too perilous. Conditions seem benign, but I nonetheless maintain my habit of praying for a safe passage.

Dursey Pier

A spine of rock called Lamb's Head hides my next goal. This elongated hump-backed finger mimics the island it blocks but allows passage via a narrow sea route that leaves me gasping. Jon had forewarned me to follow this lane-sized cut if conditions were suitable. Two great flat plates of purplish limestone tower towards their grassy tops above. In awe of my surroundings I do not immediately notice the panoramic view of my lunch-stop appearing in front of me. The full length of Dursey Island's southern side greets me as I exit this enchanting rock gully. At the start of the twentieth century this six kilometre island had a population of over 200, but nowadays boasts only five residents. With many holiday homes in regular use, and thanks to its cable car delivering 20,000 visitors annually, its main thoroughfares are kept well worn. I pull in at the rarely used slipway and hoist myself above the tiny pier to bask on the short grass, kept trim by the island's free-roaming sheep.

An impossibly bright sun beats down from high above as I delight in some snacks, relishing the 40 kilometres already bagged. I spend almost an hour on Dursey until finally deciding to continue through the sound and strike out across to the next finger. I will be nearing 60 kilometres if I make it to Derrynane on the Iveragh peninsula in County Kerry.

I end the day pulling into the idyllic Derrynane beach. A tiny jetty extends from the shore as small sand dunes back the strand. The place is populated by a scattering of families. As the tide is at its height, I stick to camping on the sand. I do not fancy getting caught by a watery night-time visitor. I find a cosy spot beside a low embankment only 20 metres from the water's edge, and decide it will do nicely as home for what is forecast to be a balmy windless night. My tent pegs slice easily into the warm golden powder as I beach camp for the second time of the trip. After such a long-distance day I forgo cooking, heading off instead to nearby Bridie's Pub for some cod and chips. Eating *al fresco* on this hot sunny evening is heavenly.

Derrynane with campsite on beach barely visible bottom right

Wandering back to my tent, I witness the golden disc of the sun slip behind the distant horizon. What a fantastic day on the water I have just had. With the Mizen astern I am now firmly on our western seaboard. The American continent lies beyond my left shoulder with only the mighty Atlantic separating us. I will slowly scratch my way along our colourful west coast to Malin Head, and from there it should be plain sailing, as they say. It is almost too much for me to take in, so I stick to the present. I climb into my tiny abode, wriggle into my sleeping bag and check tomorrow's forecast on my phone. On discovering it to be a continuation of today's, I smile, turn off the tiny screen, and settle into my first of five nights in Kerry.

Coffee maker at Derrynane camp

I wake up to another picture-postcard day. I strike camp and head off across Ballinskelligs Bay aiming *Murchú* at Bolus Head. A large bay to my right hides the distant town of Waterville, a significant spot on the legendary Ring of Kerry route. Hundreds of tourist buses snake along this circuit every season. The route delineates the Iveragh peninsula, and is peppered with colourful towns and amazing views. Since 1980 the Ring of Kerry Charity Cycle has joined the buses. This hugely popular, one-day event has grown from an initial 46 riders to over 8,000, all endeavouring to complete its 175-kilometre loop. Interestingly, measuring one tenth of my own circumnavigation, it reminds me of how slow my kayak is.

Bolus's bulky headland resembles a half submerged dinosaur lying across my path. A single road runs along its flank like the lateral stripe of a fish. With difficulty, I scan the slopes for Cill Rialaig, a pre-famine village that laid in ruins for decades until Noelle Campbell-Sharp, an

Bolus Head

artist, philanthropist, editor and publisher, organised a group of locals to rebuild it as an artists' village. Since its unveiling in 1992 it has been offering free residencies to both up and coming and established artists. Having visited it once, I am keen to find it, finally spotting its camouflaged cluster of small stone buildings looking out over my path.

As I near the steeper sides of Bolus Head, an odd shimmer appears on the white metallic sea. Frissons of wind are hitting the water in the lee of this bulky promontory. It puzzles me as no winds were forecast until the afternoon when the sea breezes kick in. As I continue, scatterings of light catch my eye, resembling creatures racing across the surface. Occasionally one collides with me as it passes. I assume they are tumbling down from the headland and as soon as I round it they should be gone.

I continue to the corner of the head where the silver sea beyond seems more active. Once around it I expect a one hour paddle to cover the eight kilometres to Puffin island, barely separated from the mainland. As I inch my way past the land's snout and out of its lee, I am met with a surprise. The full force of a fresh breeze blows directly into my face. An un-forecast ten knots is churning up the sea into a confused state, cutting my rate of progress in half. With nowhere to hide, I simply must press on. The number four on my deck-mounted speedometer taunts me as this was never in my calculations. I resign myself to putting in some hard yards.

Two hours later I am below the great grey cliffs of Puffin island. Unfortunately, my celebrations need to be postponed as I am seriously in need of a break. After three uninterrupted hours in my boat, most of it banging into the swells, my bladder is demanding attention but I refuse point blank to relieve myself until I exit my kayak on dry land. Unfortunately, I find myself with no obvious place to land due to steep cliffs plunging directly into deep water. In fact, the area I paddle into is a towering cul-de-sac with high grey limestone walls on three sides and a completely sheltered area of calm water at their base. About a hundred puffins are scurrying about, no doubt reacting to the unexpected arrival of the green torpedo. Sadly, thanks to my uncomfortable state, the beauty of this scene cannot be fully appreciated. I need to address the job at hand, which I literally do a few minutes later at a boulder beach. The sensation of relieving myself after such restraint borders on the orgasmic. Finally, I wheel myself around to properly take in my whereabouts. From my Puffin Island stop I examine the route from Bolus Head. It had been an unexpectedly tricky section with no get out on offer. I make a mental note never to get complacent.

Portmagee, County Kerry

Me and two buddies stopped here four years ago on our way back from the Skellig Islands. Situated 15 kilometres from the mainland, the Skellig Islands are a big prize for the sea kayaker. Rising skyward out of the blue ocean, they are a breathtaking sight, especially from close range though a landing is not always possible due to the uninterrupted Atlantic swell. Only the larger of the two, Skellig Michael, was ever inhabited, with its nearby smaller neighbour, Little Skellig, playing host to some 35,000 pairs of gannets. Over the centuries the colony has painted their home with white guano giving it the incongruous look of an alpine peak jutting out of the depths. The larger twin-peaked iteration was home to a colony of monks over 1,000 years ago. How they managed to get there, land and build their beehive huts is a bewildering thought, only fully registering when you get there.

When we three kayakers arrived we were greeted by an irate warden in charge of the tiny landing spot. She was insistent that we not come ashore. She reminded us this privilege is only granted to those arriving on the few permit-holding boats from Portmagee or Ballinskelligs. As a UNESCO heritage site it has gained further notoriety after it was a *Star Wars* filming location, making seats on these boats much sought after. I remember feeling quite queasy and in need of a landing and hence unimpressed with the irate warden peering down from her perch on the pier. I tried another tack, mentioning a leak in my boat, which I had, and the need to effect a repair. 'Go to one of the tourist boats waiting offshore,' she spat. My queasiness never subsided on the return trip, so our stop-off at Puffin Island was another one of great relief. I remember clambering ashore and lying spread-eagled on the grass. Thankfully, many years later, today's arrival, apart from a full bladder, is less uncomfortable. Though not ideal, I will happily exchange that for seasickness any day.

Stage 14

A Tarantino-Type Twist
Off Dingle's Peninsula

I push on to Portmagee as colourful, Skellig-bound boats ply their trade to the lonely destination. When I land, the place is abuzz as boats await departure. Expectant passengers are suitably excited, realising their luck in securing a seat to this other-worldly place. I reflect on what lies in store for them so far out on the ocean. I hope that each one will have the privilege of climbing the 600 steps towards the heavenly site of the monks' beehive huts.

My desire for food is heavily influenced by what I see being delivered to the waiting customers outside. Fish and chips are my personal trip's *plat du jour*. Duly delivered, I take my place among the tourists who populate the quayside tables outside. The place resonates with vibrant chatter in the early afternoon air. All the comings and goings of a busy harbour impact my mind after my solo morning spin. My senses are heightened thanks to my recent confrontation with the unexpected wind, so I soak up the atmosphere and ring my B&B host on Valentia Island.

Valentia, clearly visible across the narrow channel, is accessed by a bridge nearby. Knightstown, its main town and my destination, lies eight kilometres further up the channel. Made famous for its daily weather reports issued by Met Éireann, ironically these reports now come from Cahirciveen on the mainland. They have kept the Valentia Island moniker due to the original location of a telegraph station located there for over a century. In 1858 the first telegraphic cable between Europe and the North America arrived here. Valentia Island

Valentia Island Lighthouse

had the added bonus of relaying the weather to London. Using 2,700 kilometres of cable, laid on the seabed by *The Great Eastern*, the biggest ship of its day, this was the stuttering start to transatlantic communications. It was not until the 1960s, when satellite communications were established, that the station closed its doors.

I reluctantly leave my quayside perch, hop into *Murchú*, and begin paddling along the island's flat inside channel. Rural smells reach me on the water and I enjoy the ease of the passage. Close to shore I pass under trees hanging lazily in the calmness. Slowly Knightstown appears, another sensory reward after all my day's efforts. I skirt the marina well within earshot of the hustle and bustle of holidaymakers. The ferry shuttles the 500 metres between the mainland and here. I see its blue and white bridge gently disconnect from its slipway on the mainland. It is picture postcard stuff.

I pass the town and continue, as per instructions, a couple of kilometres towards The Horizon Lodge B&B. Cathal, the proprietor, will be keeping an eye out for me from his yellow bungalow thirty metres up the hill. He recommended coming ashore directly below and bringing my kayak up from there. I take him at his word, blissfully ignorant of what this will actually entail. The northwesterly aspect of this side of the island means all the houses are drenched in the strong evening light. I search the hillside in vain until I hear a voice from above. It is Cathal. He weaves his way down the very steep semi-overgrown slope to the rocks below. He hails me over, pointing to where I can get out. I am in disbelief. The rocks at the shoreline are the size of small cars heaped against each other. My sense is that this endeavour is impos-

sible, especially after having paddled well over 100 kilometres in
two days. My arms are tired, and
heaving a fully laden expedition
kayak around is no joke. Cathal
is insistent. A battle of wills starts
up. The more I suggest the futil-
ity of this approach, the more he
seems determined to do it. He
informs me that the other option
available is via the nearby beach
and up the main road to his place.
He emphasises that that option is
a much longer drag. I mull things
over and then realise that he is
prepared to put in a considerable
amount of effort to make this

Sunset, Valentia Island B&B

thing a reality. I capitulate. We
then embark on the cumbersome task of moving my kit and kayak
over the rocks onto the overgrown hillside and up to his house. On
finally reaching his house we high five each other and I turn about to
face the great vista above the golden ocean. In hindsight I have to agree
it was worth the joint effort.

I meet an interesting character over the following morning's breakfast. Tom, an ex-fisherman from Donegal, is training to be a coastguard
radio operator at nearby Valentina Coastguard station. After his three
month stint he will be returning to his native Donegal to work in its
Malin Head station. He shows huge interest in my trip having heard
my calls on the radio over the past few days. He quizzes me about my
safety equipment, my navigation methods and my plan for the day.
I point north over the ocean, explaining I will be finally leaving the
Iveragh Peninsula and heading directly to the Great Blasket. Lying off
the Dingle peninsula, this will be the final of Ireland's southwestern
'fingers'. Once there, I will be skirting its northern flanks and landing
near Brandon Harbour, a distance of around 44 kilometres. It is lovely

to meet someone on the other side of my radio transmissions and our exchange is frank and helpful. He promises to link up with me when I am near Malin Head. Since that is still hundreds of kilometres away I put it to the back of my mind as I continue loading *Murchú* for another adventure on the ocean.

My return to the ocean is via the main road and my trusty wheels are pressed into service again. I strike out and pass close to the squat low-lying lighthouse marking the northern entrance to the channel. I am in open water again, crossing between two giant fingertips pointing westward into the Atlantic. These enormous digits are the geological remnants of the pre-Cambrian era. This upheaval left the southwestern region's valleys open to being flooded by the sea, their adjacent higher ground remaining above sea level. It created a huge amount of new coastline in the process. They afford me the opportunity of short-cutting across their extremities, the completion of which is due later today. Here's to a good day bagging the full set.

Pre-departure, Great Blasket Island

Landing onto the Great Blasket is a huge milestone for me. Most of us who went through the Irish education system pre-1995 were forced to learn, through Irish, of the hardships endured by one of its former residents, Peig Sayers, a legendary storyteller. As an islander originally from Dunquin she left school at the age of 12 and moved to Dingle to work as a servant. After being engaged by various families, she eventually married Pádraig Ó Guithín, an islander, in 1892, moving afterwards to live on the Island. They had 11 children, of whom only six survived. She recalled 1920 as the worst year of her life when her second youngest died in a cliff accident while two of her other children emigrated to the United States. Her husband passed away the following year. Thanks to her power of recall, hundreds of local legends, ghost, folk and religious stories were collected and have become legendary. She is said to have been the best Irish female storyteller ever, one of the few historical characters known by her first name, a moniker she shares with her autobiography – *Peig*.

Great Blasket Island, County Kerry

The Great Blasket, or An Blaiscaod Mór in Irish, uninhabited since 1954, now boasts a small shop/cafe manned for the brief summer season. It also has a few restored holiday cottages. Boats from nearby Dingle deposit clusters of visitors to its tiny pier. I pinch myself as I near this stunning geographical waystop on my trip. A pod of dolphins cross my path as I bear down on this humpbacked island. Taking its place among a plethora of nearby islands, I am paddling into a scene worthy of a National Geographic photograph. After my four hour open water crossing, my eyes feast on the vivid landscape surrounding me. Approaching the beach, the clear water creates a tropical, non-Irish feel.

Landings prove tricky on steeply sloping beaches because my kayak is 18 foot long and I need to deposit at least half of it onto the sand to execute an easy exit. With the steep incline I will have to work hard to achieve this. If I fail, my only means of exit would be to drop out of my kayak into deep water beside the beach. No thanks. From about thirty metres out I sprint hard directly at the white ramp. My green bow slices into the perfect white grains of sand and *Murchú* rises skyward at a strange angle. She grinds to a halt. I quickly snap off my spraydeck, jump up and exit as quickly as possible, not the easiest thing to do after four hours of confinement. I drag her clear of the sucking backwash, chuffed with my crossing and my first landing here.

I stand on the wide, empty beach, take on board the grand vista, and enjoy my whereabouts. I recall leaving Crookhaven before the Mizen, two days and 120 kilometres ago, and soon, after my stopping here, I will be rounding the most northerly peninsula of our southwestern seaboard. I can already see the Sybil Head gateway in the distance so I know I am on the verge of bagging the full set of five protrusions.

Up the grassy flanks I see ramblers spreading in thin lines across the island. I spot a cafe's white walls shining like a lighthouse on the hill above. I climb the steep slope to dine *al fresco* in the warm sunshine. I decide to experience being here, rather than get side-tracked into conversation, as this moment is particularly special and I want to keep it to myself.

People are excitedly coming and going at the cafe, the hub of the island's activities. I am a little disappointed that the only fare on offer is tea from a disposable cup and a Mars bar or bag of crisps, but it fails to dull my mood. A large rusting church bell sits on the grass nearby. Against it leans a roof slate on which a simple message is painted. It speaks directly to me and brings a smile to my face. It reads, 'Nothing is worth more than this day'. I take a photograph with my phone to link the message to my blog. This shows that beyond the rusty bell, the expansive grassy slope falls away to the white beach below. A scattering of smaller islets punctuate the scene. The day so far is going perfectly – little do I realise what lies ahead.

Reluctantly, I descend the grassy incline to *Murchú*, waiting patiently on the beach below. A young couple with two children are drawn toward me, well toward *Murchú* actually. We chat briefly, soon discovering a mutual acquaintance from Skerries. This provides a connection, after which we engage more enthusiastically, culminating in

Great Blasket Island's 'cafe'

their offering assistance with my departure. I am chuffed, as launching solo from such a steep slope could leave the stern of my boat 'high and dry' with me neither in nor out of the water. Much like the threat on my arrival, I could turn turtle before being fully afloat. Their combined efforts push my boat into the sea whereupon I wheel about 90 degrees and wave in gratitude. The kids are delighted to help and I like to think I have created a wee memory for them to look back on.

Departing this idyllic scene, I turn my sights towards Sybil Head. I am bound for Smerwick Harbour, 18 kilometres and three hours paddling away. This headland marks the western end of The Three Sisters near Ballyferriter. When viewed from inland, they appear like the apex of a majestic three pointed circus tent, but their backside hides a nasty offering for my passage. These 'half hills' have no northern slopes; instead, descending from their summits are sheer black cliffs plunging vertically into the depths below. As I inch my way towards this giant wall, I notice an unease in the ocean. Being the most northerly of the promontories, it has been blocking swells coming from that direction. Now, with nothing between me and Iceland, a moderate swell is arriving unchecked. It is slowly dawning on me that my idyllic day is changing drastically. My stomach begins to react to the haphazard nature of the sea's surface and the randomness of my kayak's movements. Paddling under the shadow of these dark escarpments, in these conditions, so late in the day, is becoming uncomfortable. Over the briefest of time my day has taken a Quentin Tarantino-style leap. I am entering the worst area of clapotis I have ever experienced.

It dismays me how suddenly my *mal de mer*, and dizziness, take hold. Soon, I am struggling to stay on top of the situation. I peer left, scanning for smoother seas offshore. I clap eyes on a small fishing boat nearly a kilometre away writhing hideously on the buckling horizon. Not good. With no escape to my left and vertical cliffs to my right, plus a reluctance to turn back, it is make or break for me and once again my expedition hangs in the balance. I shout, plead, cajole and direct positive messages into my own head as I struggle to maintain control of my kayak. It is being tossed about like a bucking bronco at a fairground.

I am straining for all my worth to simply hang on. My defences have been breached. I am exposed,

With the ominous cliff curtain stretching ahead for six kilometres, I simply must stay committed. My life depends on it. There is no pattern to this dilemma. I am calling on my instincts, my years of paddling and my involuntary reactions to keep me upright and moving forward. Unfortunately all of these, along with my speed, are being whittled away under the weight of seasickness. I stubbornly battle on. Minute by sluggish minute, I persevere. My paddles swing wildly into support strokes as rogue iterations catch me unawares. Am I moving? I pick waymarks in the cliff in order to measure my progress, just like I did previously off Mine Head months earlier. As my pace slows it feels as though I am on a conveyor belt, barely moving along the foot of these unfriendly cliffs. The process is an unending battle of wits between me and the ocean. After what feels like hours, I slide, miraculously, through a break in the cliffs. I exit the madness into the calmer waters of Smerwick Harbour. Booming waves thunder clap both sides of the small entrance. I take them as applause for surviving the day's

Feoghanagh, Smerwick Harbour

late challenge. I crawl into this delicious shelter and slump forward towards my deck. I ask myself, 'What the hell was that all about?'

I slowly slice through the flat water at Feoghanagh, eventually allowing *Murchú* to rest on the hard mud. Ironically, I am almost completely surrounded by low lying countryside inside the near circular bay at Smerwick. The sea has breached the cliffs here, carving a wide bay into these lowlands behind the elevated coastline. It feels like being backstage after treading the boards on a high stakes performance. The steep ground behind me rises to the clifftops, and I am tired, sick and thankfully delivered. Adventures like these are personal. We all have different comfort zones and I know that during that final demanding stretch I was way outside mine. It is well-timed that my three days' paddling is complete. After 140 kilometres, I bed down happily at a friend's holiday home on the Dingle peninsula. Tomorrow I begin the long trudge for home.

After breakfast I hide my kayak behind Trish and Peter's old farmhouse, shuffling my two bulky Ikea bags of gear to the roadside. I am not about to miss the only local bus passing here today. The next door neighbour pulls out of his driveway and spots me looking at my watch. As this is the Gaeltacht, an Irish-speaking district, we had exchanged a few pleasantries using the native tongue the evening before. He winds down his window and shouts over.

'Tá fhios ag an tiomainí go bhfuil tú anseo, dúirt sé liom go mbeidh sé beagáiní déanach inniu'. ('The driver knows you are here. He told me he will be a wee bit late today.')

Well, such a welcome reassurance happily causes a change of focus. I breathe in the crisp morning air and soak up the colourful panorama surrounding me.

A big aspect of my staggered solo trip is the logistical challenge of getting to and from my put-ins. As local legend Philip King says, on his weekly music broadcasts from nearby Baile na nGall, 'We come to you from the most westerly point of Europe here in Dingle. The next stop after this place is America.' I am in the back of beyond. Getting home from here, and back again to continue my trip, will prove an interesting challenge.

Soon I see a red and white shoebox of a bus weaving its way to-wards me. Looking strangely out of place, it feels like my own person-al chauffeur is coming to get me. I climb aboard to join the handful of Dingle-bound locals for a day's work or some shopping. The driver confirms that he knew I was here and we both laugh, me at the novelty and him at my reaction. Following this circuitous bus ride to the pen-insula's legendary main town, I swap to another bus to Tralee. From there I transfer to the train. This whisks me across the country to Dub-lin where I take a lift home by car to Skerries. All my transfers, worked out in advance, happen seamlessly. I enjoy this element of my travels, and oftentimes find myself at sea, thinking about making it in time to catch my train, bus and even on one occasion, my plane.

Home for the night, Trish and Peter's farmhouse, Feoghanagh

Stage 15

THE SHANNON'S GAPING MAW

Leaving Feoghanagh in Country Limerick requires a large dollop of logistical planning to ensure the next two days' paddling have the best chance of success. My plan is for two days' paddling as far as County Clare. Day One will have me continue eastwards towards Castlegregory. I intend overnighting at Scraggan, the closest point to County Clare along this stretch. Day Two then will see me leap directly across the mouth of the River Shannon to Clare, an uninterrupted paddle of over 30 kilometres. Once settled, and with my kayak in storage, I plan to catch the Killimer to Tarbert ferry which will deposit me back into County Kerry. There I hope my logistical loop will be closed thanks to Des Carmody, a fellow pilot from the locale who has offered to collect my car and bring it to the ferry after cycling from Listowel. Our twin missions will be working in parallel that morning so my fingers are crossed for a good rendezvous. With everything in place I leave Skerries bound for Kerry, aware that my convoluted logistical plan is about to be pressed into action.

Arriving at Feoghanagh as dusk approaches has me buoyant. I unpack my kit and pop out back to move *Murchú* from its storage. My heart drops when I clap eyes on her. She no longer sports her sleek green lines but instead a mottled white spattering of rook droppings has whitewashed her from bow to stern. It upsets me that my wonderful boat has been transformed into such a sorry and neglected state. A few weeks' worth of caked guano has transformed *Murchú* into a blanched version of her former self. Unbeknowingly I had tucked her in under a set of trees behind a small wall to stay hidden from passersby. The rookery overhead was vacated at the time so I had no clue as to the amount of avian dung that would inevitably fall from above. Nothing to do but to set my alarm for an hour earlier and allow time to return my boat to its original self.

When I finally pull out of Smerwick Harbour it is after a good workout washing down *Murchú*. She is gleaming again, her glistening deck seems to wink at me as I turn the corner to face the morning sun. I am concerned about the challenging coastline which lies ahead today, as it is identical to the one which tested my arrival here. Thankfully, a handy way-stop at Brandon Creek is only eight kilometres of sunny paddling away. I start out hopeful.

An hour in and I am pleased to be visiting the site where Tim Severn's transatlantic voyage began. Using a replica Irish leather boat he was demonstrating the possibility that Irish monks, led by Saint Brendan the Navigator, could have crossed the Atlantic long before Columbus. That was in May 1976 and I was a teenager at the time, and remember following his adventure with great interest. He and his crew headed out across the Atlantic, adopting a stepping stone approach. Initially sailing along our west coast, visiting the Outer Hebrides and the Faroe Islands before arriving in Reykjavik later that year. They returned the following summer to complete the second, more treacherous, half of their journey.

After negotiating dangerous pack ice off Greenland, their thin-skinned vessel struck submerged ice which punctured its skin. As the hole was below the waterline it necessitated the stitching of a patch by one of the crew while dangling over the side. Crew member George Moloney was held by the legs as he stitched the thick leather, while being intermittently dunked below the sea's icy surface. This critical repair ensured they successfully reached Newfoundland in June 1977. They covered an impressive 7,200 kilometres since leaving Brandon and proved it was possible to cross the ocean in a hide-covered Currach, in use here well over a thousand years earlier. Severin would go on to cross most of the world's great oceans in various ancient craft, inserting some truth into the myths that had been circulating about early seafarers.

Pulling into the narrow opening, I turn ninety degrees into a cleft that hides a small pier and slipway cut into higher ground. I pull *Murchú* onto wet seaweed-covered stones, hop out, and have an amble about. I climb out of the deep cut in order to get a phone signal to ring Peter, an acquaintance from Skerries who I am due to rendezvous with soon. That will be at Brandon village after passing beneath the great bulk of Mount Brandon, whose northern flanks are being eaten into by the Atlantic. St Brendan must have been some character, as his name shows up everywhere in these parts. Having been promised an open crab sandwich outside Murphy's bar when I get there, Peter is now enticing me with a nice reward after covering the next stretch, a 16 kilometre segment underneath more north-facing cliffs. These cliffs are a continuation of those that challenged me on my previous leg, but thankfully today finds me in a much improved state.

Up ahead I see splashing where the silvery swells are choppily breaking below the cliff. Thinking it might be a submerged rock, I advance with caution. Moments later it reappears, but in a different position. I am puzzled, and due to the morning sun focus my squinting eyes across the shimmering sea that lies ahead. I am about to cross paths with a pair of high speed porpoises, both of whom are bearing down rapidly in the opposite direction. They zip past me at an impressive speed, mocking my paltry efforts at propelling myself and reminding me that I am the visitor in their domain.

I continue on, happy to contend with a lesser version of clapotis under Mount Brandon's cliffs. Not long after my cetacean encounter, I decide to swing into Sauce Bay to have a look. This great circular bay is like an amphitheatre, with steeply rising ground on three of its four sides. The remaining 700 metre opening to the sea provides a grand entrance into this geological wonder. Reminded of Russell Crowe's entrance into the Colosseum in *Gladiator*, I am dizzy observing my surroundings. Beneath these great rock constructs I paddle leisurely about on the flat and shimmering sea. I feel minuscule as I make my way to the back of this great cul-de-sac. I eventually decide to stay in my boat, such is the steepness of the boulder-strewn landing place backing the bay. After being suitably wowed, I head out to sea again salivating on the promised crab sandwich.

Brandon village lies hidden behind the cliffline I am traversing. Reaching it necessitates a swing of over ninety degrees around the sea cliffs of Brandon Point. Beyond the cliffs lies open water, flanked by the distant, low-lying shoreline to my right. The next land of note is the Magharees, six kilometres across the bay. The lowering cliffscape has been undercut by the sea and I find myself unable to resist investigating it up close. I tentatively paddle below the irregular rock canopy, which is my first time kayaking below ground since the Old Head of Kinsale back in May. While I examine the stony ceiling it dawns on me that this is potentially a risky interlude. As if by magic, great blocks of ochre bedrock hang irregularly above my head. Slowly, I put this phenomenon astern, exchanging it for the less threatening final two kilometres to the harbour and my rendezvous.

I follow the low coastline to the squat pier and slipway which encloses a flat sandy shore. Family groups are scattered about, encamped at various corners of this tiny enclave. They are by the sea wall, on the beach, sitting on benches while some are using the angled slipway as a sun bed. I notice Peter's wife Elaine and daughter Muireann approach across the sand. She explains that Peter has climbed the headland to spot me passing below and she has relayed that I have already landed. He is hurrying back to meet us as we speak. No doubt my subterranean route has denied him the chance to spot me.

Camping at Ballycurrane, Castlegregory, County Kerry

Murphy's shoreside pub squats cosily beside the harbour. It looks out towards the land on the far side of Brandon Bay which is backed by the great undulations of the Dingle Peninsula's central mountain ridge. The aforementioned open crab sandwich hits the spot as we chat about my adventures and their holiday. Peter and Elaine enthusiastically convey the uniqueness of this hidden gem which they have been frequenting for years, sometimes even visiting in mid-winter. The place, in concert with their reminiscences, has me smitten. I vow to return.

I tear myself away from this friendly encounter and head out across the bay. I am bound for Magharees, today's final destination. A small pod of dolphins circulate outside the harbour, causing an audible buzz from the pier's enthusiastic visitors. A small fishing boat heads to sea and I cheekily manage to hitch a ride on its trailing wake until the sea's chop interferes with my free ride. Buoyed up by my day so far, I skip across the bay in under an hour, landing at a small beach directly on my track. After a brief moment of relief – too much liquid intake over lunch – I bear down on Scragan Bay, today's target. I am puzzled by a solitary windsurfer gliding at a reasonable pace across the bay. With the board hidden by some intervening rocks, I cannot reconcile how he is travelling so fast in such light winds. When past the rocks, I realise the board is mysteriously elevated above the waterline, and careering along like a magic carpet. It dawns on me that I am witness to a windsurfer using the recently adapted hydrofoil system. It turns out to be local legend Jamie Knox, a larger than life character who later explains to me his enthusiasm for this new type of windsurfing. Jamie runs the local watersports centre and organised a major windsurfing event here back in the mid-nineties.

I make an unfortunate discovery not long after my arrival. My VHF has packed up. With the Shannon estuary to cross tomorrow, I need to fill the void that has appeared in my kit. I hazard a guess that Jamie may be able to help, and fortunately bump into him outside The Green Room pub. In his loud London accent he informs me that he has about twenty radios at home, most of which actually work. He is happy to loan me one if I call over to his home, which conveniently is close to my campsite. By the time I am bedding down for the night I have a fully operational, fully charged radio in my possession. It goes a long way to helping me get a sound night's sleep.

From the start of my trip back in June 2017, my days were planned with way-stops strategically placed along my route. Ideally, a mini-stop around one hour into my trip allows me to carry out any micro adjustments, get comfy, and continue onwards. Whether a stretch, a pee or just an itch to be scratched, it has always been a welcome chance to sort myself out. With the prospect of hours wedged in my boat, being comfortable is a high priority.

On Illauntannig, one of the Magharees islands

Today's only available way-stop will be after twenty minutes on one of the Magharees islands, Illauntannig. Although it boasts several ancient burial chambers, which I explore, it comes too early in the crossing to be of any real benefit. The job at hand is an exposed and challenging 30 kilometre leap to County Clare. I will be heading just short of Clare's southwestern tip, Loop Head, to the tiny harbour at Kilbaha, where a big plate of fish and chips awaits in Bernie Keating's establishment, hopefully after a successful passage.

On crossings of more than two or three hours, I am prone to having a few unwelcome visitors. The terrible trio of seasickness, headache and dizziness often creep aboard and invade my body. I mostly keep these maladies at bay by gulping meds and taking shore breaks, but the tenacity of this ailment means it occasionally breaks through my defences. This journey to County Clare is going to take around five hours, so towards the end, although hoping for feelings of elation, I am pretty sure I could be suffering instead. My predictions are correct, and although the situation is familiar it remains tough. All this, while well offshore and in growing seas, merges into a real challenge. Mick O'Meara's voice echoes in my head. 'You'll be bagging the biggest leap of the trip, Kev.' I repeat it, mantra-like, throughout.

Two hours into a blustery, cloud-covered crossing and nearing halfway, I settle into a metronomic rhythm, my ultra light wing paddles extensions of my body. Up ahead, a grey sea meets an equally grey sky with no sign of my goal to encourage me. It is hidden in the greyness. Paddling on a compass bearing, previously calculated from the comfort of my tent, I am paddling blind. I do this all the time as a commercial pilot so it does not feel completely alien, but kayaking solo with no-one keeping watch over me has a distinctly different flavour. I had chosen the bearing of 020 degrees so that any error resulting from the incoming tide or the westerly breeze would push me east into the safety of the Shannon Estuary, a far better option than drifting west where the distant Aran Islands would be the next possible landing.

Things are going according to plan. Off to my right I can make out the black base of Kerry Head peering out from under a low cloud base. This large, northwestern outcrop of the Kingdom of Kerry protrudes towards my path, but offers little comfort. Other than confirming I am on track, it is inaccessible as a possible escape due to it being bordered throughout by dark vertical cliffs.

The swells are growing. I am constantly being elevated, held there, and gently set back down to the original level. I am cutting through the swells at a 45 degree angle. They continue east, nearing their final destination at the base of the cliffs on Kerry Head. I debate whether this rocky protrusion is a help or a hindrance as I creep towards my goal. If nothing else it is a marker showing I am nearly halfway there, but that's about it.

I pass by the headland, fuzzy in the grey mist. I am due one of my hourly feeds, an essential element to longer stretches. I view these as stepping stones across the great river's inlet. I am on my second feed, with three more to go before the pub dinner in Bernie's. My fuel of choice today is a stash of Nature Valley bars, five of them peeping out from the front pocket of my life jacket like a clutch of small puppets. All pre-opened, they are ready to be grabbed and eaten. I brace myself, and tentatively release a hand from my paddles. Transferring the tasty snack to my mouth I start munching enthusiastically, while still concentrating fully on the lively sea. The influence of Kerry Head stretches far offshore and I notice the swells are building into larger waves.

Approaching Kilbaha in County Clare

Busily enjoying my snack, I am suddenly wrenched from my happy state. A piece of the bar takes a wrong turn and lodges deep in my windpipe. My body desperately tries to cough up the misdirected fragment but unfortunately the offending piece is not for budging. My coughing becomes explosive, as my body instinctively attempts to expel it. With all the effort, my eyes start watering, creating a far from ideal situation. I am now attempting to control my kayak as water wells in my eyes. Part of my brain reminds me of my situation: I am in the middle of the longest crossing of my circumnavigation, miles from any escape route, and severely compromised by a bloody biscuit. It is bizarre, whilst at the same time far too real. I know that if I survive I will be gleefully recounting this moment to friends and family for some time to come.

Eventually, the guilty fragment is expelled from my windpipe and correctly reroutes down to my stomach. My body's tension eases as my heart rate returns to normal though the adrenalin is still coursing in my bloodstream. Minutes pass before I can fully relax and return to my rhythm. I am chastened by the experience. I realise that every action has to be carefully executed when offshore and alone. Future feeds demand more care or even postponement until conditions suit. The biggest lessons are hard learned. Now where was I? Ah yes, heading for the Banner County. I refocus my attention, lock back onto my northerly heading, and continue towards County Clare.

I land into the quaint haven of Kilbaha, much relieved. I am warmly embraced by the tiny harbour as I glide across the glassy water in its lee. I land onto a gently sloping slipway, and slowly realise what I have done. A big cornerstone in the construction of my circumnavigation has been heaved into place. Mick is right, it will end up being my biggest crossing. With zero time pressure, I swap the challenge of getting here with leisurely changing into my dry kit and sitting down to watch the world go by. Six hours after leaving Kerry I am now across the Shannon estuary's gaping maw in County Clare. Bernie Keating, proprietor of the pub which essentially constitutes Kilbaha, is delighted to welcome me into his cosy establishment. He reminds me of another solo paddler, Elaine Alexander, aka 'Shooter', who camped in his garden the previous year on her passage. I am more than happy to follow in her footsteps and it gives me another welcome boost on my quest.

Arriving in County Clare

I DALLY IN THE PUB ALL AFTERNOON, eating and chatting with some locals and Bernie when he gets a minute. He proves to be the most interesting of the people there and it was a treat to watch him 'work' his pub with whomever came through his door. I ask him about a small stone tower I had spotted perched on a low promontory nearby.

'That tower was built by a local landlord in the early nineteenth century so his wife could watch out over the sea from a sheltered spot on their demesne. What's more,' he continues, 'Nothing else remains, except the legacy of him being a brutal character, a vehement anti-Catholic who forbade anyone from serving Mass in the area.' Bernie winks at me. He has me hooked, and loves it.

'Michael Meehan, a local priest, came up with a cunning plan to outwit this harsh landlord. Father Michael had a mobile altar built capable of being moved onto the beach. Its design was based on Victorian bathing machines he had seen in Kilkee.' The puzzled look on my face has Bernie raise his hand. He continues uninterrupted.

'When the tide went out, the parishioners wheeled the mobile altar below the high water mark, essentially onto no man's land, where no jurisdiction held sway. The local landlord, a stickler for rules and regulations, was hoisted by his own petard, and could do nothing but let the worshippers continue their faithful practice. For five years, local masses, weddings and funerals took place there, until permission was eventually granted to build a permanent church back in 1857.'

Next comes his *pièce de résistance*, as he leans forward as if revealing a secret. 'You'll never guess but the mobile altar is still here. It is above in the local church.' I am agog at the story which grew from my curiosity about a tiny stone tower. 'Yep, and we had it fully refurbished a few years back.'

At this stage I am intrigued, and determined to see it. He waves aside my intention to walk the few kilometres to the church, reminding me that, 'Sure haven't you done enough exercise for today, canoo-odling all the way from Kerry,' and throws his car keys onto the table in front of me.

The story completely takes my mind off the day's paddling. I ponder the tenacity of the faithful of the time. Despite my atheism, it strikes me as odd that the Catholic Church, now under such pressure in Ireland, is not promoting this iconic display of resilience within its own church. It is certainly a great story.

I drive up to the church, slip inside, and see this hidden gem still standing on its wooden wheels over a century and a half later. The church of the little ark, as it is known locally, had a wing built to accommodate the unique vehicle. Also, thanks to being gifted with Bernie's car, I cheekily continue the short distance across to the western side of this finger to view the next stretch of coastline to be tackled. I spot the vertical black cliffs of South Clare and am glad to have finished my paddling for the day. They definitely look interesting and I will store this image in my head as it promises to be a while before I return to tackle this stretch of shoreline.

Waking the following morning has me eager to reconnect with my car, hopefully being shuttled by Des, as agreed, from Feoghanagh to the Tarbert ferry terminal on the estuary's southern side. All I have to do is catch the boat from Killimer on the north side. Thankfully my B&B host offers to support my mission by transferring me and my kit bags to the ferry terminal in Killimer. Such is the vastness of the Shannon Estuary, the road distance between Kilbaha and Feoghanagh is a handsome 170 kilometres, or 270 kilometres if the ferry is not operating. Compared to the shorter paddling distance of only 70 kilometres, it has presented me with the need to call for help. People are great, and as per my plan Des arrives not long after I waddle off the ferry with my two bulging kit bags. We swap stories of our respective adventures, him relaying that his tardiness was because he got stuck behind a tractor for ages. The following morning I start the long journey home which takes most of the day.

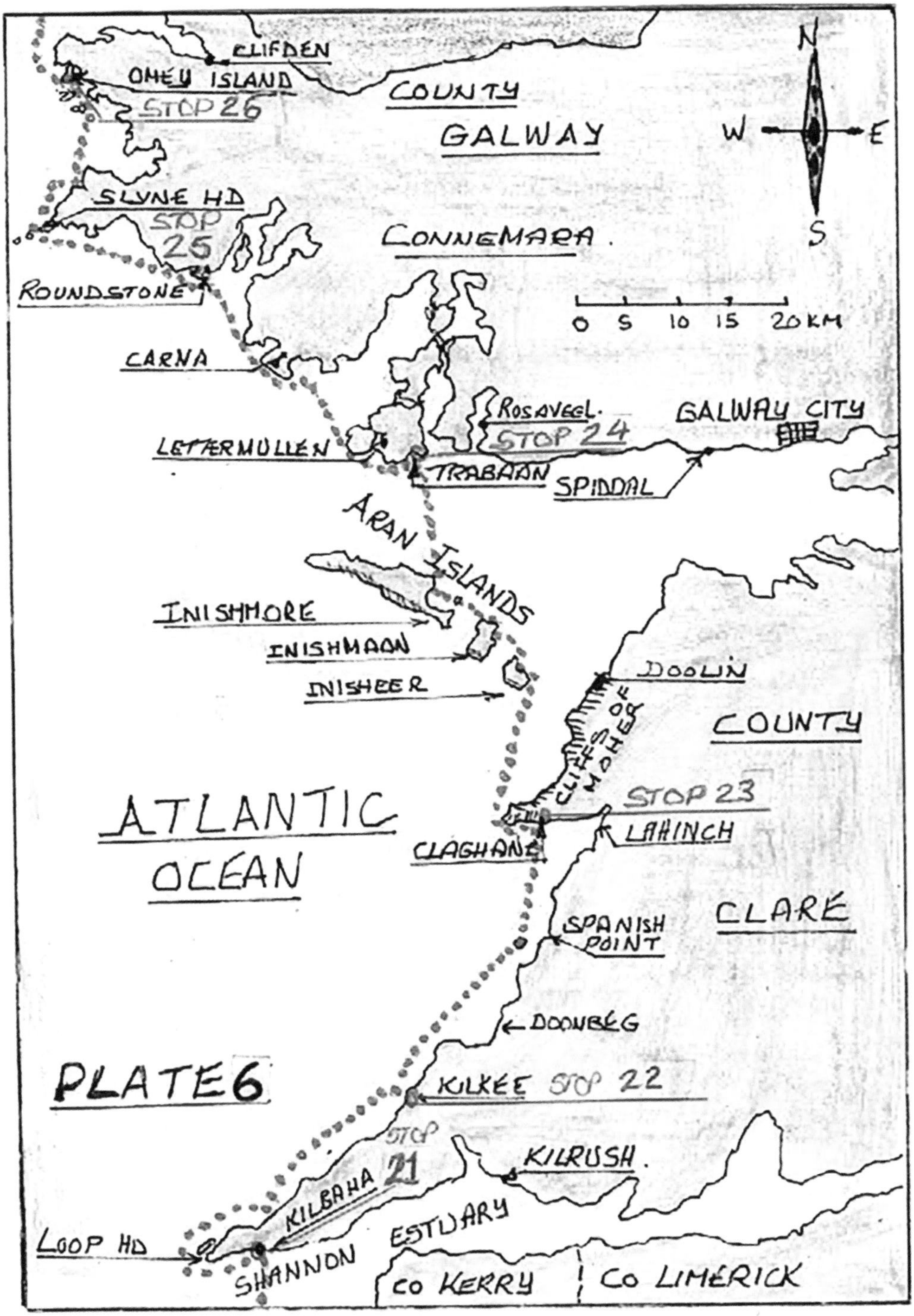
CLIFDEN
OMEY ISLAND
STOP 26
COUNTY
GALWAY
N
W
E
S
SLYNE HD
STOP 25
CONNEMARA
ROUNDSTONE
0 5 10 15 20KM
CARNA
ROSAVEEL
STOP 24
GALWAY CITY
LETTERMULLEN
TRABAAN
SPIDDAL
ARAN ISLANDS
INISHMORE
INISHMAAN
INISHEER
DOOLIN
CLIFFS OF MOHER
COUNTY
ATLANTIC
OCEAN
STOP 23
LAHINCH
CLAGHANE
SPANISH POINT
CLARE
DOONBEG
PLATE 6
KILKEE STOP 22
STOP 21
KILRUSH
KILBAHA
ESTUARY
LOOP HD
SHANNON
Co KERRY
Co LIMERICK

Stage 16

THE BLACK CLIFFS
OF COUNTY CLARE

As mentioned earlier, my circumnavigation is a sequential series of short trips tenuously linked together along the route. I examine the sea area and swell forecasts, and when satisfied, jump at a suitable weather window. I am only planning to make this great journey once, so I want to enjoy it in pleasant sea conditions as much as possible.

My next instalment is to leave Kilbaha for the Shannon Estuary's mouth at Loop Head, circumvent it and continue beneath Clare's vertical black cliffs all the way to Kilkee. As this is another stretch of coastline with minimal get-outs, it calls for more commitment. I spot a single day of benign weather coming up. As it precedes a work day, I cannot manage to dovetail it with a viable commute. Everyone at home is aware of my predicament as I reach out to friends for a shuttle to and from remote Kilbaha in one day. It is a huge task, almost 700 kilometres in total, and due to the lateness of my request I fail to secure anyone mad enough to be my one day-roadie. Later that evening, while explaining my logistical challenge to Angela, she stuns me with her suggestion.

'Sure, I'll drive you down and back. I'm keen to see, first hand, what you have been yakking on about for ages.'

I am gobsmacked by her offer, and get a palpable sense of her really rooting for me. It helps to breathe new life into completing my challenge.

A 5.00 am start has us in Kilbaha at 9.00 and I'm launching an hour later. I head west towards Loop Head, the southwestern extremity of

The trek from Kilbaha to Kilkee begins

County Clare and the outermost section of the Clare side of Shannon estuary. Incredibly, if I was to turn and paddle back towards Limerick City, the nearest bridge spanning is 90 kilometres away. It is testament to the stubbornness of this black limb that it extends to Loop Head after millennia of erosion by Ireland's biggest river on one side, and the mighty Atlantic on the other. This narrow protrusion has a disconnected piece of land near its tip. Referred to as Diarmuid and Grainne, it rises vertically on all sides and boasts a grassy flat top which mimics the land from which it calved.

Legend has it that Grainne, Ireland's most beautiful woman, fell in love with the ageing legendary warrior, Fionn Mac Cuthail. While at their wedding she clapped eyes on Diarmuid, one of Fionn's foot soldiers, and realised she wanted him instead. To this end, she drugged the wedding party and threatened Diarmuid with a spell should he not join her. They then eloped, much to the annoyance of Fionn who made chase for years. This eventually ended with Diarmuid's death after suffering a wild boar wound from which he never recovered. Several sites around the country, including this one, are named as places where the couple are reputed to have hidden.

Rounding the headland, I recall Sean Cahill and Jon Hynes, previous circumnavigators, had passed through this 20 metre wide gap, even shooting some cool footage of it. I am concentrating so hard on paddling that I only steal glances towards the opening as the explosive booms of the crashing waves emanate from within. During these glances, I spot a churning maelstrom of spray struggling within the confines of the gap. Staying well clear, I round the corner and get my first sight of west Clare's black cliffs in the distance. Not even half the height of the Cliffs of Moher, they still provide enough of a backdrop to make me feel insignificant.

With Angela, my Number One Roadie, (top) in the Loop Head Passage and (bottom) in Portacarron

I slowly make my way observing the wildlife surrounding me. Birds swing past me to inspect the strange lone traveller. They are mostly shearwaters who wheel and glide in fantastic blazing arcs, their wingtips almost touching the surface. For some reason, there are no craft on the water, and I reassure myself that my roadie, Angela, is somewhere high above along the cliff, tracking my progress north. I am bound for my first stop of the day on a storm beach not far from the Church of the Little Ark. This is the first time a roadie is mirroring my paddle on land. It is a pleasant novelty. We meet later at Portacarron, a tiny opening in the cliffs onto an almost hidden beach. My elation rises as I spot Angela clambouring down the rocky

Swimming in the Pollack Holes, Kilkee

hillside nearby. The psychological boost of having my soulmate with me today is real. Later on, I negotiate the rocky shelves protecting Kilkee Bay. I am buzzed.

The rest of this big day is made all the sweeter after we decide to have a swim at Kilkee's famous Pollack Holes. As this is our first time seeing these unique swimming spots, we head off in excited anticipation. We stride across the horizontal rock on the foreshore, and slowly these rectangular depressions come into view. Unusable when tides are high, we pinch ourselves at our good fortune. Dozens of holiday makers are swimming and chattering on this deliciously golden summer evening. We change into our swim kit and join the party.

The swim proves to be the great reset needed on this epic day. We are delighted with ourselves and amble over to the Hickie's Pub for some grub. We watch the Irish women's hockey team get thrashed by the Dutch, but thanks to Angela's support I am now within striking distance of Connemara in County Galway, my next three-day instalment. In the meantime we turn our attention to getting back to Skerries in time for my next day's work. By then we will have covered over 800 kilometres driving, 35 paddling and a delightful 150 metres swimming. All in a day.

TWO WEEKS LATER I PULL OUT OF KILKEE, having spent the night at a B&B, well actually a B. I stayed at the Ocean View Bar where they rent out bedrooms *without* breakfast. It actually suits me as I carbo-load before I launch *Murchú* from the old disused slipway below at the pier. A friend's sister-in-law, Criona, appears just as I am wheeling my kayak to the slip. She thrusts a hot coffee into my hands and gives me a hearty send-off on my three-day mission to Connemara.

The vertical black cliffs of southern Clare are exchanged for a jumble of toppled rocky formations, all fashioned from the same material. I push on towards Mutton Island, lying off the small townland of Quilty. Once used for grazing sheep, it now has a few ruined houses and two lookout towers. Its grass now grows unfettered which today is a warm green carpet. With this today's only way-stop, I lay back on the luxurious grass and feel the island push into me. I bask, enjoying the convenience of this perfectly placed break.

I return to the oily, mercury-coloured ocean. Today is perfect for indulging in one of my lifelong interests – birdwatching. Small groups of black and white birds, razorbill and guillemot, are scattered round-

Departing Kilkee

Mutton Island

about. They make for convenient targets when putting in long stretches far offshore. As I bear down on a group of individuals, one or two will begin to manoeuvre away from my intended route. Slowly, this awareness carries through to the rest, with one or two frightened birds submerging for safety. As poor flyers, they are reluctant to haul themselves aloft, and today, with no wind to assist their take-off, it would take a monumental effort. Occasionally, one will attempt this means of escape only managing to run across the surface whilst flapping furiously. I feel for these birds, burning up their energy reserves fleeing from a threat that does not exist. My brain becomes occupied in a little ornithological psychology as I gain more insight into life in the wilderness.

My final landing is planned for Clahane near Liscannor, an ideal launch spot for tomorrow's passage under the Cliffs of Moher. Happily, today proves uneventful, with only the remoteness of crossing Lahinch Bay elevating some concern. Whilst squinting hard to make out this bustling seaside town, six kilometres to my right, I am struck by how different it looks from this far offshore. Even though I am passing familiar locations all day, I barely recognize any. Finally, landing onto the flagstone shore, I haul myself and *Murchú* out onto the warm Liscannor stone. This dark grey stone has gained huge popularity due to its regular shape and thickness. It has an attractive mottled surface, thanks to the abundance of fossils in the 320 million year old sand-stone. So well-formed are the layers of rock that it has been quarried as flagstones since the mid-nineteenth century. Up until the First World War, a big export trade to England existed. Even today Liscannor stone is a popular material for construction.

These rocky platforms are class, I think to myself. For all the world I am on a wide flat pavement with a few ripples and hollows adding to its character. As the road is 100 metres away I successfully press my trolley into action transferring my fully-laden kayak to the embank-ment of flat slabs by the road. In search of a camping spot, I head off along the shore-hugging road for a suitable piece of grass. As it is high summer, and the Cliff's visitor centre is nearby, many folk are ambling along under the warm sun. The occasional campervan is parked by the roadside. I notice a lack of common land, probably because of the sea inundating this area during winter storms. As I am being brought to dinner by some friends in Lahinch, I need to find somewhere safe and semi-private to leave all my kit. I trek a fair distance in both directions, and find nowhere suitable.

Not sure what to do, I haul my kayak up towards the road and trek further along the coast. Proximity to my put-in makes for a much eas-ier start to a day's paddling, so I reluctantly embark on plan B. Whilst trying to haul *Murchú* over the embankment I notice someone ap-proaching from a bungalow on the far side of the road. My kayak looks like a green missile about to be launched from its silo as it hangs at an awkward angle above the road. Here we go, I think, as the guy starts to engage me in conversation. Expecting the usual array of questions, I make a mental note of parking my frustration at being temporarily without a base for the night.

'Do you need a hand with that yoke?' he asks.

I immediately respond, 'Absolutely … that would be great. Yeah, I'm paddling around Ireland. Yup, on my own. I started in Skerries, just north of Dublin, I came from Kilkee early this morning. And yes, all my kit is in the boat.'

Meanwhile, over his shoulder, I spot his perfect, putting-green style front garden. It seems completely out of place along this exposed shoreline. I enviously admire the perfect flatness, my eyes lured away as we chat. I dislike when this happens, so out of politeness, I explain my distraction.

'I'm being very cheeky here, but would there be any chance I could pitch my tent in your front garden? I couldn't help noticing it, plus I am having difficulty finding a place close by.'

He looks at me slightly perplexed. I think that I have pushed it too far. As I fear, his reply is not what I wanted to hear. 'There's no way you're camping in our front garden.' His wife is beside him at this stage. I nod knowingly, I suppose nothing ventured, nothing gained. He continues. 'However, if you prefer to stay *in* our house, you are most welcome.'

Wow, I never saw that coming.

He does not realise it, but these few kind words from Paddy are music to my ears. No more trundling around looking for a suitable campsite. No unpacking and pitching my tent. No grabbing my sleeping gear and kit and all the other chores with setting up for the night. Plus, no need for striking camp in the morning. Instead, I am being treated to a warm bed right beside my put-in for tomorrow. The icing on the cake follows as he hands me the house keys and says, 'We also have Wifi'.

An hour later I am Lahinch-bound with my friends Sinead and Declan holidaying nearby with their two children. The seaside town is bustling with dozens of wannabe surfers messing about in the endless swells that crash onto its long sandy beach. Flags fly gently in the sea breeze as kids run about attacking their pink bobbins of candy floss.

The Lahinch promenade

With friends Sinead, Tadhg, Orla and Declan De Fritas in Lahinch

It reminds me of my childhood summers. We park on the revamped promenade. After its near destruction by storm Henry five years ago it was rebuilt with tons of additional beach defences. The mighty ocean can get very angry, I muse. After my day of oceanic isolation, my senses feast on the bustling humanity. As we settle down to some fabulous stew and good conversation inside their holiday bungalow, I am moved by *their* excitement about my trip. Afterwards, as Declan ferries me back to Cloghane, he comments on how fantastic our rendezvous has been, especially for their children Orla and Tadhg, whom he hopes are inspired by seeing me 'live' on my mission. This warms me, as I recall my own realisation, many decades earlier, that paddling around the island of Ireland was even a possibility.

Afterwards, I enjoy a late cuppa and chat with my hosts Paddy and Berr, a retired Limerick couple who hang on my every word as I recall earlier experiences of my journey. Reluctantly, I retire to my hotel-style bedroom and sink into the softest double bed imaginable after a wonderful day. Every night, pre lights-out, I recheck the updated weather forecast for any changes. Tonight, things are changing out on the ocean, so it proves a worthwhile exercise. My plans need adjustment. So despite the offer of an 8.00 am breakfast, I instead aim to be afloat by 7.30 am, as strengthening southerly winds are closing in faster than originally forecast and I need to get past the Cliffs of Moher and up to the Aran islands.

Leaving Clahane before my hosts waken feels strange. I put a quickly scribbled note explaining my hasty departure hoping they will understand. I wheel my kayak back over the flat rock to the slowly rising tide. A greyness hovers overhead as a light drizzle threatens. Yesterday's vibrant colours are replaced by today's muted palette. My put-in today is as close as I can get to the Cliffs of Moher and sits below some short cliffs, a hint of what is to come. I initially travel west towards Hag's Head, the coastline climbing all the while towards its 200 metres apex at O'Brien's Tower further north. These 10 kilometres of cliffscape are the highest vertical coast encountered so far. As the second most popular tourist attraction in Ireland, boasting over one and a half million visitors annually, the cliffs have pulled millions of euros into the Irish economy. Only surpassed in popularity by the Guinness Storehouse, they give the observer an intense experience worthy of all the hype that accompanies the place.

Minnow-like, I creep along the hem of this vertical geological curtain. It looks seriously impressive from below. My choice of get-outs are limited, either Doolin, further up the coast, or Inisheer, the closest of the Aran Islands. Either way I have a three hour stint ahead, as I swing *Murchú* through 90 degrees from west to north. I pass the impressive Hags Head, and already the cliffs have grown to 120 metres. My northerly track diverges from the cliffs, which trail off to the east. I am more than happy to have them receding into the distance.

Stage 17

WHITE HORSES AND A SURPRISE VISITOR OFF THE ARAN ISLANDS

My sights are on Inisheer, the smallest of the three Aran islands. Flat and low-lying, it stays hidden beyond my horizon, some 14 kilometres away. Essentially, I am paddling blind again and keeping a good eye on my compass. The wind, now at my back, helps me along as the promised southerlies materialise. I am paddling across the growing swells, which assist and challenge in equal measure. At only a force three, it still keeps my mind occupied. I notice the cloud base dropping, the details of the receding cliffs dissolving behind a light drizzle.

I see a smudge just above my horizon. I squint hard, looking as keenly as possible. While hoping that it is Inisheer a heavier drizzle descends and the smudge disappears. I am disappointed. I plod on, paddle stroke after paddle stroke. Waiting for better visibility so I can see my prize, I continue religiously following my compass bearing due north. The cliffs, all but disappeared now, have me paddling on a grey sea, mirroring the low cloud. Other than sea and sky, nothing else is in sight.

After some time the smudge reappears, this time as a more distinct impression. Happily it remains in view. Almost imperceptibly, I am bearing down on my goal. When some details begin to reveal themselves, my excitement builds. I catch the faint outline of a shipwreck up ahead. It is the *Plassey*, built for the British navy's war effort. It ended its days here during a 1960s storm whilst operating for the Irish Merchant Service. The rusting hulk lies beached, high and dry, on the

Approaching Inisheer Harbour

rocky foreshore. It has gained huge notoriety from its inclusion in the *Father Ted* comedy on the fictional 'Craggy Island'. It surely must hold the title as the sorriest looking tourist attraction in the country. Today though it proves a worthwhile target for me as I close in on my goal.

Inishmore, Inishmaan and Inisheer comprise a neat three-piece set, forming the Aran Islands. On a map they remind one of three increasingly-sized ornamental ducks flying across a dining room wall. Being disconnected from the nearby Burren, and straddling the mouth of Galway Bay, they are a must see for any passing tourist. Their Atlantic-facing, southwestern flanks sport sheer cliffs, while on the opposite flanks descending ground comprises a lattice of dry stone walls and houses. These walls and small cottages evoke memories of times past, luring thousands of visitors throughout the year. Known as a Gaeltacht, or Irish-speaking region, the native tongue is in everyday use here. As I bear down on Inisheer (meaning 'East Island' in Irish), I am keen to catch some of the buzz of these unique outposts.

I paddle past the *Plassey*, turn at a low rocky outcrop and slot pleasantly into the lee of the land. I am out of the wind and waves, and co-

159

incidentally the cloud lifts and the day begins to brighten. Until now, the seaward cliffs gave the impression of an uninhabited place but now I see signs of activity. Behind some sand dunes hides the island's single-strip airfield. Further along I see a beach which leads to a pier. Cottages stare down at the harbour from the rising ground. O'Brien's ruined castle sits on a rocky ridge lording over everything. The ferry, just docked, is being relieved of its cargo as a white van is craned onto the pier.

Something spherical is in the turquoise water up ahead. Thinking it a seal, I advance slowly, soon realising it is a morning dipper. She is equally as surprised as I am considering my stealthy arrival. People on horse-drawn carts and bicycles are descending towards the pier. They roll past the collection of beached currachs lying on the sand. Getting used to this sensory overload is a thrill. Unannounced, a great noise erupts, blanketing the place in sound. Sounding like a fleet of high powered motorbikes, my heart rate spikes involuntarily. Suddenly, the Aer Aran Islander aircraft leaps into the air just behind me. Wow, what an entrance. After hours alone at sea with only wind and waves as company the accumulated impact is fantastic.

Landing here into all the hustle and bustle is a strong tonic for a weary mind. I trek to a local seafront cafe, not yet open, but I do catch the eye of Daniel, the owner. We strike up a conversation, him explaining that with the tourist season in full swing, long days lead to later openings. I lay it on thick about my quest which leads to him allowing me in, and minutes later he is depositing a piping hot pot of tea in front of me. I sit there relishing the cosy surroundings. Small wall hangings and blue chequered tablecloth topped with tiny vases of wildflowers, give a homely feel. A background whirr of activity emanates from the kitchen as they ready themselves for a day feeding the hoards of hungry tourists.

I spot a maroon and white flag hanging on the wall with *Gaillimh* splayed across it. My chest swells as it reminds me that *Murchú* and I are now in the eighth of the 17 coastal Irish counties. Galway.

Táim an sásta bheith anseo. (I am very satisfied being here.)

Fásann mo fhéinchreideamh. (My self-belief grows.)

White Horses and a Surprise Visitor Off the Aran Islands

I wander back to *Murchú* and eye my kayak with a certain fondness. Our relationship is strangely intimate, considering it is an inanimate fibreglass shell, but she continues to serve me well. My plan today is to use the three Aran Islands as westward stepping stones, and afterwards navigate northwards towards the mainland Gaeltacht area in Connemara. Together they should bring even more colour into our journey.

The continuing brightening of the day creates a sun-spattered, silver sea. As my route is along the northern flanks of the islands I am out of reach of the southerly swells. Still, occasional gusts rush down the slopes slamming into me. But only when I nose *Murchú* into the channel between the islands do I feel the full force of the wind. A force four Beaufort tries to push me away from the islands and off track. I lay off a good few degrees, countering any drift. The aquamarine colour is mesmerising as I slowly crab across to island number two for today.

A small motorised currach leaves a pier and heads in the opposite direction crossing the funnelled swells racing through the sound. I liken it to manoeuvring across a busy motorway with speeding waves as traffic. Thrown into this dynamic mix are razorbill and guillemot. Their squat inefficient wings whirr past me in a blur as they run the gauntlet with the elements. I catch a glimpse of a few fulmar screeching downwind on locked wings. These great gliders ofen come in close, curiously eyeing me. These grey scimitars spend most of their lives at sea, with the result that their legs are ill-suited for land use. Their attempts to manoeuvre on rock ledges are comical but their clumsiness is more than compensated for when airborne. Their name is of Norse origin, translating as 'foul-gull', thanks to their defence mechanism of spewing foul-smelling liquid from their stomach. One kayaking buddy was the victim of this form of aggression by getting too close to a fulmar nest on the Saltees. Despite several attempts at removing the stench using various detergents in the end he had to bin the soiled kayaking kit.

I land on Inishmaan (meaning 'Middle Island' in Irish) and decide to cook up a brew to accompany some pot noodles. I nestle in the lee of low dunes backing the island's airfield. After devouring the grub, I clamber through spiked marram grass to an elevated hummock. A few metres above sea level changes my perspective considerably. I now spot the runway and a memory floods my mind. It was when Angela and I flew here in a light aeroplane. I was then a member of Trim Flying Club in Meath, and had hired a single-engined Cessna for the day. It was before children, and one of those special days we spent together. We explored, swam and ate in a local cafe run by a woman from Guatemala. At the end of the day we flew over Dun Aengus on Inishmore. This prehistoric hemispherical fort, with its open side to the cliff top, has puzzled historians for generations and is another must-see here. To fly above it was a breathtaking experience after which we wheeled around and with a golden sun behind us flew back to Trim. Today is only my second arrival onto the island by another slightly unconventional means which brings a wry smile to my face.

I strike off next towards the main island of Inishmore (meaning 'Big Island' in Irish), landing on a small sandy islet. Straw Island, barely the size of a football-field, hosts a squat lighthouse, some reefs and is skirted by a collar of sand. The light guides vessels towards the harbour at Kilronan, the main settlement on Inishmore. I land onto its sheltered north-facing beach where twenty grey seals are basking. I apologise as they scurry away into the water. They are wary of intruders. On land they appear clumsy, but in the water these powerful swimmers can reach depths of 70 metres, and are capable of staying submerged for an unbelievable 30 minutes. I am lucky to be forcing them downwind as any sea kayaker will be aware that their body odour has a foul smelling pungence best avoided.

My last segment today is a direct downwind run to Connemara. It promises to be a blast. I am about to experience again what the Rockpool Taran is designed for. Downwinding. Feeling some fatigue from my days' paddling, this last twelve kilometres will demand I stay on top of my game throughout. I take a last stop on Inishmore itself before heading off. I spot a white horse in a field. It wanders over to get a closer look and I grab a selfie. I will soon be escorted by white horses of a different kind once away from shore. I settle into the boat as com-

Inishmore

fortably as possible. I will be keeping my hands locked to my paddles for the next twelve kilometres so final preparations are critical.

The downwind run starts perfectly gaining speed as the wavelets grow. Their size is directly proportional to my distance from shore. *Murchú* is travelling nicely in the moderate chop which morphs into small waves with the occasional crest breaking beside me. Six kilometres in and everything is up a notch or two and things are getting sporty. The warm day helps dispel any shock from salt-laden spray that hits my face. I am putting on a good show as the speed grows and with it the buzz and excitement of the thrilling joyride. I look up at the horizon and notice Connemara slowly inching its way closer. At roughly halfway across I notice the wave patterns change as a bigger cross swell traverses my path. Despite my fatigue after putting 40 kilometres astern, I simply have to concentrate harder and keep my focus. At times like these every act is crucial. I simply must perform.

The sun is a warm golden orb off to my left. It throws amber light on the surface creating a look of bog water but I can risk only an occasional glance. I am glissading along, watching waves, crests, lulls and swells, using my ol' cerebral microprocessor to calculate each stroke position and speed. I am gobbling up the distance, but with the un-

Straw Island

ceasing intensity it is taking its toll. I have to face facts. I am getting more and more tired and the mainland still looks far away. I race along, halfway between the islands and Connemara, and the wind is being ramped up to a force four. All this with a cross swell, and at the end of a long day. I would dearly love to just lie down for a few minutes, to stretch, or even just to move about a bit, but as I am locked in I must take my medicine. My spray deck has me tightly bound into *Murchú*. My feet, hard against the foot pegs, afford me minimal wiggle room. I am the foot in a tightly bound shoe.

And then the most unexpected thing happens. Not more than ten metres away, with no forewarning, I get a major shock to the system and a frisson courses through my body involuntarily. Out of a wave to the left of my bow a magnificent beast leaps from the water. A living torpedo hangs for a moment arcing through the air, its small eye trained on me as two travellers intersect. My visitor, a powerful swimmer weighing in at half a ton, is the most beautiful sight imaginable. I never saw it approaching and am convinced it is simply curious about the strange craft racing with the waves. My visitor is an Atlantic bottlenose dolphin.

Inishmore racimg currachs

Despite the event lasting only a couple of seconds the image remains implanted in my brain. I continue quite a way thinking over what just happened. My trip has been about trying to steadily make my way around the island without getting pounded by bad weather or a hostile sea. Surviving the elements has been foremost in my mind. But after seeing the speed and vibrancy of this animal up close, I am convinced that these creatures are allowing me safe passage through their domain. Had this beast decided to ram my boat I know I would have come away second best. I am fortunate that the wildlife is behaving so well towards me and I am determined in turn to treat them with dignity and respect.

Stage 18

Cúpla Focail in Connemara

Tra Bán harbour is a narrow cut into the rocky coastline aimed directly south towards Inishmore. Like parking a car in a garage, my crossing ends here without having to adjust my course by one degree. I slide into the slender haven happy to put an end to my roller coaster run, and an accumulated 45 kilometres on the clock. A scattering of wooden currachs populate the enclosure, patiently waiting for their owners. I extract myself from *Murchú* and wobble up the slipway towards the pier where a car is parked. An older guy is leaning out of it and chatting in Irish. I had not noticed, but someone is hunched over working in one of the currachs below.

I make the decision to use my schoolboy Irish and engage in a bit of *comhra* or chat. I tell him that I have just crossed from Inishmore. He immediately shouts down to his pal below.

'*Micíl, tá sé as Inishmore, san bád beag sin*' ('Michael, he is in from Inishmore, in that wee boat.')

His companion replies with a few expletives in Irish and we erupt into fits of laughter, a great de-stresser after recent events.

He points south, staring over the skittering white horses towards the island on the horizon. I follow his finger, and surprisingly find myself seeing my achievement from a new perspective. We exchange a few more words where I explain my wish to camp here and head on to Roundstone tomorrow. He notes that I am miles from the nearest pub and makes a very welcome suggestion. He offers to return an hour later after I have set up camp and drop me to the pub. I gladly accept

Tranaun Harbour, Galway

his offer and set about pitching my tiny tent in some deep grass behind the pier, hopefully out of any wind and rain.

We trundle across the rocky landscape for longer than I expect. At the pub I quiz him, politely, about getting back to my encampment. Just tell the pub owner you need a lift back and you will be sorted, he advises. It all seems a bit vague, as I watch his small red car disappear. Situated in an isolated, barren place, the pub is enormous and looks like something built during the Celtic Tiger years. I enter the barn-like, one room establishment and my initial impressions are of a ballroom. Big enough to accommodate a couple hundred people, today only three guys are sitting at the counter. Hunched over their pints, the trio turn to observe me. I greet them, in Irish, and make my way to the bar counter.

The barman nods, silently anticipating my order. Mindful that Guinness is probably the drink of choice here, I sheepishly inquire if they stock any non-alcoholic beers. One of the three drinkers responds with *'uisce'*, the Irish word for water, leading to riotous laughter in the cavernous place. It breaks the ice, and I join their chat despite my alien drinking habits. I down a couple of cokes, explaining my presence.

They all share the view that I am a pure oddity, but nonetheless entertaining. I enjoy our interaction through Irish, mindful of how poorly taught our native tongue was at school. I dig deep for words to fill the gaps in my sentences. They accommodate my efforts and I am thrilled with the distraction after my long day in the kayak. Eventually, I mention to the barman my wish to get back to my tent. Paidí's predictions prove accurate and soon I am tucked into my sleeping bag as a light drizzle descends outside. The deep grass underneath provides a nest-like cosiness as I catch up on my blog whilst examining tomorrow's route and weather.

What a thrill it is to wake up in Connemara. The landscape, though barren and rocky, has a warmth about it. Gone are the heavy black cliffs of Clare, replaced now by the honeyed landscape of the Galway Gaeltacht. I mosey to the pier where a discarded wooden hawser spool doubles as a round table for my breakfast. Tinned fish and noodles, washed down with black coffee, prep me for the day. From sleeping bag to sea normally takes ninety minutes, and today is no exception.

I am away easily as I float from the slipway and settle onto the lazy ocean. Yesterday's wind is gone, giving way to a peaceful calm. The Galway granite gives my surroundings a friendly, accessible feel. Illuminated in the morning light, my eyes feast on the scene. I cannot help but smile as I realise I have been consistently challenged ever since leaving Valentia Island in County Kerry. The accumulated days of exposure and longer open crossings have taken their toll, and I am basking in some deliciously easy paddling.

I work my way west along a stretch of coast which comprises a collection of tightly packed islands connected across narrow channels hidden from view to my right. Golam Head is my first goal. This is where the coast swings right and northwest towards Roundstone. My route is through a scattering of more loosely packed islands. I decide to take a break here, sliding into one of the many inlets carved into the low headland. I tie my boat to a rock pillar and wander across the rough terrain to the squat square tower sitting at this natural corner in the landscape. Positioned only thirty metres above sea level, and surrounded by lower undulating terrain, the vista is vast. Thanks to my elevated viewpoint I pick out my course through the islands. As a distant backdrop the isolated ridge of Errisbeg stands head and shoulders above everything else. It appears like the humped back of an enormous dinosaur frozen in rock. This reassures me because Roundstone, my destination, sits at its base.

Along the way the sands shine the whitest yet seen due to the crystallised mica in the granite. I land on Mweenish and am stunned by the turquoise waters surrounding the island's brilliant beaches. The landscape is coated with a carpet of grass, kept in check by its grazing sheep. I continue past Mace Head, and the smaller Islands of Mason, Avery and MacDara's towards my goal. Interestingly, Roundstone's etymology is hotly debated. One theory argues that it is a poorly translated version of its old Irish name, *Cloch an Rón,* or Stone of the Seal. The other argues that is comes from the large round rock that lies outside its harbour. Either way, it is a stunning village built by Scottish engineer Alexander Nimmo in the 1820s. He was tasked with building harbours, roads and houses throughout the west of Ireland, and

Golam Head

In Roundstone with sister Joan

Roundstone is one of his gems. Several Scottish fishermen were planted here and within twenty years its population swelled to 400 supporting a nascent fishing industry. Nowadays it is a quaint village strung along the elevated sea road that passes above its harbour, which happily, is still in regular use.

A must see along the Wild Atlantic Way, Roundstone's allure is aided by two nearby beaches, Gurteen and Dog's Bay. These two long strands back onto each other forming a sand spit which stretches out into the bay, capturing what could easily have been a small offshore island. It provides a fitting end to my three day instalment from Kilkee and a total distance paddled of 120 kilometres.

And so this stint ends with my sister Joan's beaming face radiating across at me as I climb out from *Murchú* to stand on Gurteen's golden sand. Shane from Roundstone Adventures is there too, to mind my boat until I return for my next stretch. I wind my way back to my car in Kilkee via Galway, where I spend a night enjoying some sibling hospitality. Who knows when the weather gods will smile on me again for what could be my last instalment for my second summer.

'THERE BE DRAGONS OUT THERE.' This is a quote from David Walsh's *Oileain: A Guide to the Irish Islands*, the fantastic book I continuously reference during my voyage. It is a succinct description of the area just North of Slyne Head, the highlight of my next leg. This publication travels on board throughout, living in its waterproof pouch in one of my storage compartments. It provides some interesting reading as I make my way, both along the coast and through its pages. Penned by a sea kayaker, it is in a language that speaks to me, and reveals the

White sands, Mweenish Island

secrets of seldom visited stretches of coastline. Whereas I also consult the sailor's 'Irish Coastal Pilot', searching for extra nuggets of info, it is for a different audience and not intimate enough with the coastline. Its readership has the comfort of being aboard a much larger vessel with a hold full of sails, and normally operating far from shore. With my mode of human-powered transport, my ability – or desire – to travel far offshore is limited.

I love diving into David's book and musing over the clever descriptions of offshore islands and coastline. I especially like notes on the more remote areas. As Slyne Head is roughly halfway through my journey, I have already gobbled up much of what he has written and am looking forward to seeing this place for myself. As this is his first mention of dragons, it has stirred up some trepidation. The prospect of handling what is in store around this half-submerged peninsula will soon be revealed.

Slyne Head is best known from its inclusion in Met Éireann's sea area forecast. Like most people, this is as much as I know about this

Gurteen

remote outpost. Marking the western extremity of Galway Bay, where the coast changes from an east-west to a north-south direction, it forms a natural divide between two large sea areas. With various islands, islets and reefs, all riven by channels, it constitutes a jumble of marine features on an exposed part of the coast. The island at its extremity sports a lonely lighthouse, four kilometres from the mainland. Despite being low lying, the island's haphazard geography creates a problem for mariners. It is deserving of some careful planning. My objective is to arrive with little or no tidal flow, basically at slack water when the most favourable sea conditions should exist. Punctuality, and some luck, are going to be crucial.

With Dave Walsh's dragons looming, I feel it is time to reach out to some of the experts. Circumnavigator Jon Hynes, from Kinsale, and local paddler Shane McElligot in Roundstone are the best options. Jon suggests using one of the bisecting channels if it looks okay, whilst Shane insists on steering well clear of them altogether and directs me to the main yachting channel out near the lighthouse. My reluctance to use this channel is the extra distance needed to travel out and back. As I leave Skerries behind I still haven't made up my mind.

On the day in question, midweek in September 2018, I aim to start from Roundstone, reaching Slyne Head at 1.00 pm in slack water. Travelling down from Dublin the night before on the late bus, I will be staying in a Galway city centre hostel, plan to catch the 8.00 am Bus Éireann coach to Roundstone and be on the water by 11.00 am. This will allow two hours on a westerly heading before arriving at Slyne Head.

I haul my two bulging Ikea bags of kayaking kit to the hostel at 11.30 pm. It is a perfect spot to stay as my morning bus leaves from across the road. Most of the clientele are students, hidden in their dorms asleep. I check in with the receptionist, and tip-toe into the dark dorm trying to carry my substantial kit without disturbing a soul. Manoeuvring blind with so much to carry proves too challenging for me as my two paddle bags slip and crash onto the floor, shattering the silence. I am mortified. These guys are trying to get a decent night's sleep before college tomorrow and muggins here is doing his best to prevent it. Either being very kind, or in the deepest of slumbers, no one budges. By the time I wake up the following morning I am alone. I slowly descend, not knowing who to apologise to for the previous night's transgressions. Instead I conveniently avoid the subject completely, devour the complimentary toast and coffee and mosey across the road to the depot.

I buy my ticket from the machine, sidling over to the clerk seeking confirmation of my bus's departure time. Looking at me blankly, he says I am a few hours too early. Thrown into disbelief, I explain that the website gives 8.00 am as a departure time.

'Not today buddy, the next bus for Roundstone is not till 2.00 pm.'

'But I checked online,' I blurt out.

'Agh, that website is not up to date.'

'Noooo.' I cannot contain my disbelief, as I have planned this so carefully. I thought I could depend on this state-run bus service. How can they get it so wrong? More importantly, I demand of their representative, 'How am I to make Roundstone by 10.30 this morning?' I ask him accusingly?

Coast of Connemara

His suggestion that I get a taxi, costing over a hundred euro, is not what I need to hear. He offers to ring his buddy, suggesting he could do it for a much better price.

My stress levels are up now. My whole plan is dependent on getting onto the water in Roundstone at 11.00 am. This is beginning to look, if not impossible, at least very expensive. Here I am in the middle of Galway city, 80 kilometres from Roundstone, and not keen on parting with a hundred euro before all my options have been examined.

The official seems to finally understand that my arrival time in Roundstone is critical and he suggests I pop round the corner and catch the Go Bus to Clifden. Then a short spin by taxi would put me in Roundstone pretty sharpish. He sees my eyes light up.

'You had better shift buddy, it's going in five minutes.' His gesture is particularly generous since he is pointing me towards one of their main competitors. Thank goodness my plan may hold, but I simply *must* make this bus.

I heave my two heavy bags, and run-shuffle the 300 metres to the private bus depot. I reach the Go Bus just in time, take a seat, and feel my heart rate slowly return to normal. I settle into my journey west, knowing that I have managed to keep things together, albeit in a roundabout way. With Clifden situated further west than Roundstone, it adds distance and time to my journey, but at least I am moving.

On the bus I chat with a semi-retired Galway Aquarium worker, Sean, who was heading home after a night celebrating with work-mates. As an ex-fisherman and carpet designer he has managed to combine his skills in his present occupation as tank designer in the Galway Aquarium. One of his claims to fame is designing the carpet covering the floor of the Dáil in Dublin. On hearing of my impasse, he recommends a reliable taxi operator in Clifden, which I duly book.

While on the bus I notice an essential piece of my kit is malfunction-ing. My waterproof watch is displaying strange hieroglyphics in place of numbers. As an integral part of my trip I need to find a replacement right away, hopefully in Clifden. Minutes after arriving in the town I exit a pharmacy as the proud owner of a garish, light blue, supposedly waterproof, watch. Fashion needs to take a back seat today, where just getting started seems to be a challenge.

On the road to Roundstone we traverse a barren upland area where my attention is drawn to the weather. The low cloud being pushed by a fresh southwesterly is pricking my thoughts about what might be happening on the ocean. No doubt it will be wearing a new palette of colours, and by the look of things will be of a more sombre tone.

Descending into the stunning hamlet of Roundstone, part of me wants to dally in spite of the soft rain that is falling. A heartwarming sight greets me as I catch sight of my green kayak sitting on Orla's car outside her Bog Bean Cafe. My spirits lift further when I spot her prepping for the day through its glass door. Once inside, a hot coffee washes down a delicious chocolate brownie in jig time. She tells me that since I left my kayak two weeks ago, Shane has taken up my offer to give it a test run. Amazingly he has decided to order one for himself. I love it.

Being tight on time, Orla promptly delivers me to Gurteen Bay. Her kindness continues with a parting comment, 'If you don't make Omey we can come collect you, wherever you are'.

This is such a reassurance to me as I know my arrival at Omey Island, 40 kilometres away, is not guaranteed. Her gesture helps take some weight off my shoulders.

As quickly as possible I pack my gear into my boat on the damp sand. Coarse grains stick to my kit as the drizzle continues. My normal sense of optimism eludes me. The sea is not as inviting as when I had landed here previously. I go through the step-by-step packing of my trusty chariot: compartments crammed with personal kit, water bag filled, snacks in pockets, new watch attached, chart on the deck, compass mounted, spare paddles on deck and paddle leash attached. This procedure requires due diligence before every solo outing as errors can be dangerous. I have had to actively avoid chatting with passersby in order to keep myself focused on my prep for the day. Thankfully, the poor weather dissuades anyone from strolling along this sodden stretch of sand.

Finally, at 11.30 am, I ease *Murchú* into the grey waters. Ringed by a horseshoe bay my wing blades dip once again into the Atlantic. I feel relief to be on the water and have not considered too much what lies ahead as I pull away from the beach. I am only a half hour behind schedule, roughly on time, but I will be a happier paddler when I have Slyne Head behind me.

Stage 19

THE DRAGONS OF SLYNE HEAD

Heading west from Roundstone feels like moving away from civilization, since the coastline, littered with uninhabited islands and islets, pushes me away from the mainland. As it recedes into the hazy distance few man-made structures remain visible. The land, trailing out into low lying hummocks, is a benign backdrop to my paddling. Earlier sections of coastline have been stacked with great cliffs and ominous looking headlands, but for now all looks manageable. How looks can deceive.

I push west, stopping onto a tiny island for physiological reasons, and a chance to collect my thoughts. In spite of my advancing years, I am resisting the temptation to pee in my boat. The balance of staying hydrated and not overloading my bladder is a delicate operation. So far I have managed to stay civilised, and as a consequence, dry.

Eventually, I see the long arm of Slyne Head appear as a grey line drawn on the horizon. I spot a single raised structure, an isolated, lonely lighthouse near the tip. As I slowly approach the peninsula, I find myself on a calm sea. Comparing my mental picture of Slyne Head from Google Earth's aerial views with what I am seeing, I cannot believe my eyes. Only when very close do I begin to see the narrow channels cleaved through the low lying headland.

I peer through the first opening. It is quite close to the base of the finger and, if passable, will be the shortest route to the far side. It runs for 100 metres and resembles a narrow lane between two rows of buildings. Beyond the channel I can see land in the distance on which swells are breaking. On first inspection the way through seems safe enough but I decide to watch for a few minutes in case a hazard become clear. A short-cut at this part of the headland would be a bonus, saving me time and distance. If I had to go further out towards the end of the finger, it could add over an hour's paddling to my journey. I then notice a disturbance halfway down, coming from a side channel out of view. Like a large truck passing a junction at full speed, a tumbling wave trundles across the lane and my intended path. My stomach lurches. Cripes, this short-cut is definitely out.

I continue out along the headland in search of a friendlier opening. I am a window shopper on the high street, searching for a desirable purchase. I then happen upon a short and narrow gap which I watch carefully for a while. No breaking waves appear and I think I may have found a safe passage. I inhale deeply and start to push my long fibreglass needle through the fabric of the rocky headland. The way is too narrow to affect a turn so I am committed. I am within touching distance of the smooth wet rocks that flank both sides of the slot. Through the aperture, I see the swell crash against a jumble of rocks further up the coast. I push on, breaking through to the other side.

Instantly I am dumbstruck by my new reality. Like summiting a ridge and seeing the opposite flank, a new and completely different vista presents. My mind quickly processes everything. With the shelter of the headland gone, the Atlantic is inundating any and every obstruction. Nearby on my right flank a nasty rock-strewn shoreline is being bashed by breaking waves. Spiked reefs to my left are being impacted by the swells. Great sheets of spray fan into the air. With other reefs up ahead and further out to sea, the place looks like a battlefield. From every quarter white explosions pull my attention and I worry about a distraction from the job at hand. Paddling my kayak, I am manoeuvring through a garden of rocks as big as houses as swells career across my path on their way to the shoreline. I have suffered another Tarantino-type twist to my days' paddling. I am about to meet Dave's dragons.

I keep paddling, *Murchú* being more stable when moving. I spot a sheltered cove not two kilometres away. This is my new goal. Slyne Head might be astern, but I am not out of the woods yet. Seconds later,

Slyne Head

something off to my left catches my eye. A new element of nature is rearing its head. A large wave is lifting itself skyward on an intercept course with me as it nears the end of its transatlantic journey. Then I realise it is first in a set of three waves bearing down on me. Expletives are uttered. I am in their line of fire and if these waves change from swells to steam rollers of white water I will be consumed by the resulting watery avalanche. I will be whipped up and swept along, joining them in their death throes on the nearby rocks. Damn it, I had not waited long enough observing the gap. I can do nothing about that now, but this is not good.

I take a deep breath and push *Murchú* up close to her top speed. I must try to outrun the three shadows that are coming at me. After years of surfing I am acutely aware of the danger I am facing. I have seen big waves break off our coasts, even searched them out so I could

179

gleefully slide down their faces in specially designed surf kayaks. But that is exactly what I do not need here. I need these rogues to behave themselves and not turn into watery steamrollers.

I am completely exposed. I keep a tiny bit in reserve just in case I am caught by one of them, to give me some spare oxygen to handle that scenario. Ninety per cent of my effort is transferred into maximising my forward speed. Thankfully, the Taran's acceleration saves me. I manage to move quite a distance before I am lifted skyward by the first heaving swell and get a sneak preview of the next two behind it. I clear the first wave and gently slide off its back into the first trough. The same is repeated for the next two. I breathe a huge sigh of relief that my luck held. With two kilometres to go before I can fully relax I continue onwards, adrenalin still coursing through my veins.

The distance left to travel is thankfully much less daunting. I am so relieved that I nearly lapse into a dopey state of exhilaration which morphs into a realisation that I am not fully out of the woods. Eventually, I land into calm waters. I then start giving thanks to many things: passing Slyne Head, my kayak's fantastic acceleration, my own skills and experience, and also a serious dollop of good fortune. I land onto a tiny sheltered beach and even though I'm feeling mighty grateful, I am still only halfway to my destination. I still have a few smaller headlands to negotiate.

After a short breather, I resume in my now even more-loved kayak. I have a couple of wave-washed headlands to negotiate next. I paddle offshore to avoid large breaking waves. At the second of these non-descriptive headlands a dark shadow looms over me as I turn back towards shore. I react instinctively by bracing into the wave as it passes, cresting over me like an umbrella. Thankfully it is only the toppling lip of a fairly benign swell, and as quickly as it arrived it is gone, shore-bound, crashing onto the shallow waters with its compatriots.

I land, drag my kayak up the tiny beach, and settle into a short bit of rest and relaxation. Time to take stock of how today's accumulated challenges are affecting me. My energy levels are definitely depleted. The high adrenalin passage combined with my earlier transport challenges has me knackered. I do not think I can take many more surpris-

Turk Island, last stop before Omey

es. Unfortunately, being tentless my only options are to call Orla and ask to be rescued or continue to Omey and the promise of a warm bed for the night. In the end, I decide on the latter as the course of least resistance and impact to my overall mission. After Omey, the next ports of call are the inhabited offshore islands of Inishbofin, Inishturk and the Clare islands. As each of these are challenging paddles, I am seriously considering storing my boat on Omey for the winter.

The second half of this leg is a dreary slog across the western reaches of Mannin and Clifden Bays, where thankfully the swells behave allowing me to settle into the rhythm of putting in the strokes. I spot Omey, a dull white scar delineating a beach and a possible landing site. Fingers crossed it is waiting for me like a parking space in a car park. I cleave *Murchú's* bow into its coarse sand, and finally relax. After my deliverance, the peculiar joy of being on solid ground after a test at sea is palpable. Despite my fatigue, I am elated. I drag my boat across a field to reach the island's only road. Then, securely strapped and finely balanced on its trolley, I man-haul it over a kilometre to my promised base.

Omey is almost unique among Ireland's Islands in that you can drive or walk there at low tide. The connecting ribbon of sand sports speed signs for the adventurous motorist. In fact, since the Wild Atlantic Way has come into existence, a steady stream of cars can be seen congregating at the small mainland car park as they wait for the tide to recede allowing a brief visit onto Omey.

I arrive at my accommodation which overlooks a west-facing beach close by. It is in an idyllic setting, although the gloom of the fast approaching dusk is stealing the day's vibrancy. I dig into my kit for the keys. This is the holiday home of a friend's mam which I am delighted to occupy as part of my Atlantic passage. After trying each key in

Arriving in Omey

every door, I am stumped. I cannot gain entry. I grab my phone, its depleting charge echoing the fading light, and ring Ian.

Unfortunately, with no answer and not having a tent my only recourse is to revisit every door, with every key, once again. This time, however, something different happens. I set off an alarm which now echoes inside. I am drifting into that strange realm of denial, having to deal with another challenge just when I was thinking I was home and dry. In fact, I am not even dry and I begin to notice my body temperature dropping after the day on the sea.

My phone rings. I jump. It is Ian.

'Hi Ian, Thank goodness.'

I explain everything. The doors, the keys, the alarm. Initially, I am greeted with silence. Finally, he asks a question. 'What colour is the front door Kev'.

I sheepishly respond, 'Red?'

Ian's booming laughter explodes from the phone. 'Ah japers Kev, that's not our house, our door is yellow, you're next door'.

Time for a swim on Omey Island

The Omey Road, uncovered

I head back up the next driveway to open the correct door and immediately set about changing out of my wet kit and rustling up some hot grub. Unfortunately, being baffled by the shower's controls, I wash under a spray of cold water. Funnily enough, it perks me up as I afterwards bask in the warmth of the house. Just as I am about to sink into a large armchair, I notice the beam from a car creeping cautiously up the long driveway. Being on a sparsely populated island cut off from the mainland, this puzzles me. I open the door and see a garda walking towards me, his cap tilted back off his head.

'Hello there,' he says. 'Have you heard any disturbances around here over the last while?'

Not having seen a soul since landing I am briefly puzzled. 'No, why?'

'An alarm was going off in the house next door and we are here to investigate.'

Sheepishly, I reply that it was me, describing my earlier arrival. Happy with this, he explains that as the tide is rising they had better get back to their mainland base in Clifden while they can. And with that he joins his companion in the car and disappears as quickly as he had arrived.

I stand there watching their light beam carve its way through the night. It is already 8.00 pm, and I am dearly hoping this is the last drama of an interesting 24 hours. I veg out, watch TV, eat some more and sort out my kit. I glance at the forecast and realise that my next two days paddling will have to be postponed, perhaps even until next year. I post on my blog that these are my thoughts and almost immediately an artist friend, Dave, messages me. He plans on being in nearby Clifden tomorrow morning, returning to Skerries after depositing some of his paintings to one of its galleries. He offers to ferry me home if it suits. Slouching in the armchair whilst watching the weather forecast on RTÉ, seals my decision. With a freshening westerly coming, this could be messy. From Waterford to Omey over the summer of 2018 is as far as I am going to get. Next year's opening salvo will be across several stretches of open water, stopping on Inishbofin, Inishturk and Clare islands before landing on Achill island which is essentially the mainland again. It is easy for me to overwinter *Murchú* here. My plan is to visit during those winter months to closely inspect my vessel and spend a night walking the island to view the next stretch to be tackled.

The next morning I commit to this decision by crossing over the sandbank on foot and watching the rising tide slowly cut me off from Omey. I set out to walk the ten kilometres to Clifden, being picked up by Dave just outside town. We share a rare and unexpected day together as we chat, eat and swim, all the while waiting for the tide to drop allowing us access back to my waiting kit. Hilariously, he decides to run the gauntlet to the island before the tide is fully receded, the salty sea being parted by his squat silver car.

In making it halfway up our western seaboard I am positioned at the same latitude as Skerries but on the opposite side of the country. This is heartening, as for the first time of my trip I will be north of my starting position. Soon I will be into Mayo, with Sligo and Donegal the last remaining counties before going 'over the top' at Malin. I am still somewhat rattled after my scare at Slyne Head but at the same time am growing in confidence at being able to get the job done.

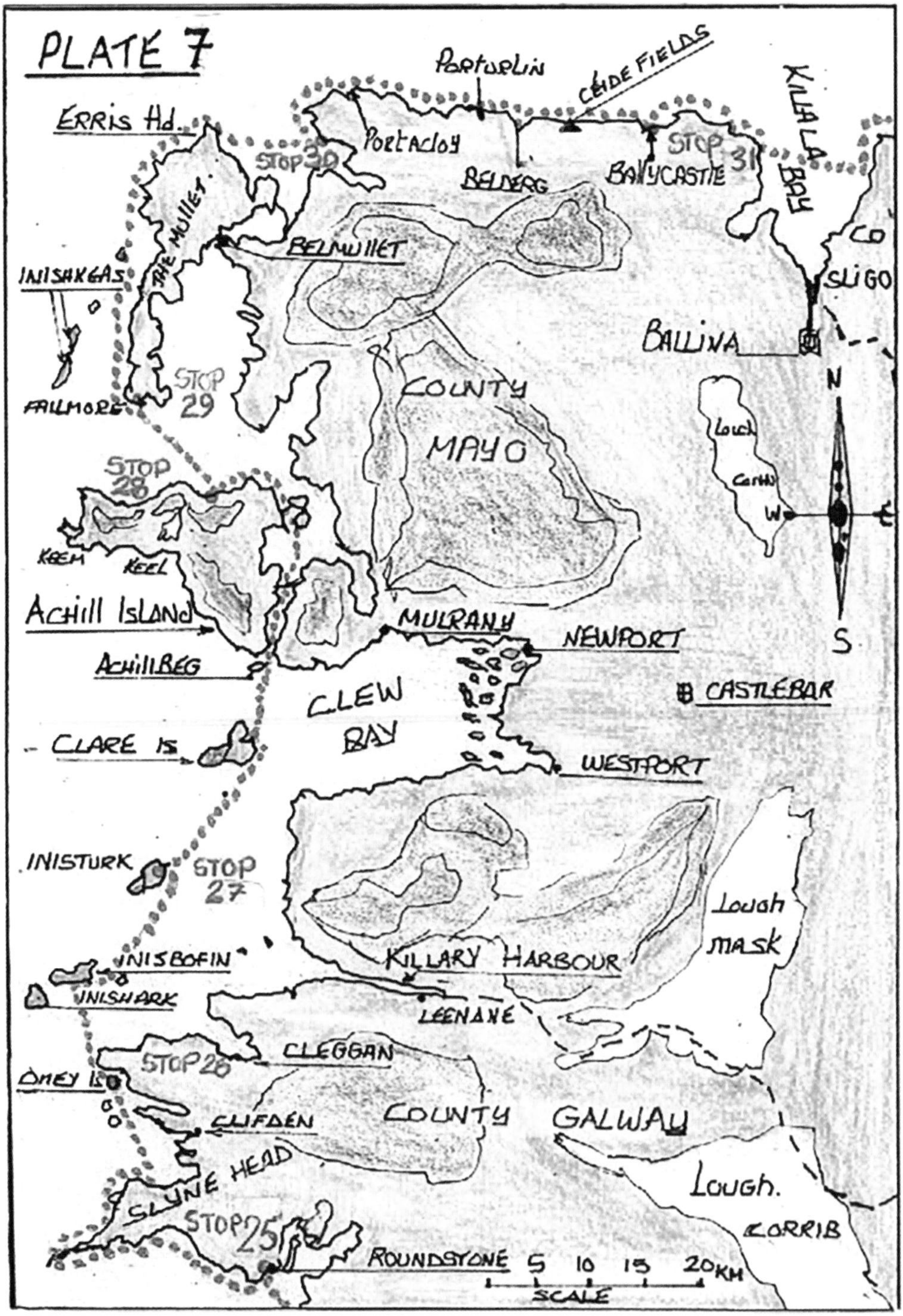
PLATE 7
ERRIS Hd.
PORTURLIN
CÉIDE FIELDS
KILLALA BAY
PORTACLOY
STOP 30
BELDERG
STOP 31
BALLYCASTLE
THE MULLET
BELMULLET
INISHKEAS
SLIGO
BALLINA
STOP 29
FALLMORE
COUNTY MAYO
N
Lough Conn
W
E
S
STOP 28
KEEM
KEEL
Achill Island
MULRANY
NEWPORT
AchillBEG
CLEW BAY
CASTLEBAR
CLARE IS
WESTPORT
INISTURK
STOP 27
Lough mask
INISBOFIN
KILLARY HARBOUR
INISHARK
LEENANE
CLEGGAN
STOP 26
OMEY IS
CLIFDEN
COUNTY GALWAY
SLYNE HEAD
Lough.
CORRIB
STOP 25
ROUNDSTONE
5 10 15 20KM
SCALE

Stage 20

ISLAND COMMUNITIES FROM OMEY TO ACHILL

The following spring, April 17 to be precise, and after an early bus to Galway and another to Clifden, I am taxiing across the hard sand to Omey Island. I am getting started earlier this year on my third and final summer negotiating *Murchú* back to Skerries. Late spring, for me, is an optimistic time of year. Wildflowers are popping up carpeting the island's patchwork of small fields. The winds, blowing in off a glistening blue ocean, are pushing swells onto the island's exposed western shore. *Murchú* is still where I left her after my mid-winter visit, and as ever is ready for action. Unfortunately, with the strong winds I am considering postponing my departure. I chat briefly with Angela who applauds my wisdom and encourages me to soak up the place. I wander along the shoreline marvelling at the transformation since my brief trek west in January. It was Baltic back then, with gales blasting out of the northwest making walking a precarious pursuit.

I pass an old abandoned caravan, still securely anchored to *terra firma* with a collection of ropes and stakes. It was the home of the island's last permanent resident, Pascal Whelan who died in 2017 on his 75th birthday. He had emigrated to Australia at 19 to work as a plasterer and while on a film set stumbled on a new career. When one of the stuntmen refused to perform a fall, he volunteered, igniting a career that boasted teaching Peter O'Toole to swordfight, and also doing stunts for Paul Hogan in *Crocodile Dundee*. He lived out the last 30 years life in this sad-looking home. *The Irish Times* printed a poignant photo of his funeral cortege crossing the sands to the mainland.

Highway to Omey is open

I revisit the tiny beach I landed at six months earlier, and thanks to its seclusion, grab myself a rare skinny dip in the electric blue water. I continue skirting the island's perimeter until I reach its only road which stops abruptly at the water's edge. Unlike Moses who parted the sea for the Israelites, I have to sit and wait for the ocean to slowly uncover my route across to the mainland. I lie back on the hummocky grass and breathe in the salt-laden air dreaming of the pub grub dinner at Sweeney's Strand bar. Later that evening I wander back before the tide returns, settle back into the house, happy that the following day's forecast looks promising for an early departure.

What a difference a day makes. Despite being mid-April, it is mid-summer out west. Well, that is until I dip my hand into the water and realise the seasonal change has not happened in the ocean. The water is shockingly cold. Unfortunately, with six months of limited paddling my muscles hurt and my back is feeling the strain. I bemoan the unexpected loss of my sea legs too and realise that my challenges are many.

I notice that I am particularly conscious of being back in *Murchú*. Though delighted to be climbing the western latitudes again, it is taking some time to get reacquainted with my chariot. After my winter hiatus, getting back into its rhythms comes slowly. With *Murchú* only due back in Skerries after completing the circuit, my winter paddling has been aboard a different animal altogether, a short and stable day-tripping Avocet.

I arrive at Inishbofin and glide into its large natural harbour. I land under a collection of small homesteads and disembark. My early start has me here early, too early, as at 9.00 am everywhere is shut. My assumption that the place would be buzzing proves inaccurate. I reposition myself further along the inlet below the ever popular Murray's Pub and Hotel. I am hopeful that I can wrangle some breakfast there. A young couple are cleaning tables and chairs outside, so my hopes rise. I discover they are opening in an hour, so I go into plea mode, explaining my circumnavigating objective and how desperate I am for a cup of tea. Coincidentally, the guy reveals that his aunt did the same trip years ago. Without realising it, I have been talking to the nephew of legendary sea kayaker Eileen Murphy, a long-time acquaintance of mine. That swings the deal. Minutes later, Joe delivers a piping hot pot of tea, which helps wash down a good chunk of my day's provisions.

I ease into my early morning break and enjoy the quiet for two hours. I am allowing the tide to drop

A well earned cuppa on Inishboffin

189

letting the north-going flood establish itself. This conveyor will speed up my day's paddling. Having made myself a promise to 'stop and smell the roses' during my trip, this break fits in nicely. My attention is drawn to nearby Inishark, Boffin's sad and smaller neighbour. Inhabited for centuries, its fate was severely compromised in 1949 when three young islanders were drowned whilst travelling to Boffin for Mass. This, along with another young man drowning shortly after, was the death knell for an already dwindling island population. Interestingly, the lack of a good harbour also compromised the island's viability. Its port is in a dangerous cove that could only be used during certain tides, and then only by experienced locals. Whatever chance it had as a viable colony has passed, with the last 23 residents being evacuated in 1960. I vow to return, by kayak, and pay the place a visit.

I stroll back to *Murchú* after paying a very important visit to the men's room, thanks to overdoing it on the tea. I view the island's large natural inlet in a new light. Having made Inishboffin easily accessible by boat, mine included, it has been transformed into a hugely successful destination off our coast. Magically, the first of the day's ferries appears from behind the headland at speed, and slides into its embrace. Its arrival heralds my departure. Passengers stand agape along its flanks, like a line of curious mannequins, drinking in their new surroundings. They will soon be deposited onto the pier further inside the natural cove. I sense the beginning of the island's buzz. The ferry's wake tumbles along the pebbly shore. Mission-bound, I leave this slice of heaven and pass below the sentinel castle, and head back out to sea.

Three hours later, after a stop off on Davillaun for a photo opportunity, I am on Tranaun Beach in Inishturk. I had been hoping to recreate a photograph featured in *Oileain*, my guidebook, and simply could not pass up the chance. It was taken by fellow circumnavigator Sean Pierce and shows Davillaun's storm beach tucked into a tiny opening, which for some reason just stuck in my mind. The image, one of many I feasted on over the previous few years, kept my dream alive. While I progress on my quest, I have a distinct feeling of travelling inside Dave's book. Like so many promotional images, though, the scene is difficult to recapture. Still, another box is ticked as I turn a page on my journey.

A stop in Davillaun (top) and Inishturk Harbour (bottom)

My first impression of Inishturk is isolation. Lying 15 kilometres out to sea, it is the remotest among Ireland's inhabited islands; Tory in Donegal misses out by only 500 metres. An irregular four by two kilometre rocky place, it boasts character and harshness in equal measure. It is a testament to the tenacity of its inhabitants that there is anyone living here at all. Situated halfway between Inishbofin and Clare islands, it is a perfect stopping point for this trip. Two friends of mine, Teddy and Aisling, wanted to get married here, but finally opted for the mainland due to the unreliability of ferry services in rough weather.

My heartbeat rises as I bear down on this mid-ocean oasis. Off to my right is Mayo's highest peak, Mweelrea, or Cnoc Malo Reidh,

View towards Clare Island

meaning 'bald hill with smooth top' in Irish. Despite its flattish top giving the impression of an upturned basin, it is still impressive, claiming the lofty title as Connaught's highest point. I land onto one of Turk's tiny beaches for my much loved stretch, before continuing, within touching distance of shore, to the island's hidden harbour. A few currachs lie sleepily on the grass by a long slipway. A small cluster of whitewashed cottages huddle around the tiny inlet, giving the feeling of being watched by faces unseen. I vainly imagine the word spreading about my arrival. A trio of kids skip into view with a healthy looking guy in red and green Mayo jersey ambling along after them. I learn he is one of two Mayo county players out here promoting the Gaelic Athletic Association with the island's youth.

Inishturk is home to the most amazing football pitch in Ireland. This unique creation was hewn out of the rocky hillside and filled with a layer of topsoil from the mainland, a reflection of the strong work

The most amazing GAA pitch in Ireland

ethic that survives here. Since 1998 Inishturk is one of nine islands that compete in the All-Island GAA Football Championships. As those who have emigrated are allowed to compete, great homecomings for the stars and their families are the order of the day. Locally, this Championship is referred to as the *real* All-Ireland.

Laden with my kit, I climb the steep windy road that leads to my B&B. Philomena, the woman of the house, or *Bean an Tí* in Irish, welcomes me to Tranaun House. One of only two such establishments on Turk, she supplements her income as the island's postmistress. Everything here has an intimate feel to it. She looks at me slightly bewildered and is possibly miffed that she never spotted my arrival. Her lofty vantage point, essentially a sentinel post, allows her access to all the comings and goings at the harbour. It does seem odd that I stole past her unnoticed, and I think I have risen in her estimation because of it. She leads me to my lodgings.

Frilly peach cushions, pink flower-spattered wallpaper and purple curtains hang in sharp contrast to the ruggedness of the terrain outside. She explains it was her daughter's room, left 'as it was' when she departed for the mainland to study. Despite my saccharine surroundings, I am 100 per cent happy with the warm bed and feel very much at home. Philomena invites me downstairs for tea and scones, and a full interview. I discover she is originally from Achill Island, my next port of call. I mention my friend Sabine, and that I hope to stay with her tomorrow, and she excitedly tells me she knows her. I have the distinct impression that very few things escape her notice, except stealthy kayakers of course.

It is time for a scan of my surroundings so I head out into the B&B's manicured front garden, a little patch of incongruous quaintness. Perfectly cut grass and tiny flowers provide a contrast to this rocky place. My eye catches six, yellow-tipped oars sweeping in unison across the water below. Being hauled by three fit-looking men, it is one of the currachs I spotted earlier in the harbour. Moving at a solid clip, the crew look impressive as they take off into the baking heat of this spring evening. I am instantly reminded of our currach-building programme in Skerries.

Over the past year, a group of us sea kayaking pals have got together, under the guidance of designer Shane Holland, to construct one of these traditional Irish boats in Skerries. Dating back hundreds of years, this type of craft is typically made by creating a lattice of wooden ribs and lats into a simple frame, all covered with a fabric skin. Once complete it is waterproofed by applying bitumen or tar. Thought to have been used by Ireland's first settlers 5,000 years ago, it is often referred to as the poor man's trawler. For centuries they have been the main mode of local transport serving the many inhabited islands off our coast, specifically off our western seaboard.

I pass a pleasant evening well above sea level admiring my next port of call, Clare Island, 15 kilometres away. Peering hazily from behind it lies Achill, Ireland's largest island. For me, the latter holds the distant promise of this instalment's final destination. The impressive cone of Croagh Patrick stands majestically to the northeast and looks far closer than the 30 kilometres that separate us. To the southeast I am looking directly into the gaping mouth of Ireland's only fjord, Killary Harbour. The stillness of this golden evening's ocean creates the optical illusion of a gigantic mirror. It is mesmerising, as though a map and not the real thing is laid out before me. Distances are foreshortened thanks to strong sunlight and clear air. A noticeable shrinking of the distance across to Clare Island is a tease. I know only too well the effort of hauling a fully-laden boat across that much ocean. Still, it fills me with a wonderful sense of anticipation to see some of tomorrow's route on display for me.

I wander to the local pub, which doubles as a community centre, anxious to meet some locals. Inside, perched on a high stool is a guy in his forties, the pub's sole client. We fall easily into conversation and I soon find myself chatting with Gus, an islander, who splits his time between here and the mainland. We are joined by the young barwoman who joins in enthusiastically. It gives me an inkling into life in such a remote place, where the pace is slow and the interest keen. Luckily for me, Gus is a sailor with intimate knowledge of the waters in these parts and he reassures me that no hazards exist on my next stretch. I can only dare to imagine the great swells he has seen arriving here off the Atlantic. He particularly mentions the western and exposed side of Turk as stunning, but not to be visited by a small boat in anything other than the calmest of weather.

Rising early, I set off on a ramble to the famous and unique football pitch in the centre of the island. Hidden between a rise and a ridge, it seems as though I am on a wild goose chase until I finally clap eyes on it. Resembling an oversized putting green plonked into the rocky landscape, surrounded on all sides by the rocky hillside, it is a perfect amphitheatre. I wonder what it would be like to climb up these rocky slopes to gain a vantage point on the scene being played out below. I can easily understand why it was part of a TV advertising campaign for one of the GAA's many sponsors.

This creation resonates with my own quest, and it elevates my spirit as I trip lightly back to the waiting breakfast at Tranaun. I am about to find out why the pub was so sparsely populated yesterday evening. There are three of us sitting down to an intimate breakfast around a small square table. I join a regular visitor plus an elderly priest. We are introduced, and I soon learn that most of the island's population attended his Mass last evening. Due to dwindling priest numbers in the Catholic Church, the island depends on visiting clergy to support the population. This elderly man has been carrying out his duties for over 50 years and is well known by all who live there. I daresay he would notice any of his flock who were missing. As a non-churchgoer, I feel his curiosity at my absence from the event, but choose to avoid getting into a heavy conversation over breakfast so neither of us gets indigestion.

Suitably replenished, I bid farewell to Philomena, promising to pass on her well wishes to Sabine on Achill. I amble downhill to the small harbour, my eye constantly drawn to the shifting conditions. I notice the early morning calm is slowly giving way to a light south-westerly breeze. Almost imperceptibly at first, the visibility drops. I know this new phenomenon will colour my day's paddling. Whilst squeezing into my drysuit I am distracted by the awakening ocean and hamfistedly burst through one of my wrist seals. I throw out a few expletives. This seemingly innocuous event could mess up my day. The drysuit, a full-bodied waterproof cocoon, should retain body heat by keeping me dry. Now that I have broken a wrist seal, the suit's *modus*

Departing Inishturk

operandi is compromised. Should I be unfortunate enough to fall into the ocean, my suit will draw in cold seawater and sap away my body heat. In fact, these suits are rendered almost completely useless once punctured. The dry suit *must* stay dry.

The option to stall proceedings because of this mishap enters my mind. I weigh up my ability to tackle the day's various challenges, starting with the first and riskiest segment, the downwind run. Am I confident in my skills and fitness level to control *Murchú* on a 15 kilo-metre, downwind, rollercoaster? This basically boils down to my con-fidence of staying in the boat come what may. The opposite side of the argument, that is, not proceeding, throws up all manner of logistical challenges. Being on an island with a limited ferry service means post-poning would be difficult, and as this is the first instalment of the sea-son I am keen to get a good start. This has particular significance since I am hoping to make it back to Skerries before year's end. I am leaning towards going for it. I let my brain mull it over for a while. Finally, the balance falls in favour of going, and once the decision is made things crystallise rapidly in my mind.

Methodically, I continue packing my kayak, check my deck-mounted kit is well sorted and tentatively exit the harbour mouth. I notice the crossing wind has continued to build, pushing ever growing wavelets to the northeast. Coinciding with my direction of travel, I aim to milk this seaborne gift along 15 kilometres of open water to Clare Island. My only way-stop, the rocky islet of Mweelaun, lies nine kilometres away. The haze swallows first Clare Island, and slowly thereafter Mweelaun, meaning I will again be following a compass bearing. I am ready to steer 040 degrees on an adrenaline-fuelled run. Today's paddle has a simple goal: stay right side up, and if I do capsize stay in and roll back up. Ending up in the ocean is *not* an option today. Basically, I am on a tightrope with no safety net, far offshore with defective kit and the wind building. I am taking a calculated risk to keep the show on the road. My circumnavigation is hanging by a thread. Let the show begin.

I take a few deep breaths and head out into the scurrying waves. Having started from the lee side of Inishturk the sea initially comprises only small wavelets. Further out in more open water I begin riding some reasonably sized waves with my speed building accordingly. If I had company and we were riding these white horses like a band of warriors, I know it would be a thrilling, white knuckle ride. But that is not the case today. Scurrying alone across a cold April sea, with dodgy kit, feels like I am surfing for my life, and in many ways I am.

The isolation is briefly interrupted by screeching shearwater careering downwind at seemingly impossible speeds. These scimitars simply add to the urgency of my high speed dash this morning. I bear down on Mweelaun, its shape slowly solidifying out of the murk. Reminiscent of the photographer's developing tray where images form like magic, this isolated rock gradually reveals its true character to me. It reminds me of a mini Rockall. No vegetation, steep sides and far from anywhere, it is a forlorn sight. The swells bluntly smack into the dark monolith, painting it with spattered whitewash. From a distance there seems to be minimal disturbance, but as I hone in I see what is really going on. I will soon be up close and personal to an age-old battle of wave versus rock.

Slowly it dawns on me that a much anticipated breather is off the cards. I had been hoping to grab an early break from the demanding run, to briefly escape from the galloping white horses and take on some sustenance. I experiment by arcing *Murchú* into a great sweep and coming to rest under the lee of the wet rocks. Only when head to wind, do I realise that the wildness of this lonely place has an unexpected feature: its own high-volume, and thumping, soundtrack. The waves are doing their damndest to erode this stubborn plug, and the noise from their struggle is impressive. On a more stable platform I could linger to watch the spectacle more closely, but for now I must busy myself with staying right-side-up on the restless surface. This lonely battle, between ocean and rock, is a metaphor for my mission. I am fighting my own battle with the Atlantic. With great care, I take on some much needed food in a risky, but necessary, manoeuvre. After a paltry five minutes, I am back up to speed and scurrying away towards Clare Island again.

Clare Island's impressive mountain, Knockmore, grows in front of me. After two hours of concentration, *Murchú's* slender green bow cleaves the flat sand of the perfectly sheltered main beach. I remain in my boat, steady for the first time since leaving Turk, and breathe sighs of relief. After my successful downwind run I land my eyes on the colourful landscape surrounding me. I delight in luxuriating in the complete safety, stationary on the wet sand of this east-facing cove. To my left, Grace O'Malley's castle stands squarely above the small harbour. At twelve o'clock, backing the beach, the land rises gently towards the base of the aforementioned summit, a lofty 462 metres higher than where I sit. Behind me the rectangular expanse of Clew Bay recedes towards its many inner islands with Croagh Patrick overseeing all from above.

Grace O'Malley's stout castle reflects her strong character as leader of lands and sea in this area during the late 1500s. She took over that role after the death of her father, Eoghan O Maille. Being a week's trek from Dublin, the occupying forces found it hard to control this remote area of Ireland, essentially allowing her free reign. This earned her the infamous title of Pirate Queen and a reputation as a woman of great power and influence. Her name has morphed into its present iteration of Granuaile, with the flagship of the Irish lights named in her honour.

Passing Grace O'Malley's castle

As English power in the region grew, her two sons and half brother were kidnapped by the governor of Connaught, Sir Richard Bingham.

Grace sailed to England to petition the queen, Elizabeth I, to release them. They met in Greenwich, and since the English monarch did not recognise her as Queen of Ireland she refused to curtsy. The Queen's guards also discovered a knife hidden in her dress which did not bode well for their exchange. However, communicating in Latin, as neither spoke the other's language, the pair displayed a respect for each other. Grace managed to have Bingham removed from his post and her relations released, all conditional on her ceasing her support for the Irish Lords rebelling against the crown forces. Grace lived a full life of 73 years, and lies buried at the island's abbey at Kill.

After my brief stopover, I adjust my track northwards aiming at the southern entrance to Achill Sound. With my circumnavigation not including offshore islands, I am taking advantage of shimmying through inner channels as the opportunity arises. With Achill the largest of Ireland's islands, its channel weighs in at an impressive 20 kilometres. Being first connected via a bridge in 1887, the island boasts an impressive coastline of 128 kilometres, the circumnavigation of which is a real jewel in the crown of the sea kayaking world. Diametrically opposite my present position at its northwestern tip lies Achill Head, the crux point for this challenging loop. That is off the cards for me today as I aim instead for the sinuous inner channel meandering as far as Michael Davitt Bridge in Achill Sound. Aside from the circulating flows at the channel's entrance this is an undemanding stretch of water and

A stop on Clare Island

Approaching Achillbeg

will be warmly welcomed. Swapping the open ocean for a backdrop of fields, mountains and homesteads will be a peaceful end to my day.

Two kilometres into the crossing I begin to realise an omission during my way stop on Clare. An ability to paddle comfortably is being compromised by a growing inner pain. In denial, I attempt to ignore it by keeping my eyes fixed on Achillbeg, the smaller island partially blocking Achill's channel. Slowly, my unease grows and I am beginning to sweat with occasional shivers rippling through my torso and legs. I think back to launching on Clare Island and spot the seeds of my own destruction, an overfull bladder. After rehydrating there I never thought to react to the faint whispering of nature's call. Seeing as I am cocooned in my 'semi' dry-suit, I am determined not to submit to my body's urges. I try moving to a more comfortable position, but unfortunately these craft are designed without wriggle room. Any movements simply compound my problem. Alas, only by emptying can a full bladder be relieved.

I struggle to maintain composure as I propel myself across the waves. Clare Island's cliff top lighthouse stares down mockingly as

I slowly edge my way away from the island's lee and strike out for Achillbeg. This is, literally, a holding pattern. Eventually, I catch sight of Achillbeg's tiny beach, my planned place of deliverance. I land, and with some difficulty climb to a semi-stooped position on the sand. I haul myself, drunk-like, towards a rock wall and manoeuvre into a safe position for a long release. This strange pleasure has me almost seeing stars and continues for quite some time. Today, I seem to be lurching between being compromised and being relieved, this one of my own making. I decide to continue towards the Sound. A few curve balls are crossing my path; it is such a pity I threw this one myself.

The inner channel of the sound is the perfect sequel to my earlier tests. Its languid movements are sluggish compared to those of the ocean. I arrive under the island's sole connecting bridge at Achill Sound in a surprisingly depleted state. With 30 of today's planned 45 kilometres under my belt, I am happy to take a reasonable break. Hoping to catch the incoming tide to here, and the outgoing one through the Northern Channel, the flow indicates I am a bit early. In search of a coffee and a roll I head off to Lavelle's Supermarket. At the door

Atmospheric Achill Island

I bump into the assistant who is shutting up shop. When I suggest I will settle for a coffee, she informs me that the machine has already been turned off and cleaned. She looks over my shoulder and points across the bridge to a large building surrounded by parked cars. 'Try there,' she suggests.

Alice's Harbour Bar and Restaurant is a large establishment on the mainland side of the bridge and with no other options I wander across. This is my first time back on the mainland since leaving Omey for dinner three days ago. I enter Alice's cavernous dining area

Almost nightfall near Golden Strand, Achill

which is bustling with all manner of clientele from family groups to tourists busily tucking into their afternoon meals. The kind proprietor grants me permission to perch at the bar despite being dressed in my kayaking kit, not the norm for this place. Soon I am devouring an enormous plate of fish and chips washed down with piping hot milky coffee. I strike up a conversation with a guy in his twenties, who is curious about my attire. I happily recount my day's activities to which he shows great interest. As a keen local GAA player he understands my passion, but not in that arena. Each to his own I suggest, his being far outside my own realm of possibilities. We chat further and then after a day almost entirely alone I soak up the hubbub watching kids scurrying about chasing each other. Their unbridled joy is infectious.

MY HOSTS TODAY ARE VERY PATIENT indeed as my estimate for landing and manoeuvring my boat onto the road, and up the incline to their house, will be out by over an hour. Towards the end of my paddle I feel drained and when spotting a boulder strewn obstruction at the back of Golden Strand, blocking my way to the road, my heart drops. Nothing else but to unload my kit and transport everything separately beyond this obstacle and repack it all into the boat. Then with my trusty trolley pressed back into service I slowly make my way along the kilometre incline from Golden Strand to Sabine's cosy cottage. My memories of the two kilometre trek on the Hook Peninsula come flooding back to me. I arrive at their house, pretty fatigued, and glad to have this year's first instalment for 2019 in the bag.

When inside and changed, I sit down with Fionn and Caoimhe, Sabine's adult children, to a piping hot stew washed down with some fantastic fruit tea. I am impressed with their restraint. They had all waited for my arrival before diving into the earthenware pot of wholesome goodness. They are eager to hear tales from the sea and, wide-eyed, hang on to my every word. I am buoyed to have arrived, self-powered, onto the island of my past and to be welcomed by friends.

It has taken me three days to get *Murchú* from Omey to Achill, and I am well chuffed. Looking out through Sabine's window I catch a glimpse of the Mullet Peninsula, and despite its taunts as my next instalment, I barely register its existence. That is all for another time when I will be taking on the notorious Erris Head from where I will turn eastwards for Sligo. I am starting to recognise a belief that I will be able to complete my trip along our West Coast and top out at Malin Head. After that I feel the rest of the north and east coasts should be manageable. I am only now beginning to honestly believe that I may in fact complete what I started. I will be heading to Dublin in the morning, with a licence to extend the line on the map stuck to the wall in our kitchen. I have managed about ten centimetres in three days. Here's hoping I can close the loop before the year is out. With these as my final thoughts, I settle down into a deep and luxurious sleep.

Stage 21

THE MULLET PENINSULA
IN WEST MAYO

Three weeks later, after first crossing the country by train to West-port, and then by bus to Achill, Sabine picks me up and ferries me to her house. From her whitewashed cottage, overlooking my next passage, the traverse to the Mullet peninsula is laid out before me. Nearby Sliabh Mor, or 'big mountain' in Irish, towers over everything adding drama to the location. Thankfully, my beach commute is downhill and an hour and a half after tearing myself away from my host, I am afloat and headed northwest to Faulmore, on the southern tip of the Mullet. The sea is iridescent and the afternoon warm. Houses shine brilliantly on the slopes off to my left, as the intensity of colours reflect the climb towards midsummer. The descending orb of the sun throws sparkles onto the shimmering carpet ahead. I am mesmerised at the sight.

After two hours in the boat I haul myself up a small slip and begin eyeing where to set up camp. Located at the end of a country road, any further west and I would be on the exposed side of the Mullet. The grass hereabouts has been shorn by grazing sheep and resembles a softly sloped putting green. After a while I notice an older guy making his way along the gravelly shoreline just below my lodgings. I strike up a friendly conversation with Patrick, a local, who shows great interest in my exploits. On discovering he is an ex-fisherman I quiz him about tomorrow's journey. He basically confirms the information gleaned from *Oileain* about the tidal flows. I thank him for the reassurance and mention to him that I could do with taking on more freshwater. He

Faulmore, Belmulett with Achill in the background

points to the closest house saying Sean will be home in a half hour, and that he could sort me out.

A little later, I ramble up the long driveway and meet Sean, who turns out to be descended from a family from the nearby Inishkeas. He invites me in for a cuppa, and soon I am happily munching on some biscuits under the watchful eyes of his two children. I am moved to hear that his daughter Kea is named after the islands of his forefathers. His wife joins us in what turns out to be a pleasant Q&A session. I learn about their ancestors and what it's like to live in this remote spot, and in exchange they learn about my quest. With the house perched on elevated ground a great panorama of the Atlantic fills their windows. The two Inishkeas can be seen on the horizon.

Hosting a population of 350 in the 1900s, the Inishkea islands were abandoned in the 1930s. In October 1927, a flotilla of Currachs were night fishing when an unexpected storm hit, devastating the fleet and drowning 48 of the island's menfolk. Several of the capsized boats were washed up on the nearby shore. The shockwave suffered by the islanders left a wound that could not be healed and the population were permanently rehoused to the mainland shortly afterwards. As ever, I am privileged to meet such friendly folk and reluctantly leave to head back to my base.

Back at my camp, I put on a brew and tuck into some noodles and tinned mackerel. Such is my hunger it tastes like manna from heaven. When ensconced in my sleeping bag I reexamine the charts and compare them to tomorrow's section in *Oileain*. On my next stretch, I will be climbing up the latitudes with the Mullet to my right, and a string of islands to my left. The notorious Erris Head is tomorrow's critical point, and I am dearly hoping for safe passage. This is where I will be swinging *Murchú* onto an easterly track and beginning the long traverse across the north Mayo coast towards Sligo. I complete my blog, switch off my headlamp and descend into a deep sleep.

IN THE MIDDLE OF THE NIGHT I HEAR a voice, a woman's voice with a strange accent. I hear my name being called. Being semi-awake, I wonder if it is my wife or daughter so it does not cause me undue alarm. The voice increases in volume and is carrying a tone of panic. Someone is clearly trying to get my attention. In the black of night this makes me most uneasy. Someone keeps calling my name, asking if I am inside. I mumble a few words, completely baffled by the whole affair.

'Oh, thank goodness,' the voice exclaims.

'Sorry?' I ask, puzzled.

'I met a friend of yours today who told me you were kayaking across, I just wasn't sure you'd made it.'

'Oh, yeah, I did, I'm fine, you're very kind,' I reply, still puzzled.

Reluctantly, I offer to emerge from my chrysalis to meet her in person.

She is having none of it and is very contrite. ' No, No, No, don't do that, I am happy now, I am so sorry. I just had to be sure you were okay,' her voice now brimming with relief. 'Get back to sleep now, and eh, best of luck tomorrow.'

And that was that, from rude awakening to speedy departure, I am guessing the whole affair took under two minutes. So here I am, wide-eyed and awake, staring into the dark silence in disbelief. A car grumbles into life. It seems like it is inches from my tent. It crunches the gravel outside as it begins to head back up the road. The fading rumble mirrors my descent back into dreamland.

My morning preparations, as ever, set me up for the day. The sequential stuffing order, and associated mental map, forms a big part of a solo sea kayaker's *modus operandi*. If I need to land and grab my first aid kit, I need to find it immediately. Or, if during a stop I need to replenish my drink system, my stock of water bottles must be close to hand. I continue my ritualistic sorting, whilst taking the odd glance back out across the sea. Yesterday's passage from Achill, now consigned to memory, stretches out behind me as I ready myself to advance. Like a long drawn-out pit stop I am about to be spat back onto the circuit at my planned seven kilometres per hour. These thoughts have me emboldened for the day ahead. I notice a rumble and glance back up the country road to see a small white car descending in my direction. It pulls up beside me and a familiar voice wishes me a good morning.

It is Hannah, my night visitor, who has come to see me off. Her act of contrition is by way of some gifts which she lifts from the back seat. She hands me a delph plate covered in foil. While pleading for forgiveness, she removes the foil to reveal a full Irish breakfast. I am flabbergasted. Unfortunately, I am completely full after my own early feed but still manage to down some rashers and eggs, plus a very well cooked sausage. Not content with this, she then places a large slab of chocolate in my hand.

We exchange a few pleasantries and off she heads back up the road to her busy life as a teacher in the local school. As I slip my boat into the ocean I am warmed by this generous gesture, struck again by the kindness of strangers. As I pull away from the slip I spot a porpoise scurrying about less than 50 metres away. I take this as a sign of a good day ahead and turn onto the western side of the Mullet tracking along its long sandy beaches.

I continue directly north and watch the unfolding land and seascape roll past me. Inishkea south and north flank my first five kilo-

Inishglora

metres, leading to a crossing to Inishglora and its companion islets. This is where I intend to stop for my customary stretch. I will have a pleasant 15 kilometres in the bank at that stage. Initially, Inishglora proves a bit of a conundrum as it is a hummocky hill, contradicting my guidebook's description of it as a 'low lying featureless place'. When travelling by kayak on the ocean, the horizon lies only ten kilometres away, and anything low lying will not be visible until well within range. I am puzzled by this growing landmass on my path. Getting closer, it starts to grow horizontally, finally extending its right flank all the way to the mainland. Completely flummoxed, I continue paddling, occasionally consulting my map just to confirm the correctness of my navigation. When only four kilometres out I spot a dark line running along my horizon and realise I have been overlooking Inishglora all the while. My sights have been locked on to the hilly southern part of Erris Head which lies behind my flat, lower target. With my faith in *Oileain* renewed, I finally close in to a rocky landing, climb out of *Murchú* and step onto the island of legends for a mid-morning break.

One of the myths about the place was that its climate supposedly preserved the bodies of the dead. It was widely believed that one's lineage could be viewed in the faces of the many generations laid out, above ground, on the island. In the sixth century Saint Brendan the Navigator founded a church here and in deference to this holiest of men local fishermen briefly dropped their sails as they passed the island.

The Children of Lir feature in an ancient Irish myth associated with Inishglora. Bodb Dearg was an Irish king, a rival of Lir, ruler of the seas. Bodb gave his daughter Aeb to Lir to appease him. This union bore four children, a girl and three boys. Sadly, Aeb died leaving Lir distraught. Bodb decided to send yet another of his daughters, Aoife, to Lir. Shortly thereafter Aoife grew jealous of the children's love for their father and decided on a plot to kill them. Lacking the courage to carry out the deed, she used her magical powers turning them into swans instead. She banished them for 900 years around Ireland after which they would be free. They spent 300 years in Lough Derravaragh in Westmeath, 300 in the Sea of Moyle, the channel between Antrim and Scotland, and 300 in Sruwaddacon Bay near Erris in Mayo. When the 900 years had passed, they flew here to Inishglora for the remainder of their days. Sadly, today, only a few herring gulls are the extent of any avian activity visible on the island.

A rocky inlet, North Belmulett

I continue northwards, slowly reeling in Erris Head. A high blue-sky arcs overhead. Soon I will be swapping the sandy beaches for jagged cliffs as the land climbs skyward towards my crux point. As this headland has no get-outs, I dive into the last landing available, a long rectangular opening in the coastline. Little do I realise I am about to find myself in another spot of bother, and completely my own making. I slot my kayak onto a long shelf, tie her up, and wander to the rock-strewn storm beach at the end of the opening. I go walka-bout while sinking my teeth into Hannah's large slab of chocolate. The melting sweetness in my mouth transports me away from my salty challenge. I am looking forward to clapping eyes on Eagle Island and its iconic lighthouse soon. In the meantime I am savouring the sense of remoteness of this corner of northwest Mayo.

I STAY IN THE ROCKY COVE LONGER than expected and end up paying a price. I discover my kayak is now sitting well above sea level. Perched neatly on a shelf and approaching waist height, I stare at it in disbelief. I must get her back down to the water. Too heavy to lift, and with unloading taking ages, I look for another solution. I decide on the tried and tested method of pivot-walking. Alternatively lifting the bow, and then the tail, it requires careful assessment of the boulder strewn ter-rain as I walk *Murchú* with what is essentially an 18 foot gait. I begin

the sequential procedure. I lift the bow and place it in a new lo-cation, moving then to manoeu-vre the stern. Due to its fully lad-en weight I put my hand around the hull to lift it. Slowly, she pivots amidships, see-saw like, as she starts to leave the shelf. I am winning. Just a wee bit more and she will be at sea level and ready to go. Suddenly, the boat lurches, the tail swings up and across slamming into the rock, dragging me with it. A searing pain comes from my hand which I realise is now trapped between hull and stone.

Erris Head sea corridor

'Jesus' I yelp, as an electric shock of pain emanates from my hand firmly jammed behind the boat. The heavy kayak has see-sawed into this position and the leverage has exerted a large force jamming me in place. All the rocks here are encrusted with a carpet of barnacles peppered with the odd limpet. Sliding my hand free is a non-runner. Any attempt to extract my limb meets with increased agony. My kayak has the stubbornness of a solid tree trunk. I have got to release my hand from its grip. The pain continues unabated until I somehow manage to briefly lever my kayak out of position to free my aching appendage. My relief is followed by shock at what I see. In the middle of the back of my hand is a cone-shaped depression, created by an unfortunately positioned limpet. My heavy kayak has tried to punch a hole through my hand. The end result resembles a stigmata.

My immediate reaction is that I will not be able to continue paddling and will have to find an alternative method to extract myself from this rock-backed bay. I look in disbelief at the impression in my hand and am amazed it has not penetrated right through to my palm. I immerse my hand in water hoping for some relief and maybe some restoration. I try massaging it and then slowly realise my good luck. While not back to normal, nothing seems to be broken as the limpet has forced its way between the metacarpal bones. I have some soft tissue damage, but considering the pain felt this is minimal. I am lucky to have downed some chocolate during my break, preventing me from slipping into shock. Minutes later, almost unbelievably, I return to the ocean. I once again take note of the continuous care needed when travelling solo in remote places. With each paddle stroke I submerge my injured hand into the cool water gripping my blades tightly to help my sorry hand. Slowly, it returns to near normal, albeit with some bruising. Despite my atheism, and not for the first time, I feel incredibly blessed.

Stage 22

Passing Erris Head en Route to Ballycastle

Exiting the deep bay I spot the legendary lighthouse situated a few kilometres offshore. Eagle Light stands on a humpbacked island and carries with it some amazing stories. The first dates back to 1836 not long after its construction. As this island is close to the continental shelf huge waves are generated over the steeply rising seabed. During a severe storm a rock was thrown up the cliff and broke glass in the tower which stands 60 metres above the high water mark. The second tale dates back to 1861 when its light room was struck by a rogue wave, smashing 23 panes and damaging equipment inside the building. The light keepers could not gain access to the tower as water cascading down inside prevented them from opening the access door. They had to drill holes in the door to release the water and gain entry.

Getting past Erris Head is a pleasant anti-climax. I can easily visualise it with a swell transforming it into a serious hazard to circumvent by kayak. Reefs, islets, spikes of rock and tight channels, not to mention a 90 degree turn in the coastline, constitute important ingredients for some watery chaos. Not since rounding Slyne Head in Galway have I seen such a collection of hazards packed neatly into one small area. I am chuffed to pass by under benign conditions. My early morning porpoise sighting was a good omen.

My next get-out is a strangely named place called Danish Cellar. This descending cleft in the cliff sports the narrowest slipway to, hopefully, allow me exit for my customary stretch and look about. I haul my kayak onto its trailer and move it up the steep incline, just enough

Erris Head passage – a piece of cake

to clear the tide. I chock the wheels, tie up to a large protrusion, and continue upwards to investigate. When up at road level I discover the trailhead for the Erris Loop walk complete with its information sign.

I notice the cleft broadening into a wide depression bisected by a narrow country road. Like beads on a string, several cottages are dotted along its inland meanderings. I hear laughter up ahead and spot two men tending nets beside a house. On seeing me in my kit, they promptly engage in conversation, asking if I had come around by Erris. When I confirm that it was me their interest heightens, leading to an enthusiastic exchange. This is one of the great bonuses of travelling the watery highway.

'You're a lucky man to get conditions like today,' one of them comments, explaining that Erris is no place for any vessel, big or small, when the sea is misbehaving. I seem to be tapping into an ancient network that still links the seafaring community off our coasts. I can only imagine the sights these guys have witnessed over their lifetimes at sea.

I sidle back the steep slipway, heartened by the exchange. It is my first since meeting Hannah this morning. Have I really been chatting with myself for the interim? How I have not driven myself mad is anyone's guess. I seem to be developing a positive relationship with myself which is helping to cover the distance. A deep trust is growing within as I handle the myriad challenges that face me on a daily basis. And now I have Broadhaven Bay to finish today's work. Ah yes, life is good.

Danish Cellar

The nine kilometre crossing to Benwee Head takes almost two hours, mostly because of the freshening northeasterly. I catch sight of a passing skua, which bring up memories of Dad. These triggers go off without warning, bittersweet moments that lead me down old alleyways in my mind. It is funny, but random things often evoke the strongest of memories. I fondly remember our shared interest in wildlife, birds especially. Sadly, I do not think he ever clapped eyes on a skua, probably due to its habit of remaining mostly offshore. Now this species holds a tangible link to him, having spotted one on the day he died last year.

A splash of water unexpectedly returns me to the job in hand. The last chunk still has to be negotiated and I need to stay focused on the seascape I am traversing. The final few kilometres of any day are definitely worth paying attention to, especially given the cumulative effect of fatigue which can creep up unawares.

Eventually my kayak trades its buoyancy for the support of Rinroe Beach. Glowing in the early evening light, and with my day's mission complete, I instantly relax. As plenty of daylight remains, I scan my surroundings, still sitting in my boat in the middle of the cove. A golden moment, on golden sand. Behind this slice of paradise is where I will set up camp for the night. I have a nice 44 kilometres clocked up, a marathon plus two, so I am content. The beach is west-facing, deeply recessed and protected from most swells by the distant Erris peninsula. It is a perfect safe haven for me. I move my kit up onto the sheep-shorn grass banks behind the marram to set up camp. To my dismay, I spot a pile of rubbish amongst the long spiky grass, the first I have seen since landing. Upon closer inspection a neatly stacked pile is revealed, evidence of enthusiastic beach cleaners. This raises my gratitude for my temporary residence, which I realise is otherwise spotless.

Rinroe derives from the Irish, 'An Rinn Rua', the 'Red Tip', which I assume refers to the russet coloured rocks that line this beautiful cove. While arranging camp an English couple trundle up in their white camper and park a respectable distance away. I allow them to settle into two bright deckchairs where they are in semi-worship of the setting sun. I wander over for a neighbourly chat and am offered a welcome

Beach guardians in evidence on Carrowteige

cup of tea. Both in their sixties, they are following their noses around our beautiful island. As we are both camped near Carrowteige, in a remote corner of County Mayo, we have the whole place to ourselves. We exchange a few pleasantries, then I wander back to my camp, tuck into my nosh and retire inside my tent for the night.

DAY THREE OF THIS INSTALMENT IS PLANNED to cross under the high cliffs of the north Mayo coast from Broadhaven Bay to Ballycastle. With limited get-outs, this challenge needs to be negotiated carefully. Almost the whole coastline here is elevated, comprising rising and falling land backed by some fantastic sea cliffs. A few openings will allow me to take breaks, but for the most part this is a committing stretch. After 12 kilometres I can pull into Portacloy, followed half that distance again by Porturlin and then after another 13 kilometres to Belderg. This final stretch into Ballycastle will take me under the site of the famous Ceide Fields interpretive centre. More about that later.

I call Malin Head Coastguard at 6:45 am, relaying my whereabouts and my intention to make Ballycastle by evening. They confirm all is copied, and with favourable weather forecast, wish me safe passage. Minutes later, as I am getting into my kayak, my phone rings. Puzzled about who could be ringing at this early hour, I take the call.

'Hello, who is this?' I query.

'This is Malin Head Coastguard. Is that Kevin?'

'Yup, is everything okay?'

'Just confirming that you hope to make Ballycastle today?'

'Yes, that's my destination.'

'In Antrim?'

Ah, now I understand. He is located quite close to the bigger of the two Ballycastles on the island of Ireland. He most likely does not know about the one that lies 44 kilometres away from me here in Mayo.

'Ah no, I'm not that fit. The one in north Mayo is my goal today.'

'Ah I see ... well that's alright so,' he chirps, 'you had us all guessing up here… safe travels.'

Stags of Broadhaven

And with that, I shimmy *Murchú* afloat to see what the north Mayo coastline has in store.

I leave Rinroe beach, head west and turn the corner towards Kid Island. You would think this a small insignificant island, but my first view of this 'massive lump' leaves me reeling. Near-by, some enormous cone-shaped stacks rise menacingly out of the water to heights between 50 and 100 metres. Great escarpments rise skyward to my right, and with the island only 250 metres distant on my left, they describe a gateway to the dramatic coast-line of north Mayo which recedes into the distance. I am winding my way through a geological minefield of great proportions. Whilst navigating these hazards a sighting on the horizon stops me in my tracks. The Stags of Broadhaven. Five, tightly packed, tooth-shaped cones of rock, looking like a herd of oversized elephants, are gathered offshore. Even at a distance of six kilometres, they are huge. From a kayaking perspective, it is widely known that landing onto any of the Stags is impossible, without first exiting your boat and swimming ashore. Seeing them today for the first time defin-itively reinforces this.

My day continues to fill with all manner of breathtaking vistas with Portacloy next. I enter a kilometre long, finger-shaped bay, backed by a flat sandy beach. I am feeling a bit queasy thanks to a dollop of cliff-in-duced clapotis, or crapotis as I now like to call it. I hop out and enjoy a walkabout on this incongruous piece of low-lying land. Farms and homes dot the landscape. As my next leg to Porturlin harbour is only a short hop, a brief lull is enough. I press on.

Landing on Portacloy

An hour later I pull into Porturlin, a working harbour flanked by a collection of houses on its western slopes. An elongated inlet, it has a scattering of colourful boats moored just inland of the pier. Looking for fresh water, I call on a house above the pier and end up waking a young guy named Patrick, who is happy to oblige. He also offers me a cup of tea and we both park ourselves outside his bungalow, basking in the bright morning sun. I learn he is soon to be married. I mention that I have been for twenty years, and he wonders if I have any advice. Feeling less than qualified to impart any wisdom, but mindful of the cup of tea he has put in my hand, I rack my brain for a nugget. I eventually suggest to keep talking to each other. Men have an awful habit of keeping things under wraps, whereas it's best to have things out in the open from the get-go. All easier said than done I add, but he is appreciative all the same. I bid him goodbye after a fair exchange. Tea for tips.

This pleasant exchange helps take my mind off the challenging coastline I am soon to revisit. My next stop is Belderrig, 13 kilometres away, an even longer stint than earlier. I have the possibility of a stop onto a cliff-backed stone beach at half distance, so fingers crossed I can make a landing there. I may be in need of it. I continue eastwards past another monumental rock curtain that dwarfs me and *Murchú*. I slowly come to the conclusion that a sizable chunk of Mayo must lie at the bottom of the sea as I seem to be making my way along the remaining half of a great range of hills removed by some giant cleaver.

Up ahead is Illanamaster, another lofty island separated from the mainland by a narrow canyon. I enter its channel and am plunged into shadow. The towering canyon is staggering and I almost capsize looking for the top. Up ahead, a bright beam of sunlight spills onto a patch of ocean which is almost encircled by the next promontory. Interestingly, a strange quivering action is taking place there, much like rain splattering onto a puddle. I am puzzled since I have not seen a cloud all day. Maybe a stream is leaking from the cliff above or a shoal of fish are running. Cautiously, I paddle forward into the mysterious phenomenon. What I witness is the smallest area of high frequency

Storm beach near Illanamaster

clapotis I have ever seen. The strange geometry of this canyon has led to some small wavelets interfering with each other, creating a miniature version of this dreaded phenomenon. I continue towards the cliff-backed opening, hopeful for a short break on a storm beach.

A storm beach is formed when rocks are piled high after multiple storm waves have torn lumps from the coastline. Smoothed, rounded and washed clean, these grey mounds of stones, despite having no sand, are misnamed 'beaches'. They can measure up to 30 metres vertically, have steep inclines and can be notoriously difficult to land on by kayak, especially when travelling solo. The stones range from pillow size right down to pebbles. As I paddle into the small amphitheatre, I am already trying to gauge the steepness of what lies ahead. I decide to run the boat high onto the rising stones and jump out. I have no intention of a half-cocked effort that ends with a capsize. I reverse away from my target, settle myself, and start a full blooded sprint to ensure *Murchú* climbs far enough out of the water for a safe exit. Thankfully, my speed leaves me above the waterline where I can exit my boat, grab the deck lines and prevent her from sliding back into the sea. I drag her to a flatter section of stones, sit down and take a breather.

Being enclosed on three sides by cliffs, with the only egress via the ocean, I commend myself for being one of the few humans to have landed there. Seeing as my circumnavigation is more about smelling the roses than racing ahead, this gem of a way-stop has been in my sights for a while. By boating standards, the shallow draft of the sea kayak makes it one of the few sea-going craft capable of visiting these hidden corners, and for this I am grateful.

As I survey my surroundings something unusual catches my eye. Between me and the sea, a pile of rocks, perhaps twelve in all, are stacked neatly into a vertical tower. I am surprised I failed to spot them earlier. I smile wryly as I realise my unique visitor status has been compromised. I imagine a scene of several adventurers observing the stacker carefully creating their piece of isolated random artwork. A bit arrogant for me to pat myself on the back so quickly.

One hour later I am guiding *Murchú* into Belderg, or 'Red Mouth' to give it an English translation. This wide bay has a small working harbour tucked into its western shore. Its pier is full of machinery, spills of oil and a few old fishing boats perched on rusting cradles. After my passage along some pristine coastline it is both an arresting and depressing sight. This once fine facility seems to have suffered from years of neglect. Bright sparks from someone welding shine from one of the boats. I decide to take a wander about and spot the lone worker. Hidden under his black protective helmet, intent on his work, he nods me a quick hello, returning immediately to his task. I continue ambling about, noticing a set of concrete steps leading over the stout quay. Behind the pier is another set of steps lined with stainless steel railings, descending to a landlocked swimming pool formed in the rocky foreshore. Called Pol a Sean tSaile, or 'The Hole of Old Seawater', it provides safe swimming though only after it is replenished by a high tide.

Belderg, North Mayo

Stage 23

UNDER THE PYRAMID
AT CEIDE FIELDS

My final 13 kilometre segment to Ballycastle continues under Mayo's dark cliffscape, and clocks up another day's total well above forty. The unusual site of the pyramid-shaped Visitor Centre at Ceide Fields, peering over the dark cliff at my halfway point, reassures me that my day's paddling is nearly complete. This futuristic interpretive centre looks into Ireland's deep past thanks to a discovery of stone walls in the 1930s by a local school teacher, Patrick Caulfield, who was out digging peat in the area. In the 1970s, Patrick's son Seamus, who was studying archaeology, initiated a more detailed examination of the site, which was dated at 5,500 years, during the Neolithic or Stone Age. This would make it the world's earliest example of a closed field system, a claim challenged by other dating methods, placing it during the more recent Bronze Age, 2,500 years later. Either way, the unearthing of this ancient sight revealed another seam in the layered history of our island's ancestors. The incongruous, pyramid-shaped centre draws tens of thousands of visitors to an otherwise neglected area of north Mayo. It boasts a panoramic viewing deck above the elevated coastline. For all I know, voyeurs could have been peering out at me as I clawed my way eastwards.

After dealing with the miles of reflected chop continuously coming from the cliffs, an unwelcome guest is taking hold. It feels like a dead weight is bearing down on me and I am filled with a pressing desire to just lie down, cover my head and make it go away. My old nemesis, seasickness, has come aboard to pay a visit and is making this last segment a considerably greater challenge than it should be. It has been a while, but still, there is no denying its presence. Some would say that with such a susceptibility I was mad to have embarked on this mission, and right now I am inclined to agree. However, in a crazy sort of way it offers me an opportunity of personal growth by dealing with it, alongside whatever else the ocean might drum up. Growth happens where we are vulnerable, and this is definitely my 'soft spot'.

Closing in on the opening to Ballycastle, several day boats are heading out to sea. Small groups, armed with fishing rods, are venturing out in search of some quarry. They provide a welcome distraction for my sore head, as well as heralding my proximity to this sheltered inlet. I make my way inland spotting a shallow reef near the pier, occasionally erupting into a perfect breaking wave. I give this feature a wide berth as it could easily upend me within a few hundred metres of my landing. I'd rather not provide free entertainment for the people onshore.

Ballycastle harbour is teeming with all sorts of activity when my bow clunks onto its generous slipway. My kayak will be looked after

Arriving in Ballycastle

My sister Mary, Ballycastle roadie

by a legendary paddler, David Horkan. I spot him about to embark on a group trip to a blowhole further back the coast. He tells me that they will meet a guy there who will fly a drone into the large blowhole and capture some footage of the paddlers from above. David is a go-getter who lives life at an enthusiastic pace. I quickly empty my boat, pop it onto his roof rack and watch him lead his group to their exciting rendezvous.

A year to the day since Dad passed, it is my sister Mary who ferries me to our brother's house in Sligo. We three share an evening in his memory, thanking him for imbuing in us a thirst for adventure and a fondness for the sea. Mary is a keen open water swimmer who has recently taken to triathlons despite her dodgy knees, and Mossey is a surfer who settled near Enniscrone, home to some of Sligo's outstanding reef breaks. He is firmly embedded in the local fabric of similarly-minded folk who have swapped the rat race for a more stress-free way of life. It is a far cry from the suburban upbringing we all shared.

My brother Mossey in Easkey

A MONTH LATER, WEDNESDAY, JUNE 19th, my jeep crunches the gravel of my brother's driveway. His booming welcome lifts my spirits after a day strapped into various driving seats, the Airbus, which I had flown to Paris earlier that morning, and my car which now sits outside his bungalow in west Sligo. My goal this time is a one day sortie from Mayo to here. I intend getting *Murchú* in place for navigating the great bight of Donegal Bay at a future date.

Mossey ferries me to my put-in the following morning. We collect *Murchú* from Ballina and continue westwards to Ballycastle. I am distracted by the leaf-laden trees swaying in a freshening breeze from the northwest. Already, my mind races ahead visualising what might await me offshore. My stomach lurches involuntarily.

It is 8.45 am when I resume my quest. I leave Ballycastle pier and strike out on an easterly bearing towards my tenth coastal county, Sligo. I am especially keen to clap eyes for the first time on Dún Briste, or 'Broken Fort' in English, which lies off Downpatrick Head, my first significant milestone. This flat-topped, 45 metre high sea stack resembles an enormous black forest gateaux rising vertically out of the ocean. With layered sides of dark sedimentary rock it mimics the nearby cliffs from which it calved in the late fourteenth century when a sea arch collapsed, leaving the isolated sea stack still surviving today. Heeding the advice from David Horkan, well familiar with his home waters, I will be giving it a wide berth, especially with a two metre swell forecast.

Being a month since I last sat into *Murchú*, it takes time to reacquaint myself with her movements. This is especially noticed in the sporty conditions that are developing. Ballycastle pier's flat water is a distant memory now, as moving out from its shelter the swells build, crossing under the boat with ever growing amplitude. As I close in on Downpatrick Head the swells continue to magnify, throwing me into an absorbing tussle. Occasionally, I surf down a wave at speed, followed shortly thereafter by an attempt to turn broadside along the same swell. I am continuously pushing hard on my rudder pedals as I grapple with *Murchú's* movements. I need to concentrate and keep things simple.

Despite Dún Briste looming off to the right, my focus on the boat's varying trajectory is so intense that it is unsafe to steal a glance. I must not end up like Lot's wife, who looked back and turned into a pillar of salt. My peripheral vision picks up its great mass, the base of which has churning swells creating a frothing mass of foam. Great booms rebound off the blunt cliffs as waves return offshore, confusing the seas further. I am at the pinch-point of this dark headland and know I am nearing the limits of my ability. Up ahead, a less agitated sea state comes into view. I continue arcing southwards putting the swells dead astern and giving me a welcome push for the next few kilometres. Finally, I enter Rathlacken Cove. Its small pier and slipway sit tucked below some gently sloping fields. I am in need of a break after the early morning rodeo

Entering Rathlacken Cove

Rathlacken pier

ride. With a rickety 14 kilometres in the bag, it is time for some sustenance on solid ground. Little do I realise it but they are just a warning
for the day ahead.

A large black anchor and stone plaque sits in a cutaway of the embankment abutting the pier. Erected in memory of an Italian barque,
the *Teresina Stinga*, it was carrying coal from Scotland to Buenos Aires
when she was lost here in 1887. Another reminder of the perils faced
when travelling by sea, especially when under canvas. Rumours
abound that for every hundred metres of our coastline there is a shipwreck. It does not help my peace of mind, since I am propelling *Murchú*
with much less power than a sail. I find myself involuntarily looking
down at my two hands, thankful they are capable of transmitting the
energy needed to keep my mission alive. I put them to good use by
tearing the wrapper off my staple snack, the peanut-laden Cliff bar.

Passing Benwee Head I am waving goodbye to the majestic coastline of Mayo and turning my sights towards the low lying flaggy shore
of County Sligo. Traversing Killala Bay I am a good eight kilometres

Stunning views, North Sligo to Easkey

off Enniscrone beach, barely visible to my right, and have an even greater distance to cover until my next stop. I muse over a different landing at nearby Kilcummin over 200 years ago. This was when General Humbert and over a thousand French troops arrived in support of the 1798 Irish rebellion against the British. Unfortunately, the rebellion had already been quashed but that did not stop them from winning the Battle of Castlebar. They were subsequently beaten into submission by the occupying forces.

Coming in to land on the low-lying, rocky shore of east Killala seemed easy from the Google Earth views last week, but bearing down on it with a nice swell running is a different matter entirely. As I reach the shore the swells are rising into long steep ridges. Initially not a problem, things changes as they begin to crest over and break into tumbling masses of white water. If one of these rogues catches me in this boat it will be a hair-raising ride all the way to whatever lies waiting inside. With no beach to speak of I negotiate towards shore in a zig-zag collection of dashes and turns, like a rugby player trying to

Sligo landing, east side of Killala Bay

avoid a grounding tackle. With the tide low the rocky foreshore that finally greets me is covered in a glistening mustard-coloured carpet of bladderwrack, a type of seaweed sometimes referred to as sea grapes. Some maintain it has health benefits, especially for stomach problems!

It is heartening to take my first few steps on Sligo's healthy seaweed and I turn around to examine the waves still breaking, some of them quite far offshore. I have just crossed the U-shaped Killala Bay, the only major indentation in an east-west coastline that extends 80 kilometres from Kid island out west to Strandhill in the East. Soon I will make my way back onto an easterly track as I bear down on Easkey. Paddling back out through the blue swells is easier than my trip in so I find myself heading north a few kilometres waiting to decide on when to turn east. On land, the 'corner' is a non-descript collection of low lying fields bordered by short stone walls. It belies the action that is taking place out at sea where the waves have arranged themselves into long parallel swells marching like lines of troops towards shore.

The coastline of Sligo is a haven for surfers, thanks to its perfectly shaped seabed. Formed of limestone during the Carboniferous period, the underfloor slopes out to sea at the perfect angle allowing waves to break optimally for surfing. It also means that when swell size increases, the breaking waves simply maintain form and begin cresting further out towards the horizon. For me, this means I need to keep a constant lookout over my shoulder to see whether any of these incoming rogues decides to break before reaching me and causing me all sorts of bother. As a one-time surf kayaker, I know only too well the power contained in one of these beasties. As I make my way east, kilometre by slow kilometre, I have the distinct feeling of running the gauntlet. I am hoping for a clear run over my final nine kilometres to the Commons at Easkey.

Several times along this stretch I get too close to shore and run the risk of being 'caught on the inside' by one of the larger waves. I adjust *Murchú's* trajectory away from land into deeper water. The swells continue to build, and ahead great cascades of tumbling water pummel the flat limestone slabs. Each swell elevates me above my surroundings, giving me a better view out to sea. It seems an age before I finally catch sight of Easkey's black pier and its adjoining castle. I dream of being back on dry land on this fabulous sunny afternoon. Easkey, when seen through the eyes of a surfer, sports two significant breaks, both of which are 'going off' as I approach. This means they are forming and breaking suitably to surf on. I continue tentatively, searching out a small east-facing indentation in the flaggy shore for shelter. My hands tire from a day gripping tightly onto my paddles.

As I approach I realise I have never seen the Commons from this perspective before and find it almost impossible to match the scene to my land-based recollections. Compounding this is an angry looking barrel wave which is breaking at the cove's entrance. The swell is tripping over a shallow reef causing a gnarly tube to form. It is something I simply must avoid.

I weigh up the situation, noticing a gap between this tube and the rocks off to my right. From what I see, the wave does not extend this far and a small opening presents me with an opportunity. It may be the only safe way of making it to shore. Today's efforts, now a respectable 45 kilometres, looks like it will be finishing with a full-blooded sprint.

Easkey Commons

I hang about, observing the swells that pitch dramatically into their short-lived barrels. I decide to go with my gut. I give myself a hundred metres run-in from outside the gap. The Taran, a fast boat by any standards, needs consistent energy to reach and maintain top speed. A bigger set passes by, my cue to get *Murchú* moving.

Adrenaline helps my tired limbs as I completely commit to the task. The noise of the churning spiral fills my ears, but I ignore it, maintaining sight dead ahead. *Murchú's* slicing bow carves towards deliverance. My heart pounds as I will the initial surge of energy to maintain her speed. This beautiful craft does not disappoint as a glance to her deck shows a speed over 10 kilometres an hour. I slowly realise I am adjacent to the hazard. I keep going a little longer, eventually easing off the accelerator. We glide, spear-like, into the taut surface of the Commons haven. Like a rider after a clear round, I smack *Murchú's* foredeck in appreciation. I stop paddling, let my heart rate recover, and then notice the salt-encrusted burning on my face. It had not even registered while being so occupied.

Finally, I land *Murchú* in this surprisingly pastoral setting. The land rises from here into a scattering of small fields dotted with homesteads. It is a scene worthy of a Constable. The enjoyment I feel in my new surroundings are a reminder of the weight I have been carrying during the day's paddling. It dawns on me that the pull of these challenging situations is followed by the heightened appreciation of the relief afterwards. It is my gauge as to how difficult it has been for me to overcome the test.

'Jeepers, Kev, that's a pretty impressive stretch today, there's a decent swell running.'

That is my brother Mossey's opening remark when he arrives to collect me. I cannot hide the smile on my face. Being a surfer, he speaks with authority on the ocean, so his comment lands solidly with me. I quiz him about the curling wave at The Commons. 'Ah, that's Temple Rock, it would really chew you up in a yoke like that'…

We both look over towards the continuing barrels. Mossey bursts into a booming laugh when he sees my shocked expression. I have survived a close call, once again.

Boat storage near Easkey

PLATE 8
0 5 10 15 20KM
SCALE
N
W
E
S
INISHBOFINE
Gola Island
BUNBEG
Bloody Foreland
STOP 38
Owey Island
CARRICKFINN AIRPORT
STOP 37
DERRYVEAGH MTNS.
ARRANMORE ISLAND.
STOP 36
ROANINISH
CO DONEGAL
INISBARNÓG
ARDARA
BLUE STACK MTS
STOP 35
GLENCOLUMKILLE.
RATHLIN O'BEIRNE Is.
DONEGAL
KILLYBEGS
SLIEVE LEAGUE CLIFFS
STOP 34
ST JOHNS PT
ATLANTIC OCEAN
DONEGAL BAY
BALLYSHANNON
MULLAGHMORE
INISHMURRAY
KILLALA BAY
BEN BULBEN
CO. LEITRIM
STOP 32
ROSSES POINT
STOP 31
STOP 33
SLIGO
BALLYCASTLE
EASKEY
STRANDHILL
AUGHRIS
ENNISCRONE
BALLYSODARE
KILLALA
COUNTY SLIGO
CO MAYO
BALLINA
OX MTNS

Stage 24

BIG CLIFFS FAR AWAY:
DONEGAL BECKONS

A week later, on a baking hot June afternoon, my train pulls into the picturesque station at Collooney in County Sligo. Flowers are in full bloom as trees in full leaf sway under a light breeze. I am linking up with Valli Shafer, a creative spirit and partner to an old friend of mine who lives nearby. She splits her free time between sea kayaking and clambering up vertical rock faces. A local crag called Happy Valli is named after her thanks to the many routes she pioneered there.

We are heading back to my brother's in Easkey, collecting my boat, and putting-in where I finished a week earlier. The *we* today is different.

So far, we normally referred to me and *Murchú*, but today stretches to include Valli in her bright green plastic sea kayak. Having her alongside is my first experience of company on this trip and is an unusual, but welcome, distraction. As we push against the breeze near the midpoint of our traverse, I make a discovery about my travelling companion. In the middle of this wide bay Valli declares that she hates bee-lining. She prefers to wander the shoreline instead and discover things close-up. Her journeys are akin to a ramble through an art gallery, viewing the sea arches,

Ready to head out with Valli

235

With Valli near Easkey

deep caves, sea stacks and pillars that populate the northwest of our island. She tells me in no uncertain terms that she simply does not like this other type of paddling. I love her directness, part of being German I conclude, and apologise for my *modus operandi*. Seeing as we are out here in the middle of this wide bay, nothing can be done to change the situation so we just paddle on, knowing each other a little better after the exchange.

We persevere into the wind until we make shelter behind the warm rock of the sun-bleached headland near Aughris. A great cave has slowly been revealing itself and Valli, determined to offset her monotonous paddle, disappears inside. The constricted swell lifts and drops her boat as she slips from my view. With my boat's wide turning circle, I decide to hang about outside. When she finally reappears, a broad smile is painted across her face. I find it amusing that a brief foray into the darkness has brightened her day. I smile too as I realise how accustomed I have grown to my own company. Accommodating someone else into my mission is a new element to be considered.

With Valli's marine potholing complete, we circumvent the headland and land at Aughris Beach. A thatched cottage, complete with red door and matching windows, is the only building here. This is Aughris Beach Bar, staring out to sea across a scattering of caravans, tents and motorhomes, all parked on the grass backing the beach. It

With brother Mossey and Valli in Aughris, County Sligo

was the go-to place back in the 1980s after a day's kayak surfing in these parts. Groups dine *al-fresco* on brightly coloured picnic tables as kids scurry about in the warm evening light.

My tiny tent is installed next to a small hedge outside the bar. It offers limited privacy while at the same time plenty for me to see going on about the place. We retire to the bar where my brother Mossey, Valli and a few others have gathered among the holidaymakers, all enjoying the vibrant buzz of the place. We form a cosy knot in the dimly lit bar as outside the sun drops low in the sky. It is a welcome distraction for my slightly tortured mind which occasionally drifts to tomorrow's crossing. I thank Valli for her company today, give her a well deserved hug, and wave to her as she heads off for home. Back on my own again, I will have another wide opening to traverse. The mighty Donegal Bay waits patiently for me.

Campsite in Aughris, Ben Bulben in the distance

THE FLAPPING TENT ROUSES ME AS THE bright sunshine raises the temperature of my tiny home. I am slow to see what the day has in store. The clinking of delph and a rich scent of frying draws me from sleep. I emerge from my cocoon, stand upright and inspect the day. A bright sun in the east paints long shadows across the grass as a sea-full of white horses gallop, uncharacteristically, westwards. Below the sun sits the blunt massif of Ben Bulben looking haughty above the dancing ocean. I ponder the high level cloud forming overhead, an indication of an imminent change. I turn to the job at hand, quelling my hunger with noodles and canned fish, all washed down with strong black coffee.

The force four easterly herding the whitecaps across the bay is thankfully at the lower side of the forecasted four to six. With a 40 kilometre paddle across the bay looming, I pray this is as strong as it gets. I am keen to go, but wariness slows my preparation. I keep staring at the sea trying to estimate what is happening. I am in two minds and beginning to doubt myself. Overhead, some strange cloud formations are illuminated in the morning sun. They are puzzling, especially since the winds are coming out of the less common eastern sector. The

Coastguard's helicopter appears suddenly out over the sea, adding more drama to the scene. I turn on my VHF and learn that it is a local training exercise. Knowing it is in these parts provides me with an unexpected boost in confidence. I am tilting in favour of putting to sea.

I liken today's mission to a three course meal. Beginning with a 13 kilometre starter to Magherameenagh Point in Sligo, a convenient protruding finger of land coinciding with my route, followed then by an 8 kilometre snack to Inishmurray Island, and finally a 21 kilometre main course to Teelin Harbour, beside Slieve League cliffs. Another accumulated marathon distance will then have passed under my boat and I will be into Donegal, the last of Ireland's western seaboard counties.

Off to my right, the impressive table tops of Ben Bulben and Dartry Mountains look proudly out to sea. These flat-topped, vertical-sided uplands are skirted by sloping bases, reminding me of those mesas featured in Hollywood westerns. Ben Bulben's impressive form was created when glaciers cleaved into the plateau that predated the last ice age. Its American cousins had wind and water to do the work. Needless to say they are impressive features and provide an interesting flank to my giant leap across the bay.

Leaving the cosiness of the cove at Aughris is difficult, especially as today's mission is mostly over open water far from land. Reluctantly, I sit in the cockpit and delay my departure. I scan my surroundings and look north to Donegal which resembles a light grey whale sleeping on the far horizon. From here it looks almost impossibly distant to reach by kayak, something I dismiss by adjusting my gaze to my first landfall, visible across 13 kilometres of bouncing ocean. I heave *Murchú* off the wet sand and take my place among the charging whitecaps. Two hours later, I am fully awake and pretty wet, and swing into a wide gravelly cove for my first break. An older couple, strolling over the flat grey stones, approach me and we exchange a few pleasantries. She goes for a dip and I chat with her partner while munching on a snack bar. Rested I depart, this time for the pancake-like Inishmurray Island, the only stop until I reach my destination some 30 kilometres away.

Inishmurray, an isolated outpost off the Sligo coast, is steeped in history. Ranging from a sixth century monastic settlement to a thriving poteen distillery, it was finally abandoned in 1948 having at one stage supported a population of over 100. It lays claim to a very interesting and slightly chilling superstition. St Molaise set up a monastery here in the sixth century, the remains of which are still to be seen. In front of one of the altars are intricately carved stones with supposed mystical powers. Referred to as Inishmurray's cursing stones, they were once used to wish good or bad fortune on individuals. This was done by making the wish and rotating the stones clockwise for good and anti-clockwise for ill. Woe betide if an unwarranted curse was cast. It would be redirected back to the person who created it.

I land on Inishmurray's flaggy shore to briefly interrupt my northbound course. The wet limestone tests my footing as I stand up. Slieve League boasts the second highest cliffs between Britain and Ireland, and with them as my goal the *Father Ted* sketch about the 'big cow far away and the small cow near' comes to mind. Though their proximity has been halved since I started out from Aughris, the dim light leaves them looking as distant as ever. The sun and breeze are diminishing and the greyness drains the beauty from the day.

I leave the island without having explored it, which showed my increasing disinterest in proceedings. My arms were heavier than normal and the pewter-coloured sea sloppily undulates under the boat. Its hypnotic rhythm worms its way into me as I embark on the day's longest passage, a 21 kilometre trek across open water. By the time I finally slide into Teelin Harbour, I am carrying a heady mix of nausea and lethargy. My head is sore and my brain cries out for solid ground. I stop paddling, slumping forward to rest, allowing *Murchú*'s momentum to slice through the mirror flatness of the harbour. Yet again, I am left wondering about the whole enterprise after the tough day just passed. Not wanting to torment my sore head, I postpone this nagging question, turning instead to setting up camp on a small, inviting patch of grass behind the pier. An hour later a kind local is driving me to the Rusty Mackerel gastro pub. Outside, the place is abuzz with the hum of conversation, the soft Donegal-accented hubbub bringing a wry smile across my salty face. Things are looking up already.

Gliding into Teelin Harbour, Donegal

Feeling a bit of a chill, the after-effect of my malaise, I decide to park myself inside the cosy tavern. It boasts a honeyed wood interior with bare stone walls and warm lighting. I happily insert myself in a corner ready to examine the menu. When a young member of staff arrives and hears my request, she informs me that the kitchen has just closed. My face drops. When I remind her that it is only 9.30, she merely repeats her apology. I explain that I have just kayaked all the way across Donegal Bay to get here, and I am *ravenous*. Thankfully, this leads to a slight shift in her tone. She suggests a bowl of chowder *might* be available, and instantly some salvation seems possible. Minutes later, a creamy bowl of brimming goodness arrives at my table. I dive in, hungrily devouring it with chunks of crusty bread plastered with salty butter. Then to my great surprise the manager himself appears, full of apologies and curious to meet me. The upshot of this exchange is an offer of a second bowl of chowder, this one he insists on the house.

I revisit my postponed examination of the feasibility, and indeed the wisdom, of my expedition. My mind bifurcates, taking two sides

241

of the same argument. I am honestly pitching one side against the other. Having taken on some serious sustenance in these heartwarming surroundings my mood is changing. First off, I remind myself I have made it into Donegal, my last western seaboard county, and it will be Donegal all the way to Ireland's northernmost extremity, Malin Head. This is a major turning point of the trip, and it warms me to contemplate that a few more days paddling should have me top out there. I scan my surroundings, absorbing the buzz, and my heart swells with pride at getting this far. The show simply must go on.

I HAD ALWAYS EXPECTED MY FIRST SPIN under Slieve League's cliffs to be one of the highlights of my trip. Meaning 'mountain of the stone pillars' in English, it tops out at an impressive 600 metres. It holds second posi-

A sea arch at Slieve League

tion in Ireland behind Croaghan on Achill, 90 metres higher. Whereas I avoided those cliffs thanks to an inner channel, this time I will be traversing under this great escarpment as I head west towards Malin Beg, the southwestern tip of this impressive Donegal promontory.

I sneak out of Teelin harbour, head briefly south, swing right by 90 degrees and commence onto a westerly track. My jaw is about to drop as I prepare to claw my way along the hem of this colossal geological feature. Initially, its vertical extent is only a few hundred feet, rising consistently to its apex after a small headland which initially blocks my view. Unfortunately, on rounding this headland there is no gain in elevation at all. Thanks to some morning stratus, this low-hanging cloud reveals only its lower sections, denying me sight of the towering precipice above. The ascending rock disappears, Jack and the Beanstalk-like, into the murk overhead. I feel a bit short-changed.

After travelling a few kilometres along this truncated wall, I become somewhat irritated with the experience. The appreciation of my surroundings is changing as I adapt to the day's poor weather. I

Two views of the cliff at Slieve League

243

feel hemmed in between two grey bookends, sea and cloud, as I slide *Murchú* through the horizontal slot. I am disappointed that the majesty overhead is hidden, especially since I feel so much better than during yesterday's crossing. I suck it up, continue westwards, hoping for better weather and views. Thanks to the absence of a swell I decide to go in close as a distraction. I scurry through some arches and skirt around sea stacks, deciding against stopping at any of the suggested way-stops on my route. These are tiny beaches directly abutting the cliffs and only a few metres deep. I count myself fortunate not to have stopped because afterwards I learn that the area is prone to rock falls.

Waiting further west is a much safer beach, Malin Beg. Marking roughly halfway along my short 25 kilometre trip, it occupies the back of a perfect rectangular bay. It is a breathtaking and majestic sight.

Malin Beg beach, Murchú dwarfed below

Interesting signage above Malin Head beach

From its base rises a set of 174 steps which I eagerly climb to the over-looking car park. As a discovery point on the Wild Atlantic Way this place has its fair share of footfall even during my brief stay. I notice most are content to enjoy the panorama from above. Fortunately, the cloud surrenders to the June sunshine, revealing the distant counties of Sligo and Mayo, now happily under my belt. Off to my right I see the swing of the coastline as it heads north again leaving the western extremity of Donegal's Rathin O'Birne Island and lighthouse behind. Interestingly, this island's light was the first to be nuclear powered back in 1974. Strange to think of such a remote outpost as having such a claim to fame.

Back aboard *Murchú*, the gaping mouth of this perfect bay discharg-es me into the ocean. Soon I am tracking north along the sound of the aforementioned island. The sun paints everything with a magic glow. I wheel around Rossan Point towards the flat calm of Glencolumkille Bay. A staggering sight greets me. I am surrounded by a collection of enormous geological formations that takes my breath away. The coast-line has jumped skyward creating a view denied earlier due to the low cloud. Enormous sections of rock, cleaved from the mainland, lie disconnected just offshore. Pyramid-shaped sea stacks, towering buttresses, spines of rock, islets, crags and indentations leave me agape. I feel incredibly small and insignificant. Donegal's coastal fringe stretches away into the distance, a continuation of the spectacle.

I tear my eyes away from the vista and back onto the water in front of me. I scan the small break in the cliffscape trying to figure out the final course into my destination. The quaint village at the neck of the opening, named after one of our most famous saints and scholars, Colmcille, slowly comes into view through some gaps in the rock-strewn entrance. A perfectly formed swell gently pushes *Murchú* forwards. It steepens into a small surf wave and I thrill at the free ride to the pocket-sized beach that waits for me.

After landing into another picture-postcard scene, I am struck by the intense heat of the day, more noticeable now that I have stopped moving. The sand is baking hot so I am thankful to be wearing decent footwear. I make my way to the nearby road in search of a possible store for my kayak. Such is my confidence in the continued goodwill of others I march confidently to the nearest bungalow. I am greeted by

The view from John O'Flaherty's garden

With John O'Flaherty in Glencolumbkille

ex-fisherman John O'Flaherty, who unflinchingly fulfils my expecta-tions with the offer of his garage to store my boat.

Descending via John's sloping vegetable patch leads me directly back to the beach. I decide to bring my kit this way to avoid the longer route by road. The constant search for efficiency is omnipresent. With *Murchú* resting neatly on her trolley, I enthusiastically start man-haul-ing her across the golden sand. Nearing John's patch, the sand deepens and the whole enterprise morphs into an energy-sapping slog. *Ireland's Fittest Families* could easily film an endurance event in such a location. I eventually grind to a halt, short of a shallow gully lying across my path. Annoyingly close to John's garden, I am regretting my earlier beeline decision. With my heart rate skyrocketing, I begin the familiar task of extracting all my kit and transferring it in armfuls to my oasis. After many energy-sapping excursions my empty boat alone waits to follow suit. Despite being emptied, it is still an unwieldy piece of kit to manoeuvre alone in deep sand under the baking sun. Eventually, just short of a coronary, I manage to transfer all my kit into John's generous garage.

Relieved after a very welcome shower, I finally sit down to share a cuppa with John. These minor curve balls are part and parcel of my great adventure, in a masochistic way bringing more colour to my mission. John, an absolute gent, regales me with recollections of fishing trips far offshore in storm force winds. Just inside his front door hangs an amazing photo of one of his trips aboard a large trawler in mountainous seas. The beast of a boat is thrusting skywards off the top of an enormous wave as sheets of spray peel away from her flanks. Looking at the small waves lapping the golden beach below, I am reminded of the silent heroes in our midst carrying their own great achievements lightly. Seeing how much kit I intend taking with me, John's final act of kindness is to ferry me to the bus stop at the far end of the village.

Satisfied at moving my mission from Sligo across Donegal Bay to Glencolumbkille, my fibreglass cockpit is swapped for the plush warmth of a seat on the bus home. The bus to Dublin cuts an erratic diagonal through the teddy bear-shaped island I have committed to encircle. The magnificent Donegal coastline awaits my return in a few weeks. In the meantime, it is high season and Dublin Airport will be buzzing. I will change my mode of transport from kayak to jet and a 100-fold increase in my speed to 800 kilometres per hour. Perspective is everything as I switch roles from paddler to pilot.

Stage 25

Onwards to Bloody Foreland

Two weeks later, after jetting around Europe, a family holiday cruising on the river Shannon and a long bus ride, I land into Glencolumkille aboard Bus Éireann's local service. John, aware of my imminent arrival, is unexpectedly waiting nearby, ready to ferry me to his house and my boat. I was not relishing the kilometre-long trudge with two bulging kit bags. Thanks to his generosity, an extra 40 minute cushion slots into my schedule to make Arranmore sound before the tide turns. I relax instantly.

I now take the time to fully take in this stunning place. No clouds discolour the blue dome overhead as the land surrounding me shines brightly under the high sun. Great swathes of rising ground climb to a ridge line that delineates the landside of the cliff tops. Later today, when on the water, the sheer escarpments will be revealed as I go 'backstage', tracing the hemline of another rock wall.

Looking across the beach to the sloping vegetable patch by John's house brings back memories. Only a few weeks earlier, on seeing the same sight, I was unsure how my next step would work out. After arriving unannounced and being helped by a then complete stranger, I have had my faith in humanity restored by John. I am very grateful.

I glide over crystal clear waters, elevated above the sandy seabed which extends far offshore. The dark lozenge-shaped shadow of my kayak mirrors my progress along the surface. All is going swimmingly until, unexpectedly, a breaking wave smacks into my chest, snaps me out of my daydream and forces my attention back to sea level. Time to concentrate on the sea road up ahead.

North of Glencolumbkill

Crashing swells whitewash a large monolith marking the northern flank of the bay. They contradict my earlier reckoning on their potential size during the day's passage and provide a reminder to stay alert. The plan, a marathon length paddle to Arranmore island, commences with a 19 kilometre leg to the fairly isolated island of Inishbarnog. This will be followed by another remote outpost, the low-lying Roaninish, before finally arriving into the Arranmore archipelago.

After Inishmore, Arranmore is the second largest of our offshore islands and promises a warm bed in its harbour hostel. A ferry service from nearby Burtonport helps support a permanent population of around 500. Doubling during the summer months, it still falls well short of its pre-famine population of 1,500. But thanks to the recent opening of an internet co-working hub, many people are moving back to the island. Arranmore features strongly in Three Ireland's campaign advertising their rural broadband expansion. Thanks to its stunning cinematography I am looking forward to exploring the place.

My initial kilometres are flanked by more jaw-dropping sights. A continuation of the earlier spotted cliffs, sea stacks, and buttresses pass

Inishroan

over my right shoulder. I can see why fellow kayaker Valli has this area as her favourite stretch of Irish coastline. A feeling of insignificance comes to roost as I totter along the hem of another huge irregular rock wall. As with many great things, though, it comes with a price. Exposure. The only get-out is in Port, a lonely pier 15 kilometres into my trip. A deserted village nearby adds to the area's air of isolation, reinforced by a 20 kilometre narrow road which winds its way inland. Nestled at the back of a rock-strewn inlet, its less than ideal slipway renders it solely an emergency option.

I press on, conscious that this stretch brings me out into a vast expanse of ocean. The sea is windless. An old swell lumbers by, followed by a lazy return. The soporific rhythm lulls me into a semi-sleepy state, occasionally interrupted by me shivering fully awake again. I force myself to stay present, akin to nearly dozing off at the wheel. Three kilometres short of Inishbarnog the sea is changing. I am now being hoisted even higher above the surrounding ocean, as though the sea is inhaling deeper, more laborious breaths. Despite the exhilarating feeling, I am keen that none of the ever steeping swells become an avalanche of breaking water which might throw me from my kayak into a right ol' mess. Fortunately, before this can happen I move away from the underwater bank and back above deeper waters.

After a brief stop at Inishbarnog, a nondescript and lonely island, I continue north around the humpbacked Dawros Head back out to sea for my second way stop, Inishroan. Translating as the island of the seals, my only previous visit was in 2009 whilst training for my kayak instructor's award with fellow kayaker Brian Forrest. In poor visibility, we tied our hopes to a compass bearing in an effort to find this lonely outpost. It was like paddling in surround-sound as the swells impacted the cliffs stretching away from our put-in at Portnoo. The thunderous booms sounded like explosions in a war zone. I admired Brian's confidence as he led a wary apprentice out into the mighty Atlantic. Then, as now, I land on Inishroan with a sense of relief. Sitting on a chunky rock above my kayak I allow my thoughts to return to the intervening decade. They come to rest on my friend Mark Murphy's passing and the final push he gave me to embark on this adventure. 'Just start' seems like a distant memory. Now I am adding one of my own, 'Just finish'.

Inishbarnog

Arranmore Island, West Donegal, hostel right of centre

Late in the afternoon I arrive at Leabgarrow, Arranmore's main town. Paddling into a sheltered, east-facing bay, I spot my hostel flanked by fluttering Polish and Irish flags. Taking its place among a line of shoreside buildings it looks out over the beach, smoothed flat by the receding tide. I stop paddling, lay my paddles across my lap and drift into another perfect scene. The land beyond the beach rises a respectable 400 metres, its verdant lower slopes dotted with houses. To my right, the stone harbour reaches out towards me like a beckoning concrete arm. Muscles and mind relax. I sit motionless in the centre of the crescent bay. It feels like a homecoming after a day spent at sea under great cliffs and in open waters.

Shortly afterwards I meet Sebastian, an enthusiastic Polish guy who runs the hostel. Sporting boundless energy and jammed into an undersized T-shirt, he looks like someone who pumps iron. His eyes widen as I fill him in on my day's travels. As I am his only client this evening, we spend a good while chatting. He tells me of a boat trip he and some friends are organising from the sister island of Arran in

Scotland. He exclaims in his strongly accented English, 'You perfect for this trip, Kevin, you will join us'.

Thankfully, my fatigued state helps me ward off his suggestion and I remind him of the great distance I still need to complete. Undeterred, he tells me of another project he and his girlfriend are masterminding. He unlocks a door from the kitchen into a tiny cafe soon to be opened to the public. His energy, though infectious, is preventing me from settling in so as gracefully as I can I take my leave.

I establish myself into the cosiest ground floor room I can find. Whilst unpacking my bags a great whooshing noise strikes up from somewhere in the building. My heart rate skyrockets and I find myself tentatively advancing towards the sound. I slowly open the common room door and discover the source. Someone outside is power washing the large windows overlooking the bay. The sound, magnified by the great glass diaphragms, fills the place to an impossible volume of noise. I decide to avoid this cacophony, return to my room to grab my jacket and head out for a wander.

Whilst ambling along the road I bump into Sebastian and his girlfriend, both insisting on bringing me for a quick tour of the island. Minutes later, I am well above sea level surveying the surrounding seascape and beyond. The Donegal mainland is laid out before me like a scale model with the dramatic peak of Errigal stealing the show. As I look back over the day's journey, I realise my time on the western seaboard is nearly over. I am bearing down on the third of four corners of Ireland. Donegal's Bloody Foreland will soon join the previous pairing of Wexford's Carnsore Point and Cork's Baltimore Beacon.

Later on, whilst enjoying a drink and some pizza, I fall into conversation with a fellow patron in Early's Bar. My acquaintance is an older islander enjoying a couple of early pints. On hearing about my mission he recalls a fascinating story of another lone mariner who landed here back in the eighties.

Wayne Dickinson, a 39-year-old computer technician from Florida, set off from Massachusetts in October 1983 in a 2.7 metre sailboat named *God's Tear*. Attempting to undercut the previous transatlantic sailing record by two inches, he survived some serious Atlantic storms until being force-landed in a gale at the base of the island's western cliffs. Having spent an incredible 142 days, almost five months, at sea, he was spotted struggling ashore here by lighthouse keeper Charles Boyle. Battered, bruised and unable to walk, he was helped up the steep rocky side of the island and ferried to Charles' home where he began his recovery. A doctor summoned from the mainland tended to the unexpected visitor.

A few days later, a tearful reunion took place when his mother, Peggy Dickinson, arrived on Arranmore. Since he departed, a medallion fashioned to the shape of God's Tear had hung from her neck. She had been rubbing this talisman every day in the hope of hearing from her son. Long before personal satellite communications, knowledge of his whereabouts were patchy and happened only twice during his ordeal. The first, three months in when a passing freighter spotted him off Newfoundland, and a month later in mid-Atlantic when another ship reported a sighting. *God's Tear* was completely wrecked during the grounding, taking with it Wayne's log and passport. The sole element of the trip remaining was Wayne himself. I sat gobsmacked, my story teller smirking at the reaction visible on my face. I buy him a drink, a fair exchange for the tale of adventure just relayed.

Wandering home afterwards, I notice a slight southerly wind touching the treetops over the road. I wonder what might be in store for tomorrow. Later, while settling into my cosy bunk, I mentally replay the day's paddling to where I find myself, on this fine island off the Donegal coast. Tomorrow, for the first time on the trip, I have a flight to catch. Not only that, but it will be taking off from a strip of tarmac laid over a sand spit, only 14 kilometres further north. Sure, what could possibly go wrong?

With my departure from Carrickfin Airport due for 2.00 pm, I am up and away by 10.00 am. After devouring a serious amount of Crunchy Nut cereal and toast, I swallow my travel sickness meds and cross my fingers again. From my breakfast table I see a force 4 southerly with whitecaps and waves trundling up the sound. Luckily for me, this coincides with my direction of travel. The forecast, a force 5 to 6 from the same direction, has me keeping a watchful eye on the sea.

The cloud, now low, allows a soft drizzle to coat everything. No one is about yet so my departure is a lonely, slightly nervous affair. I push out past the pier, turn left onto a northerly track and slowly edge my way towards mid-channel where the wave train is at its strongest. My speed increases, rising sporadically to 14 kilometres an hour, double my normal speed, as waves continuously lift and thrust me forward. It reminds me of my last great downwinder between Turk and Clare islands. This morning my attention is being similarly seized. With the waves topping around the metre mark, their speed and steepness making them such a welcome, albeit challenging, prospect.

As I move from the shelter of Arranmore, I am becoming more exposed to another possible fly in the ointment, the open Atlantic. Watery hills, heretofore blocked by the island, are trundling across my path, slowly hoisting me well above sea level and continuing on their journey towards the mainland to my right. Basically, the smaller northbound waves are thrusting me forward, whilst great eastbound swells are slowly raising and lowering me. I am having difficulty fully processing the dynamics, especially my ever-changing visual perspective. Whilst all this is happening my speed tops out at 16 kilometres an hour making my boat feel as though driven by an outboard engine. *Murchú* is humming with my paddles bouncing off the surface like skimming stones. My paddles are stabilisers, leaning onto the surface like water skis. Everything is at a high tempo, my sluggishness banished as I eat up the distance and bear down on the gap between Owey and Cruit islands, my turning point and an eagerly anticipated easing of tension. From there I can track east towards Carrickfin while under the shelter of land. But that is all eight kilometres away and I am near a lee shore where the great Atlantic swells are crashing onto rocks.

I continue screeching along, face wet from spray and mist. Some sweat too, such is my work rate. I am aboard the green torpedo plunging headlong before the waves and it is class. Stay focused. Keep straight. Use the rudder pedals. Relax a bit. Watch that bigger wave. Tighten the grip. Glance at the speedometer, 12 kilometres an hour. Cool. Shoots to 15. Back to 10. Always double digits. The gap ahead is nearing. Speed is my golden ticket. Watch the bearing. She is turning left. Get her back. Push the pedals. Keep her tight on track. Here we go again. Another crossing swell. Lowering back down. Speed is intense. Concentrate. Owey is closing in. Maybe two klicks. Keep her straight. Adrenalin is waning. Drill deep, if it asks, just give. No holding back. Nearly there.

Suddenly there is a difference. Imperceptible, but it is there. It is definitely easing. The cross swells are blocked. The gauntlet has been run and I am nearly through the gap. My heart rate slowly drops. I slice around the edge. I am turning under Cruit, and finally I am on a safe heading. Yes, I *can* relax. Jesus, that was absolutely insane, and though the water is calming, adrenalin is still coursing through my veins. Slowly, easing my grip allows my heart rate to slow as things start returning to normal. I paddle languidly along beside wet hump-backed rock as soft drizzle settles on *Murchú*. I continue towards the sodden beach, spotting my deck mounted speedo which tells me the 14 kilometres were covered in a little over an hour. Today's paddling has been compressed into an adrenaline-fuelled downwinder. What a way to start my day as I arrive early to my destination, leaving me plenty of time to catch my flight.

Later, I am hoisted skyward aboard Stobart Air's commuter plane and immediately swallowed by the low grey cloud. Incredibly, after 40 minutes we touch down at Dublin Airport and I am thrust back into civilization with a bang. It is an assault on the senses and my brain is slow to adapt. Despite working here for nearly forty years, the place feels strange to me as I am still reeling from this morning's Atlantic express. I collect my two bulging IKEA bags from the revolving carousel and walk, trancelike, to my car.

TWO WEEKS LATER, AFTER A RED-EYE FLIGHT to Amsterdam, I make a quick dash to my car, swap my pilot's uniform for civvies, and then return to the terminal as a passenger. My intention is to catch a flight back to Donegal's airport to resume paddling. I am blessed with good fortune as during its approach the aircraft heads out over the Atlantic to wheel around for a landing on the southern runway. It affords me a birds'

Carrickfin Beach to the airport, a 200 metre commute

eye view of Bloody Foreland and nearby islands all embedded into a cobalt, waveless ocean. Today is a far cry from my previous arrival, after a white knuckle downwinder under leaden skies. Within an hour of landing, and not 500 metres from the terminal, I am retracing my path across the flat sand of Carrickfin beach to my put-in. *Murchú* sits on

Carrickfin Airport

her trolley as I soak up the warmth of this sun-kissed afternoon. My aim, after three days' paddling, is to put our northernmost point, Malin Head, astern, leaving me on the Inishowen Peninsula's eastern flank. The northernmost milestone on my trip is finally in my sights.

I strike out, severing the perfection with my kayak's bladed bow. I try hard to create minimal disturbance as I pass out of the shallows and wheel north inside a series of islands. Seven in total, they provide

258

a welcome channel for me to navigate inside. Having land on my left means no rogue ocean swells can cause me any bother, allowing me to concentrate on the scattered archipelago. With the tiny islets of Go, Inisfree and Allagh soon behind, I am level with the legendary island of Gola. This island, uninhabited from the mid-sixties until the late nineties, now boasts a small population, boosted seasonally by an ever increasing number of temporary residents in renovated homes.

I paddle by Inishmeane and Umfin, and on towards the last of the string, the slender island of Inishirrer. Translated from Irish as 'Outer Island', it measures no more than 500 by 1,500 metres, and incredibly supported a small population during the early years of the twentieth century. Now abandoned, it constitutes the last island on the west coast for me. As I begin to leave it behind I catch a glimpse of something yellow moving slowly across the surface a good distance away. After several minutes I make out the familiar rhythm of paddle strokes and realise I am about to bump into another lone sea kayaker. The paddler adjusts course and minutes later we grab each other's deck lines and dive into enthusiastic conversation. He is Jonas Loffler, a German, who

With Jonas Loffler off Inishirrer

regularly holidays in Donegal with his daughter and wife. With a wry smile he tells me his plan today is to find some real Atlantic waves. I cannot help but laugh as we both look at the mirror-like conditions surrounding us. He wishes me well and promises to catch my blog on Facebook later that day after his quest for swells.

Uneventfully, I pass Bloody Foreland, rounding the corner towards Inishbofin, which translates as 'Island of the White Cow'. Lying only two kilometres off Magheroarty Pier it is inhabited for most of the year by descendants of the original islanders. I land onto the island's long slipway. Nearby, a few children are catching crabs. Their shrieks are infectious and it is a scene that could date back a half century or more. Situated on the eastern, sheltered side of the island, the small village hosted an island festival here last summer. This I learned from two women who are supervising the crab catchers while chatting away in strongly accented Donegal Irish.

Minutes after I arrive, everyone suddenly disappears. It slowly dawns on me why there is no one outdoors. Being a calm and balmy evening my arrival has coincided with a summertime menace, a tiny

Bloody Foreland slipway, Tory left of centre

Camping on Inishbofin

creature who punches way above its weight. The midge. These tiny, biting insects measuring less than 3 millimetres, have arrived in abundance and I spend the next few minutes trying to cover up as much exposed skin as possible. While being bitten, I rummage through my gear, swap short for long trousers and tuck them into the longest socks I can find. I hastily pitch my tent, cook my grub, and retire to my tiny indoors. Before I settle in for the night, I set about the task of murdering the few critters that have snuck into my tiny cocoon. As the sun sinks lower I steal a glance through my tent flap towards the mainland. I catch a last glimpse of cone-shaped Errigal standing proud among its chunky neighbours. Having this iconic summit in my southern quarter is a nice reminder that I am finally encamped on our northern seaboard. The morning will bring me as far east as I can manage.

WHAT A DIFFERENCE A DAY MAKES. Lifting my tent flap reveals a surprisingly blustery day. Yesterday's clear skies are gone and a layer of heavy grey cloud presses down from above. The mission today is a series of open water stretches above a string of north-facing headlands. Templebreaga, Horn, Rinnafaghla, Melmore, Ballyhoorisky and Rinmore Point will leave me bearing down on the much visited and picturesque Fanad Head. Beyond here is the 10 kilometre-wide mouth of Lough Swilly which allows the Atlantic Ocean to wander inland. Here, a 40 kilometre snaking inlet stretches as far as Letterkenny, separating northwest Donegal from the Inishowen peninsula. With no fixed plan, my intention is to continue east, rounding Fanad, where a decision on whether to cross to Inishowen or camp nearby will be made.

I leave the enchanting isle of Inishbofin and strike out across a wide bay. The mainland's long crescent of sand gives way to a stony beach cut into the opposite headland. The gloom and chop contradict the season. I can hardly believe we are still in August. After an hour and a half I land in choppy conditions for my customary early break to collect my thoughts. My anorak is tight around me and my cosy beanie replaces yesterday's peaked cap, all in an attempt to stop my body heat leaking away into the elements. I leave the cove cautiously anticipating Horn Head which lies just out of sight of my first way stop. I look back across the churning sea and catch my last view of the northwest corner of Ireland, Bloody Foreland. I turn and continue heading east.

Rounding this uniquely shaped headland I am dwarfed by 180 metre high cliffs plunging into the ocean. Unfolding before me, Horn Head slowly reveals the origin of its name. A lower section of cliff rises up, horn-like, before sloping into the sea away from the main rock walls. Like an enormous fish hook this feature must have aided early mariners in identifying their exact whereabouts along this imposing stretch of coast. As David Simpson, a previous circumnavigator, recounted of this place, 'A most impressive headland, but scary biscuits'. I agree, as today the head is capped with a dark rain cloud adding to its sinister look. Thankfully, I pass under it safely and strike out on another beeline, this time across the top of Sheephaven Bay bound for the Rosguill peninsula. The clouds are not hanging about, and one by

Rough seas around Horn Head

one the lower layers of dark grey stratus give way to blossoming blue blotches. Over the course of a few hours they miraculously merge and I am now below a cloudless sky.

The steep cliffs have been replaced by a coastal strip full of character. Miniature headlands, rocky outcrops, islets and reefs give way to an occasional burst of brightness as I happen upon a tiny, tucked away beach. I am buoyant, literally and psychologically, as I search the low rocky coastline for a stop-off. I wheel into a quiet bay and notice a long white cottage overlooking a tennis court-sized stony beach. I glide *Murchú* over the crystal clear waters and enjoy my lunch break. The setting is a verdant landscape covered in ferns with the occasional white bungalow. In the distance, small hills provide a perfect backdrop as they serenely sit under the blue dome. After four hours' paddling my fortunes have changed. I contemplate dressing down to prevent overheating. I just love Ireland's four seasons in a day.

Fanad Lighthouse

Continuing east I pick off the headlands one by one until I see the brilliant white of Fanad Lighthouse which marks the 90 degree turn in the coastline as it drops into Lough Swilly. I round the corner heading south under the watchful eye of the sentinel and the clutch of tourists who have been drawn here. I land on a flat beach and realise, due to the steepness surrounding it, that there is no exit landside. This means that I am not done kayaking yet, but having clocked up a handsome 43 kilometres I am considering calling it a day somewhere nearby. Time to contact Adrian Harkin, my kayaking contact on the Inishowen, for his opinion on such matters.

As a go-getter type, Adrian persuades me to take the 10 kilometres leap across the bight onto the Inishowen Peninsula. He knows it is a carrot I cannot resist, especially since he has offered to put me up for the night. I aim *Murchú* towards the inverted bowl-shaped Dunaff Head and begin putting in some hard yards. A freshening breeze is picking up again and after a full day's paddling these last few kilometres are far from easy. The water feels like treacle as I try to keep my pace going. Nearing Dunaff Head I enter an area of choppy water which dishes up a last challenge for my tired body and mind. I struggle unexpectedly as *Murchú* herself seems unhappy with proceedings, bouncing in a haphazard fashion for the first time today. Demanding a lot of me, it forces my muscles to work at a higher intensity. I notice the steep sides of the headland are reflecting back the growing swells and sense there must also be a strong current flowing under the boat. After enduring this final hurdle I plod on into calmer waters towards the tiny jetty where I am to meet Adrian.

With Adrian Harkin at Dunaff Head

Murchú and I land onto a wide area of wet bladderwrack covering the foreshore. I simply cease paddling. I am happy to have clocked up 53 kilometres and reached this strange little backwater. In the lee of Dunaff Head and partially positioned up a narrow muddy inlet I sit beside the narrow breakwater. Arriving early I stay put briefly to collect my thoughts and allow the adrenaline to leave my system. Eventually, I haul *Murchú* out and begin unpacking everything in an orderly fashion ready for my journey to Moville. Tomorrow I will head to Derry and my bus home.

Adrian's minibus bounces into view as he negotiates the tiny lane down to the pier. Full of energy he leaps out and enthusiastically welcomes me to Inishowen. His ruddy complexion, red hair and customary wry smile are a sight for sore eyes. The first thing he queries me about is why I am unpacking all my gear. When he learns that I am finishing this instalment because of the forecast, a puzzled expression appears on his face. Hold that thought, he informs me, and stop unpacking everything. We will get moving and chat on the way. Later on, as we start traversing the large peninsula, he begins his methodical interrogation.

Why am I stopping? There is a good forecast and Malin Head is only 15 kilometres away. I explain that my go-to app, Windguru, is forecasting a freshening wind, and is causing me some concern. As master of my own trip I am not keen on being coerced into a situation that makes me uncomfortable. This is especially true when it involves this infamous headland. As we bounce along country roads Adrian fumbles with his phone, searching out his own forecasting app. My eyes are fixed on the road like a rally co-driver until he finds it. He tosses it to me and what I see completely contradicts my forecast. Sensing an opening, he tells me that tomorrow is the perfect day to round Malin. He reminds me that since he made the passage numerous times I should trust his judgement. He also offers to collect me from wherever I land on the east side of Inishowen. He knows the way into my logical mind and delights at the change that is taking place in there. I am in a state of flux as the idea takes hold that my mission may be extended by another day. I do a quick calculation and announce to Adrian that a 5.30 am alarm call will be needed to make it all happen. I should have guessed that his response would be a solid affirmative. His smile widens as he senses victory, his *pièce de résistance* being that he promises to be up before me to make breakfast.

True to form, when I land into Adrian's kitchen the following morning, the smell of toast and hot coffee hangs in the air. He loves this stuff, the thing of adventures, when the norms of everyday life are thrown aside in pursuit of a lofty goal. Part of me likes it too, but today I feel nervous at the prospect of going over the top. Malin to me is akin to making it over the summit of Everest and back down the far side. All of this is heightened by the almost sleepless night just passed. I am reminded of the nerves I felt before rounding the Mizen last year, and now, at the opposite end, the butterflies are back. Outside, a crisp morning awaits, the sky a dark blue brightening from the east. In no time I am back at the tiny pier where I landed yesterday, packed and heading north towards my goal.

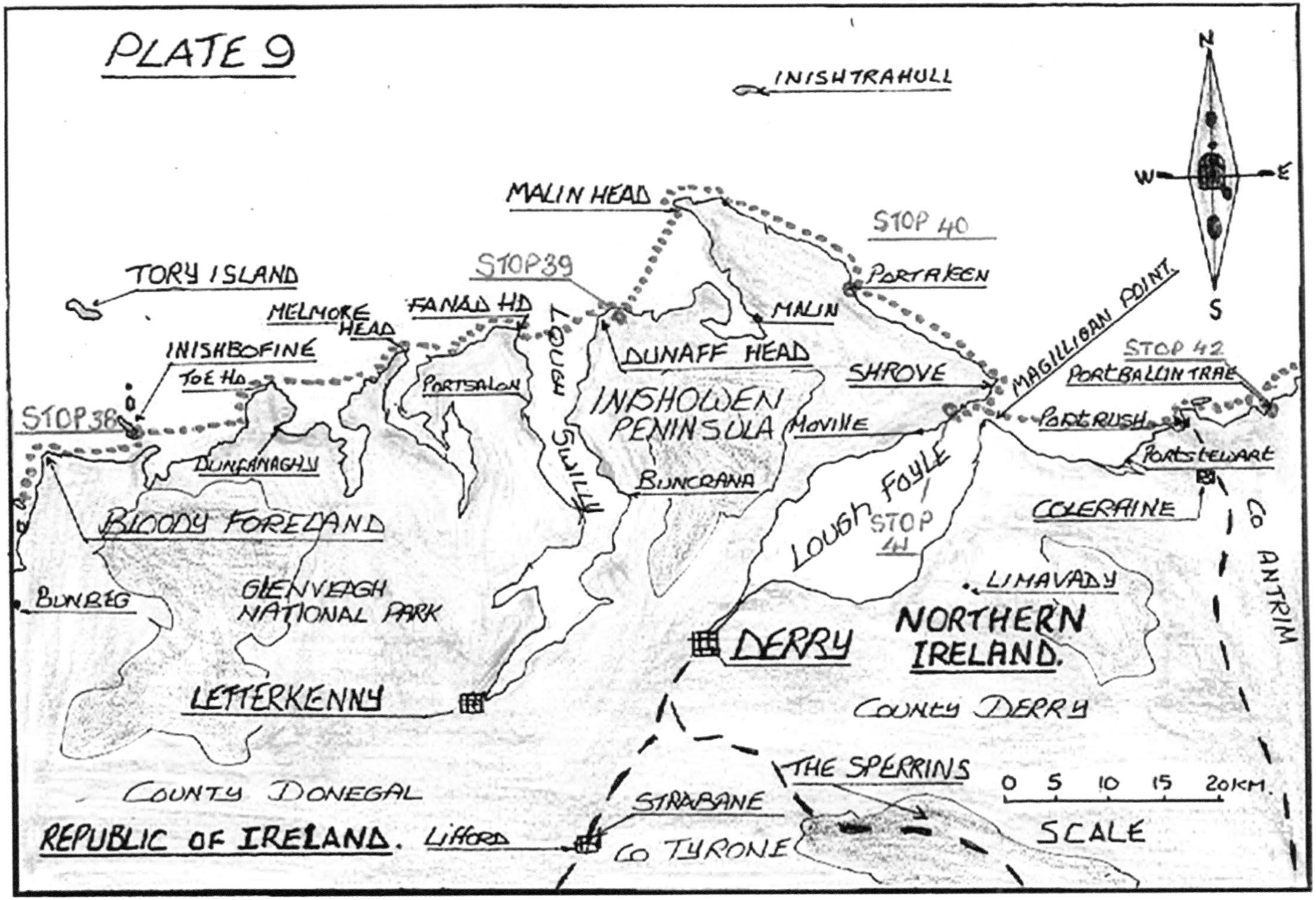
PLATE 9
INISHTRAHULL
N
W
E
S
MALIN HEAD
STOP 40
TORY ISLAND
STOP39
PORTAKEEN
MELMORE HEAD
FANAD HD
MALIN
MAGILLIGAN POINT.
STOP 42
INISHBOFINE
LOUGH SWILLY
DUNAFF HEAD
SHROVE
PORTBALLINTRAE
TOE HD
PORTSALON
INISHOWEN PENINSULA
STOP38
MOVILLE
PORTRUSH
DUNFANAGHY
PORTSTEWART
BUNCRANA
LOUGH FOYLE
STOP 41
COLERAINE
BLOODY FORELAND
CO ANTRIM
LIMAVADY
BUNBEG
GLENVEAGH NATIONAL PARK
NORTHERN IRELAND.
DERRY
LETTERKENNY
COUNTY DERRY
THE SPERRINS
0 5 10 15 20KM.
COUNTY DONEGAL
STRABANE
SCALE
REPUBLIC OF IRELAND.
LIFFORD
CO TYRONE

Stage 26

Topping Out at Malin Head

Going across to the southern tip of Malin Head takes me into very open water and for a long stretch I am over five kilometres from land. Thankfully, the winds are slight and the sea placid. It is the exposure of this segment that weighs in as my first challenge. My plan is to take a break before going around, aiming first at a narrow gravel alcove cut into Malin's expansive headland. The whole region resembles a barrelling wave when viewed on the map, with me and *Murchú* climbing vertically to the curling lip ahead. Eventually, I make land, hop out to replenish and ready myself for my passage across Ireland's Northern tip.

After several minutes I realise I feel ill-prepared and am unsure about getting back into my boat. I am just not ready to do this. This is the problem with going solo; I alone decide to go or stay. And now I find myself unwilling to return to my faithful companion sitting expressionless at my feet. I look at *Murchú* in search of inspiration. It then occurs to me that I should try to tap into this nervousness. I take out my phone, turn on the camera, and start talking. My mind is coloured by horror stories that my voice blurts out nervously. I describe my reservations to an imagined future audience thankful such an opportunity exists for this solo mission. After a brief monologue my mood improves. I have given voice to my trepidation and am ready, like Blackadder, to go over the top.

I round the ragged rocks of the headland and find myself looking into a 500 metre-long corridor, backed by solid rock. Off to my left is a section of stony land resembling a fossilised dinosaur's back. The opening is the size of a minor road and I kayak ahead in the hope it is not a dead end. I spot a swell breaking up ahead and reassure myself that an opening is causing it. I approach, gingerly, thankful to see a path out. A swell breaks over the nearby rocks which combined with the tidal flows creates a minor disturbance. I can see how this haphazard collection of islets could kick up a real storm in heavy weather and strong tides. I paddle onwards cautiously, as though entering into a haunted house of horrors. But I discover that my fears are completely unfounded as I pass by the crux point of this headland with ease.

Once past, I paddle directly east across the top of our island home conscious, like no time before, of my precise location. From great wall maps hanging in my primary school, to smaller atlases and charts, this lonely zenith has always attracted my attention. As well as being geo-

Pre-Malin Head passage, looking south

graphically poignant, it also reveals a political contradiction. The irony of being in the Republic of Ireland, or the South as it is often called, but also north of Northern Ireland brings a smile to my face. These thoughts are best parked for later, though, when I will be paddling the shores of a unique part of the United Kingdom that exists on our shared island. Topping out here brings with it a huge psychological boost. My 800 kilometre journey along Ireland's western seaboard is at an end, and I am thankful, and on this day of days, elated. Once around the top my goal is to stop at Slievebawn, barely three kilometres away, where a very special rendezvous awaits.

I turn into the hooked pier of this tranquil harbour. A mirror-smooth patch of sand adjoins the pier and slipway as two sit-on-top kayakers ready themselves for a fishing expedition. Two well-fed guys are bedecked in all sorts of fishing apparatus with fish trackers, nets, lures and VHF radios hanging from them or their boats. A mini-forest of rods point skywards like elongated bows from their quiver. They look slightly comical heading to sea with all their kit on show. I even notice their drink cups are slotted into purpose-built openings on their decks. We exchange pleasantries, a strange intersection of two very different kayaking disciplines in this remote location.

Minutes later *Murchú* is parked well above sea level as I walk inland towards my rendezvous. I pass an impressive two-story terrace on my right, the old coastguard station now divided into private residences. Built in 1912 it housed men who manned a fleet of rowing boats used to police local waters, originally for smugglers and then as a section of the British Naval reserve. Malin lays claim to a huge concentration of sunken ocean liners and German U-Boats from the Second World War.

I continue along the rising road and spot Inishtrahull, an island ten kilometres offshore, the most northerly off Ireland. A kilometre further north lies a small islet, Tor Beg Rock, which constitutes the most northerly point of Ireland. I am relishing my whereabouts up at our highest latitudes. I turn off the road towards a collection of sturdy white buildings surrounded by tightly cut grass. Inside are people I have been talking to while kayaking up the west coast. I have been filling them in on my ambitious plans of negotiating the coast, and now, for the first time, I will meet them face to face. I push open the main door and walk into Malin Head coastguard station.

The mystery behind those I have been in contact with for months, via my VHF radio, is revealed. Vast areas of ocean are laid out on wall-mounted flat screens, while a team of men sit at their desks ready to support those at sea. Their uniformed appearance conveys the training thats lies behind their responsibilities. Outside, the coastline paints a peaceful sight as indoors I am like a sponge soaking up the workings of their service stretching far out into the Atlantic. They, in turn, query me about my trip as I take in the set-up of the coastguard station. Being here is a celebration of completing a huge chunk of my circumnavigation. I have finally 'topped out', and soon I will be starting to drop back two full degrees of latitude to 53' north to my home back in Skerries.

Visit to the Malin Head Coastguard station

For now, though, I am enjoying a warm exchange with this closely knit group of guys who man this remote outpost. I owe Adrian a debt of gratitude for his timely interjection. Lesson learned: listen to local knowledge.

Chauffeur-driven in the coastguard jeep, I am soon reunited with *Murchú* back in the harbour. The slipway, hot under the high sun, is slowly being swallowed by the swelling tide which thankfully means

Seascape architecture east of Malin Head

less of a drag to the water. After a lonely morning's paddle with only wild thoughts as company, this picturesque haven is a difficult place to leave. Positioned now on the eastern side of this great peninsula I savour the moment. As Adrian has offered to collect me from wherever I land, I press on southeastwards.

With no swell about, I continue barely a stone's throw from the coastline. The profile of the land reveals a softer type of rock creating a vegetation rich, pitch-roof gradient, down to the sea. Unable to support a steep cliff, a great haphazard collection of disconnected land lies discarded along the shore. Great chunks of the mainland have calved and toppled into the sea creating an array of shapes just offshore. Small pyramids, towers, oversize shards and blocks create a cataclysmic atmosphere juxtaposed against the tranquil sea. It provides a welcome distraction to my day's continued path southeast, in easy, if slightly boring, conditions. Still, all I can manage on the day's final shift is 13 kilometres to Portaleen Harbour. Clocking up a modest 32 kilometres, I am convinced that yesterday's long paddle, followed by today's unexpected one, has eaten into my reserves. Coupled with Adrian's generous offer to collect me from anywhere along this coast, I decide to call it a day.

A colourful clutch of small fishing boats sit perched on a wide concrete platform behind the slipway at Porteelin Harbour. Beside the pier, a rusting yellow pillar supports a jib arm, primed to haul the next catch ashore. My foot is off the gas now, and my commitment to 'smelling the roses' is realised with the earthy aroma from gorse bushes that hangs in the air. Moments like these are delicious, when I find myself in the back of beyond with some time to spare. As Adrian has not arrived yet I have a look around. I climb up a mound to discover a quaint memorial to those lost at sea. From as far back as 1936 the names of those lost are remembered. Delaying a few minutes, I soak up this tiny corner of northern Inishowen, eventually wandering down to *Murchú* when I spot Adrian's van bounding down the country road.

The following morning, before catching the bus home, Adrian offers to escort me around his home city of Derry. It is my first time properly seeing the place, and because he grew up in the Catholic Bogside

Adrian has an intimate knowledge of the serious unrest that took place there. This was an area where residents were crammed together in tenements and treated harshly by the authorities leading to civil rights marches. The army and police intervened to stop these peaceful protests, which led to the tragic events of Bloody Sunday when 13 marchers were killed. In the decades that followed over 3,000 were killed in tit-for-tat shootings with society divided down religious and political lines. The Protestant Unionists were staunchly pro-British while the Catholic Nationalists were passionately pro-Irish. Thankfully, since 1994 when the Good Friday Agreement was signed, a rickety kind of peace has existed.

After a brief visit to the Free Derry Museum, a must see, Adrian becomes visibly upset, no doubt due to the traumatic memories from his youth. My heart goes out to him as it illustrates the great anguish felt by all who have suffered from blatant sectarianism for decades. On a lighter note, and keen on showing me the real Derry, Adrian takes me to a genuine Derry cafe complete with plastic seats and potato cakes, that I must admit are to die for. After such an education, both culinary and political, I am ready to head for the bus. When I eventually board the coach for home, my mind and belly are full. My dearest wish for this strained part of our shared island home is that peace will prevail.

Stage 27

OOPS, WHAT A DIFFERENCE
A TEXT CAN MAKE ...

Three weeks later I am heading north again to rejoin *Murchú* at Adrian's place in Moville. An old pal from Belfast, Ian Fleming, is ferrying me today. Sharing a name with the creator of James Bond, he is a creative type, an artist in fact, whose forte is creating pieces of the ocean breaking onto rocky shorelines. How apt. As a fellow year round swimmer, Ian, a larger than life character, has supported me on my trip from the beginning. As a great promoter of peace it seems appropriate that he will be escorting me to my launch point into Northern Ireland.

We arrive late and knock on Adrian's door. Surprised to see me, he exclaims, 'Did you not get my text?' On learning that I had not, he promptly blurts, 'The forecast is shite. There's force 5 to 6 southwesterlies due tomorrow.' On seeing my shocked reaction, he moves aside and ushers us in.

Shortly thereafter, Ian bids us farewell and we start to discuss what might be possible in the morning. We pore over my intended route and I realise that things are not going to be so straightforward this time out. After much discussion over forecasts, local topography and tidal streams we decide to plan for an early start. A 20 kilometre dash to Shrove on the southeastern tip of the Inishowen is all that seems possible. This should position me nicely for a bigger paddle the next day. As ever, Adrian is pulling out all the stops to help me on my quest.

It needs to be another break-of-dawn mission before the winds really get going. As the latter half of this passage is under cliffs it should afford me some shelter. I notice a hesitancy in Adrian's voice, which forces me to consider scrubbing the plan altogether. We finally decide to have a rain check in the morning which, unfortunately, needs to be *at* Porteelin Pier just before dawn. This means rising at 5.00 am and on the water paddling by 6.30 am. He insists I *must* be off the water by 10.30 before the wind really hits. A promised hot shower by 11.30 is a appealing carrot after my risky mission is complete.

In complete darkness we arrive at Porteelin, survey the weather, and notice that an offshore breeze has already picked up. It is not too strong, so we decide the mission is on, but it hangs by a thread. We place *Murchú* gently on the concrete beside the pier and I start packing for what will only amount to a few hours' paddling. Some snacks, drinks and dry gear, plus my usual safety equipment, all hastily stuffed into hatches. I am travelling light today. During this activity, Adrian disappears into his minibus, cognisant of me not wanting to pack and converse at the same time. He knows how easily kit can be packed incorrectly or even left out altogether. I respect his gesture.

The faint light of another day starts to spill over the distant horizon. It is muggy and a breeze blows along the east-facing pier out over open sea. My mission feels like a covert operation forcing me to hide *Murchú* from the offshore winds that are due to strengthen to almost 38 knots over the next few hours. My boat has a knife-like bow with a large surface area to achieve higher speeds. Unfortunately, when hit by strong crosswinds, it can end up being blown downwind which leaves the paddler hijacked, potentially having to 'run with the wind' or attempt the arduous task of turning back upwind. I simply cannot afford to have this happen today, especially since the nearest downwind landfall is sixty kilometres away – Scotland.

Expedition sea kayaking means getting wind, waves and tidal streams to help as much as possible. Get it wrong and it will cost. So I take off on the rising tide's conveyor belt and am soon achieving respectable speeds of over 12 kilometres an hour. I weave my way along the serrated rocky edge within arm's reach of shore. Since waving Adrian off, I have yet to clap eyes on another human being. I pass along the deserted beach of Caratra, or 'Friendly Beach' in English,

Approaching Shrove in the gloom

the name helping lift my mood. Soon, I find myself travelling in the lee of the much anticipated cliffs. I am mostly out of the wind, but the sound high above is akin to a noisy overpass as the rising wind flings the clouds to seaward. I notice that just 100 metres offshore the wind is cascading downward, slamming into the sea, like angry downdrafts from a helicopter. I keep a careful eye on them lest they drag me out to sea. I press on cautiously towards Shrove.

It takes me three hours to weave my way along this stretch, relieved when the squat lighthouse at Shrove appears up ahead. The weather is continuing its downward trajectory as rain cascades from above. As I am nearing the mouth of Lough Foyle, the wind begins eating into my progress. The shelter of the land is coming to a close as I pull into Shrove Beach for a breather and the customary self-congratulatory pat-on-the-back. I ring Adrian, suggesting I paddle the remaining nine kilometres into the teeth of the wind all the way to Moville. How silly of me to think that such a thing is possible.

Shrove Beach, Inishowen

On rounding Shrove light, I swing 90 degrees and enter the Lough. I am now heading straight into the teeth of the building wind I have been hiding from all morning. By my reckoning, a force five or six is now blowing and a great invisible hand pushes against my chest. It almost denies any progress towards my goal. The water is being torn by the wind into shuddering wavelets, their crests spraying against the boat. Fortunately, I am able to creep inside low rocky outcrops and avoid the bigger waves further out, but even here the full force of the wind is inescapable. My pace has crumbled from seven to barely two kilometres per hour. The water feels like treacle as I am reminded how tough paddling into strong winds can be. Every time I plant the blade it remains stuck in position, refusing to be drawn smoothly back through the water. Essentially, I am in a near-stationary boat, paddling as though my boat is anchored to the spot. Despite being a serious slog, it is certainly a great physical workout.

With my snail's pace, I have ample time to closely observe the low-lying shoreline lined by many fine houses. I visualise families scattered about on bright summer days enjoying a tranquil watery scene.

This only magnifies today's foul conditions as their sodden gardens lie empty and unvisited. I spot a caravan park up ahead and instantly hone in on it. Not even 500 metres into the Lough, I am already questioning the wisdom of my plan to make Moville. I am already looking for a get-out.

Needing to find a suitable spot for Adrian's van to get close, I aim for the caravan park slipway. I make a hasty landing, ringing him when ashore. Unfortunately, he cannot gain access here, and I am forced to return to hauling treacle again. Succumbing to the wind, I admit defeat at Sweet Nellies Beach only two kilometres after rounding Shrove. This marks my slowest stretch thus far, covering that distance in over an hour. My arms feel longer than when the day started but I am happy to have moved *Murchú* to a launch point for Northern Ireland. Just across the water is the infamous Magilligan Point and prison, and a unique political entity that has existed on our island for almost 100 years. In the meantime I pack up after an interesting morning's paddle, my last one on the Inishowen. That hot shower promised will be very welcome.

Bunagee Pier, Inishowen

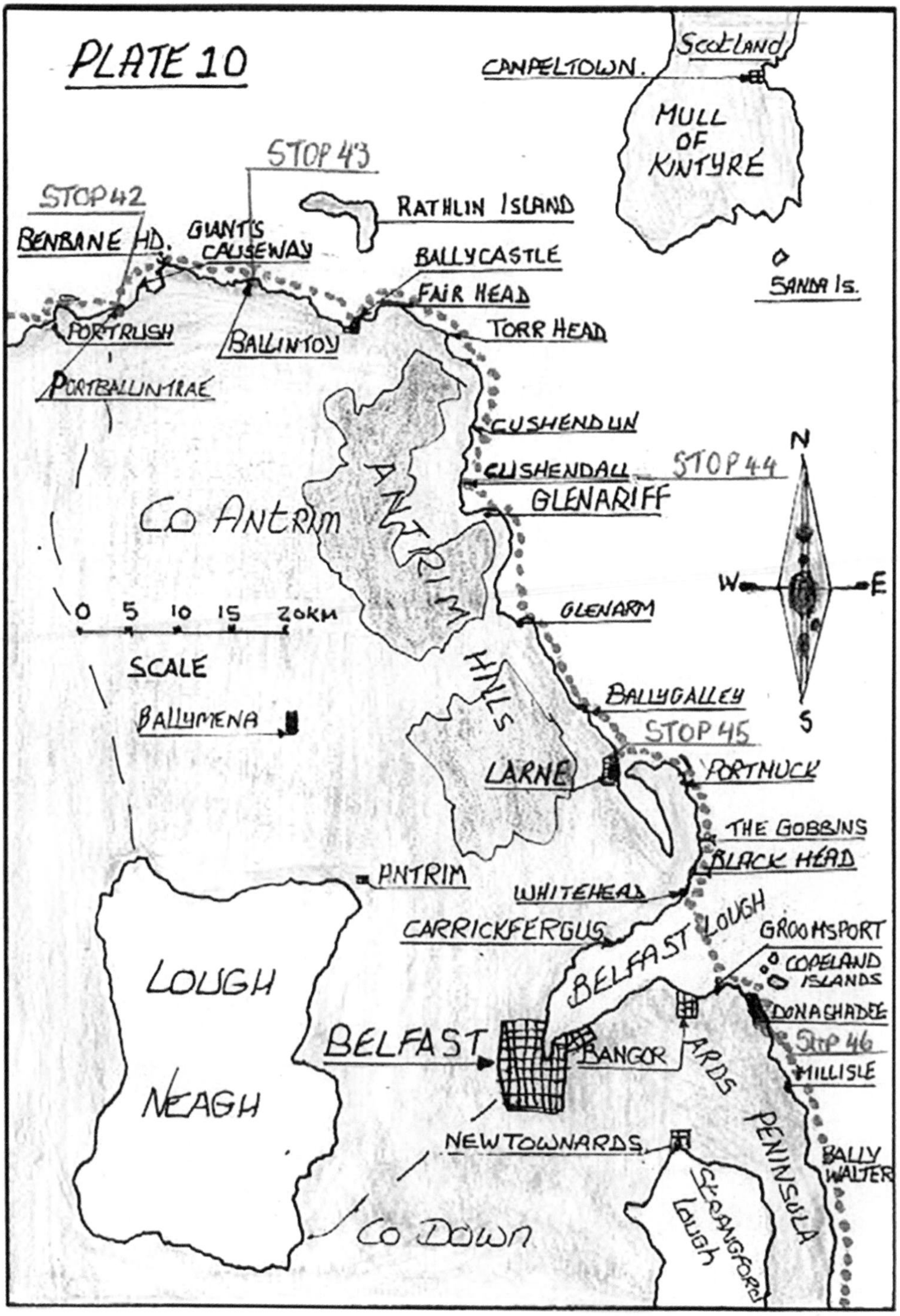

PLATE 10
Scotland
CAMPELTOWN.
MULL OF KINTYRE
STOP 43
STOP 42
RATHLIN ISLAND
BENBANE HD.
GIANT'S CAUSEWAY
BALLYCASTLE
SANDA IS.
FAIR HEAD
TORR HEAD
PORTRUSH
BALLINTOY
PORTBALLINTRAE
CUSHENDUN
CUSHENDALL
STOP 44
GLENARIFF
CO ANTRIM
ANTRIM HILLS
GLENARM
0 5 10 15 20KM
SCALE
BALLYGALLEY
BALLYMENA
STOP 45
LARNE
PORTMUCK
THE GOBBINS
BLACK HEAD
ANTRIM
WHITEHEAD
CARRICKFERGUS
BELFAST LOUGH
GROOMSPORT
COPELAND ISLANDS
DONAGHADEE
LOUGH NEAGH
BELFAST
BANGOR
STOP 46
MILLISLE
ARDS PENINSULA
NEWTOWNARDS
BALLY WALTER
STRANGFORD LOUGH
CO DOWN
N
S
W
E

Stage 28

GAME OF THRONES AND ANTRIM'S CAUSEWAY COAST

The next morning promises a better day. Finally, I will be venturing into Northern Ireland which is still part of the United Kingdom. This six county statelet was formed on 3 May 1921, the remaining 26 counties constituting the embryonic republic. It carries with it a tragic history going back centuries, with a society divided along political and religious lines. I am genuinely interested in how I will be received there.

Crossing the turbulent Foyle estuary feels like crossing an invisible border. From Sweet Nellies beach to the distant seaside town of Portrush I hope for a seamless transition into another jurisdiction. Unfortunately, a strong outgoing tide is squeezing through the one kilometre narrows between the spit at Magilligan's Point and the Inishowen Peninsula, creating all manner of irregularities downstream. I am helped out to sea by a light southwesterly and by an unexpected escort; a lone porpoise briefly shares my track before accelerating out of sight far ahead. Despite his naïveté on the politics taking place in these parts, I take his presence as another good omen.

The crossing to Portrush has me well offshore again, and with clouds starting to darken I keep a good eye on the ever-crinkling sea. Up ahead a small cargo ship appears to be at anchor. I assume it is waiting to continue up the Foyle to Derry. I adjust my track to take a closer look. It seems to be well cared for, with its black hull and white superstructure recently painted. As I bear down on her I notice the swells are rebounding in my direction creating a small area of con-

Portrush, first landing in Northern Ireland

fusion. It is my old nemesis, clapotis. I never knew that this could be created from a ship at sea and as I traverse it I maintain a state of alertness. Thankfully, I am through in a few minutes. I leave the tethered leviathan behind.

Pulling into Portrush, one of the North Coast's main seaside towns, is a welcome break after almost three hours at sea. The terraced Georgian houses stand proudly overlooking the west-facing harbour. The town is built on a narrow outcrop of land that has beaches on both sides and a grassy headland at its end. The headland gives the impression that the town is hunkering behind it for protection.

I paddle up to the slipway and wheel *Murchú* onto the pier. I am unsure of the protocol and am ready to adjust tack, come what may. I park the kayak and spot a much needed facility, the public loo. While determinedly marching towards it I am intercepted by a van. I fear that I am about to get a load of Northern Irish criticism for arriving unannounced into such a fine harbour by kayak. Nothing could be further from the truth. I am pleasantly surprised when the driver asks if I am

Kevin O'Sullivan, and realise that I am finally meeting legendary mariner, Robin Ruddock.

A sea kayaker, builder of boats, and a highly motivated teacher, Robin features almost as a sentinel for circumnavigators along this stretch of the north coast. Having followed my blog, he knew I was in the area and, ever watchful, spotted me a good ways offshore. His statement that I could surely put away a cooked breakfast has me instantly salivating. He escorts me to the Portrush Sailing Club, deposits me upstairs in their lounge, and treats me to a plate of scrambled eggs with toast and a pot of coffee. Before he leaves he suggests that because

Meeting Robin Ruddock in Portballintrae

the swells are growing I should not continue beyond Portballintrae, since challenging the Causeway Coast would not be prudent today. As previously learned, I pay attention to local wisdom. I devour the grub, basking in the warmest welcome imaginable. My porpoise escort was right after all.

FOUR DAYS LATER AFTER A QUICK FEW days flying, I am northbound again, aboard the Goldline bus from Dublin Airport. An early schedule allows me to work and commute on the same day, an essential element to my logistics today. Hopping onto the Derry train, I get a first-hand experience of the travelling public in Northern Ireland. I am happily surprised. The hubbub of conversation feels more like a pub than a train, and a group of senior ladies have us all in stitches with their humorous banter. They call themselves the 'Real Derry Girls' and are returning home after a Belfast city trip. They are not shy about sharing their stories and a great bit of banter follows. Seldom have I enjoyed a train trip more as I reluctantly disembark at Coleraine.

I spot Robin's van waiting outside the station. We drive to his yard which is full of currachs, dinghies, punts and various types of kayaks scattered about, with some getting extra attention inside his workshop. He casually relays that a few years ago he and ten others rowed a currach from Ballycastle in County Antrim to the island of Arran in Scotland to retrace St Colmcille's sixth century voyage. He is a living legend and I would love to hear more but he insists I press on immediately and put the Causeway Coast astern before the swell grows further. Within an hour of landing I am waving farewell to this gentle mariner and back on the water.

I leave the almost circular cove at Portballintrae and once out of port turn right and head across the yawning bay lying off Bushfoot Strand. A popular surf spot, this crescent-shaped beach continues towards Runkerry House, a Victorian residence that resembles a mini-Hogwarts. It adds a haunting air to the scene. With the far end of the bay marking the start of the Causeway Coast this becomes my aiming point. With no option of a get-out for another eight kilometres, I concentrate on synching my rhythm to that of the sea. My fear that the task will prove difficult is well founded.

At this stage I decide to take in where I am, drinking in the magic of this stretch of coastline. The sea road off North Antrim boasts a dramatic vista for the travelling boater. Flat-topped, vertical columns, resembling pipes in an outsized church organ, are complemented by the world famous Giant's Causeway, which disappears into the frothing ocean ahead. Created almost 50 million years ago, it boasts 40,000 tightly packed hexagonal columns mimicking a beehive's honeycomb structure. Annually, almost a million people are drawn to this site, boosting the local economy in the process. Unfortunately, I am unable to look closely at this phenomenon because the rebounding swells are creating an irregular sea which requires my attention.

Ballintoy Harbour, Game of Thrones country

It is not until I am beyond the Causeway Coast that I can relax. Up ahead, across open water, I spot my goal for the evening, the small stone harbour at Ballintoy. Featured in the *Game of Thrones*, it was the location for Lordsport, one of the series' Iron Islands. Off to my right is the Port Moon Bothy, an old fisherman's cottage renovated by the National Trust that can be used as lodgings by the passing kayaker. Sitting below a steep cliff that lies about 50 metres inland, it is best reached from seaward.

Continuing eastwards I notice dusk descending as I pass Dunseverick Harbour and White Park Bay. My destination, Ballintoy Harbour, is hidden behind an assortment of rocks that resemble giant cockroaches, half-submerged by the darkening ocean. I continue, with caution, towards the labyrinth. Bearing down on it, I bemoan the fact that my only previous visit was in calm, daylight conditions. In fading light and with the swells breaking, it is a real challenge. With so many small islets scattered about, I berate myself for not examining the Google Earth images more closely.

The dark hummocks blend into one another creating what looks like a black wall between me and the east-facing harbour entrance. So near and yet so far, I continue further east, acutely aware that I will eventually have to get down and dirty with these rocky obstacles. Finally, after a lengthy internal debate, I swing *Murchú* towards a gap, hitch a lift on a rising swell and start careering between two ominous black mounds towards shore. Her speed is alarming and I dearly hope I am in the proper channel. She eventually slows as the wave slackens into the deeper water inside. It took all of about twenty seconds but I realise my gamble was good. The sanctuary of Ballintoy Harbour is waiting for me to enter. And here was me thinking that once I had passed Malin Head it would be a flipping cakewalk.

What awaits in Robin's boathouse is a reward for my efforts. Blending in seamlessly with the harbour and fashioned from the same rock, the boathouse contains his personal store of collectibles. Old wooden sea kayaks hang from the rafters, while great whale bones, bird skulls, old oil lamps, ship nameplates, and some chairs are neatly arranged

Ballintoy Harbour and boathouse, Rathlin Island behind

Inside the Ballintoy Harbour boathouse

throughout. For me, though, the *pièce de résistance* is his wood-burning stove. I brew up hot tea and start boiling noodles and tinned fish – *quelle surprise* – salivating as I prepare. I am in warm civvies as my wet kit hangs drying overhead in this magical Aladdin's cave.

The next day I will be transiting under Fair Head, the fourth and final corner of our island, heralding my descent down the Irish Sea to home. Torr Head, lying a further seven kilometres on, offers a possible sting in the tail as it protrudes into the strong flows that race past it, either filling or emptying the Irish Sea. But that is all for tomorrow, when hopefully I will meet fair weather and easy paddling. I complete my blog, clamber up the ladder to the loft, and insert myself into my sleeping bag. I slide into a welcome abyss dreaming of perfect paddling conditions.

DAY TWO OF THIS THREE-DAY INSTALMENT has me initially passing by crystalline off-white cliffs with little swell to worry about. My main concern is the extreme tidal flows along this stretch. The gargantuan filling and emptying of the northern Irish Sea basin can be felt dozens of miles beyond the 20 kilometre opening separating Antrim from the Mull of Kintyre in Scotland. Off to my left, Rathlin Island, sitting in the path of these flows, takes up a sizable segment of my horizon, while beyond it lies Scotland. I paddle inside Sheep Island, a flat-topped monolith resembling an enormous concrete block, planted 500 metres offshore. Cleared of rats in the 1970s it has since successfully supported puffin and cormorant populations. Distinctive and imposing in equal measure, it occupies my orbit until my next milestone comes into view.

The next island is Carrick-a-Rede, and like Sheep Island it is another volcanic plug. It had been used as a base for salmon fisheries until the latter half of the twentieth century when stocks mysteriously dwindled. Connected to the mainland by a rope bridge it attracts almost half a million visitors every year. With a short 20 metre span and suspended 30 metres above sea level, it is a psychological challenge for visitors to negotiate. I remember nervously walking across it in the 1980s with both my hands tucked into my pockets, trying to be the cool guy. I was secretly shaking all the way across and back. There are stories of some who had to be removed from the island by boat after refusing to retrace their steps. Craning my neck skyward to look at this rickety construction from my new perspective almost costs me a dunking. Happily, I attract a few shouts from above as I squeeze through a narrow slot in the opening.

Bearing down on Ballycastle, a seaside town and the departure point of the Rathlin Island ferry, I bump into John and David, two older paddlers out for a morning potter. I know I am pushing towards sixty but these guys look like they have a decade on me and are still enjoying their time kayaking. Unbelievably, this is only my second time bumping into sea-kayak paddlers on the trip. The previous meet-up was with Jonas off Donegal, the lone German paddler out in search of big waves. We compare notes and soon discover a mutual acquaintance in Robin Ruddock. As ever, I need to press on and wish them fair winds and safe paddling.

During a brief stop on Ballycastle beach, a couple of toddlers make their way over to investigate the strange looking vessel that has suddenly appeared. Dutifully followed by their parents, who seem as keen as their kids about my boat, we engage in an easy conversation about my trip and the goings-on in this bustling town. It is a magnet for day trippers, with the sea, shops, hotels and harbour all bunched close together giving it a warm, lived-in feel. They assist me in finding a facility I am in much need of using, another public convenience.

Rathlin Island ferry, Ballycastle

Later on, passing under Fair Head, I am delighted to be re-entering the Irish Sea after 44 days of paddling, which means eighty per cent of my circumnavigation is complete. This angular headland is appropriately dramatic for this significant passage. Flat on top, it drops vertically down to its lower slopes which angle into the sea. Conveniently, it actually *looks* like a corner. Thanks to an increasing breeze from the south, the wave train being generated by this 'river in the sea' is impressive, so much so that I decide to stay close to shore

Passing Fair Head

and forgo taking this conveyor belt south. Unfortunately, this puts me in the path of back-eddies which are flowing back against me. Luckily for me, the coastline has many obstructions interrupting the flow and offering some shelter. Anyway, I am quite happy to be paddling within a few boat lengths of shore, pleasantly distracted by rock formations and shoreline vegetation.

Torr Head looms into view as the second element of this corner. I observe it with a certain amount of trepidation. This barb-shaped protrusion can create turbulent water, so when it is astern I breathe a sigh of relief. I continue south along the coastline where the famous Glens of Antrim reach the open sea. Most noteworthy are Cushendun and Cushendall, the second of which is my intended journey's end for the day.

Cushendun is a quaint little place situated at the far end of a crescent beach and nestled below a rising pastoral landscape. A black river slides into the sea after passing under an old stone bridge. A small collection of tiny boats are tied up nearby, all overlooked by an old cream coloured building. In case I am in any doubt it has *Cushendun* written

Torr Head slipway

on it. I paddle into the narrow river pulling *Murchú* up onto the seaweed-covered rocks and wander towards the long building. When at close quarters I notice the word *Hotel* written after Cushendun and realise why it boasts the townland's moniker. Spotting an open door, and being relatively dry, I decide to venture in.

Inside I seem to have time travelled over a hundred years, as sepia-coloured walls, wooden floors and ornate ceilings give the impression of a location for a period drama. Now operating as a public house, it was built as a working mill in the mid-1800s but saw only 20 years' service as such. It then morphed into variously named hotels, and finally to its present status. I learn that Randal Mc Donnell, grandson of the founder, is still caring for this historic landmark by meticulously keeping the old furnishings and decor as they were when it was created. My broad grin shows my appreciation at this find, especially since today's paddle has become an uneventful run southwards as far as the next Glen.

Seven kilometres and one hour's paddling later I pass the town of Cushendall. A phonetic anglicisation of the Irish name, Cois Abhann

Cushendun Hotel in a time warp

RNLI Red Bay Lifeboat Station in Cushendall

Dalla, meaning the 'Foot of the Dalla River', accurately describes the place. The town is spread along the shore and I am keen to land, get into my dry kit and do a bit of exploring. A column of shoebox-shaped mobile homes overlooking the sea gives way to a campsite which immediately catches my interest. A nice little boost to my morale is the sight of an RNLI lifeboat on her mooring just 100 metres offshore.

Within thirty minutes I am checking into my own pod, a one room, tent-shaped wooden structure with bedding, a heater and rudimentary facilities. Big enough for a small family, I enjoy the space. I opt to dine *al fresco*, munching on some fish and chips, as I wander lazily around this little coastal town. For refreshment I wander into McMullans Central Bar which turns out to be a great idea. As I sink into the warmth of the pub, well fed after a good day's paddling, a feeling of contentment fills me. I stay until the fading light and return to my cosy pod for what turns out to be a particularly comfortable, though at forty quid slightly pricey, night's sleep.

Pressing on towards Larne diagonally across the bay I soon round Garron Point under the shadow of the impressive Lurigthan Mountain.

Luxury accommodation in Cushendall

Like a worn version of Ben Bulben in Sligo, it looks out over the surrounding area. It is overcast and a weak drizzle dampens everything except my spirit, which laps up the easy coastal paddling. The highway here is a coast-hugging road, only metres above the water. I notice the sense of adventure ebbing away as I share my route with local buses, delivery vans and Joe Public, all bound for Carnlough, Glenarm Ballygalley or Larne.

A freshening breeze from astern starts to build and southbound wavelets inject a higher tempo to my day. The traffic now gets little attention as I immerse myself in the dynamics of another helpful down-winder. The waves, though small, are enough for me to extract some propulsion, my attention keenly trained to my immediate vicinity. I read the erratic patterns along the steeper sections, leaning on my blades occasionally as my speed outpaces a wave in front. I heave myself over the small rise and once again glissade across the silvery sea.

Stopping only a couple of times, mostly to stretch, take some much needed relief and consume some carbs, I clock up a moderate 30 kilometres as far as Larne. Over the last few kilometres the ferries are visible plying the waters between there and Scotland. Not since passing Rosslare Harbour in Wexford have I shared the sea with these great vessels. Larne is one of only two large ferry ports linking Northern Ireland with mainland Britain, the other being Belfast. During my next instalment I will be traversing the mouth of the deep lough that has the capital of Northern Ireland at its head.

David, a local paddler, has offered to look after my boat until the next leg of my trip. A man of his word, he pulls into view as I land onto the unfortunately named Drains Beach. Hoisting *Murchú* onto David's roof rack I experience a brief moment of concern. Larne is predominantly a Protestant or Unionist town and flags and symbols carry a lot of weight. *Murchú's* main colours, green and gold, are similar to those of the Republic of Ireland's flag. Considering that Unionists outnumber Nationalists by over two to one, I am hoping it doesn't attract too much adverse attention. Pulling into a lane we head towards the back garden of his mother's house and quickly put the kayak into her garage. 'In she goes so,' I exclaim, with David appearing somewhat relieved as *Murchú* disappears behind the metal door.

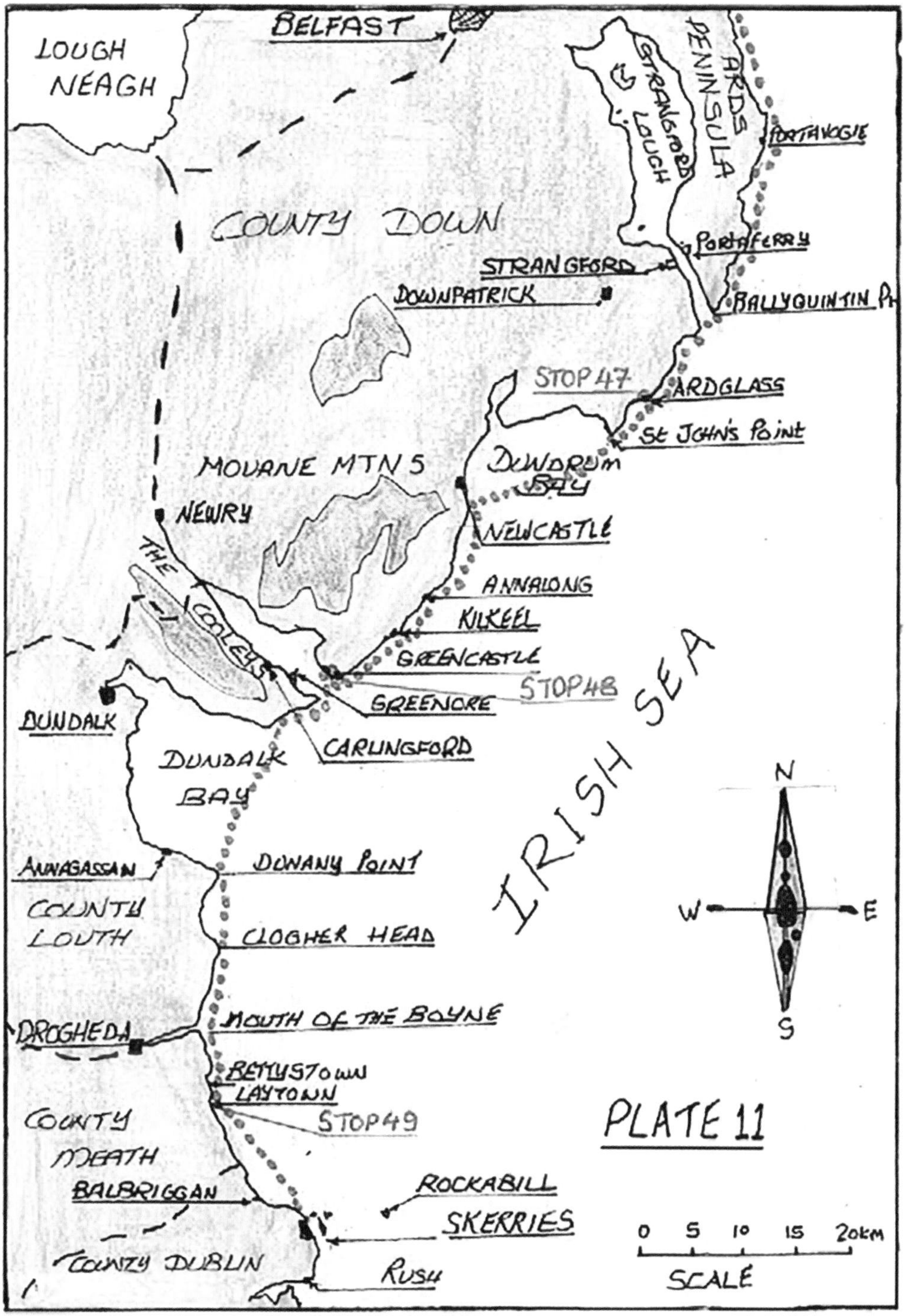

LOUGH NEAGH

BELFAST

ARDS PENINSULA

STRANGFORD LOUGH

PORTAVOGIE

COUNTY DOWN

STRANGFORD

PORTAFERRY

DOWNPATRICK

BALLYQUINTIN Pt.

STOP 47

ARDGLASS

St JOHN'S POINT

MOURNE MTNS

DUNDRUM BAY

NEWRY

NEWCASTLE

THE COOLEY

ANNALONG

KILKEEL

GREENCASTLE

STOP 48

DUNDALK

GREENORE

CARLINGFORD

DUNDALK BAY

IRISH SEA

ANNAGASSAN

DUNANY POINT

COUNTY LOUTH

CLOGHER HEAD

DROGHEDA

MOUTH OF THE BOYNE

BETTYSTOWN
LAYTOWN

STOP 49

COUNTY MEATH

BALBRIGGAN

ROCKABILL

SKERRIES

COUNTY DUBLIN

RUSH

PLATE 11

N
W   E
S

0   5   10   15   20km

SCALE

Stage 29

SLIDING SOUTH THROUGH
COUNTY DOWN

My return trip to Northern Ireland is by train to Lanyon Station in Belfast. I arrive after dark and catch a commuter bus for Larne. On stowing my stuffed bags into the hold, I hop aboard carrying my two split paddles nicely stored in their contoured black carry cases. On spotting them, the driver asks in a sharp Belfast accent if I have rifles stuffed in there. I laugh, replying loudly so all can hear that contained within are some pricey kayaking paddles in need of constant care. How things have changed in this part of our shared island and I am warmed by his lighthearted, albeit dark, comment. Arriving into Larne the driver stops almost a kilometre from my accommodation explaining there are diversions in place. I decide to haul my kit through the silent town to my accommodation, not the ideal prequel to the long days' paddling ahead.

Thanks to a punctual 7.00 am pick up by James, a Sea Cadet Commander and highly qualified instructor, I am afloat by 7.40 am, just in time to catch the last two hours of the southerly stream to Muck Island. Running strong in these parts, the colloquially-called 'conveyor' will provide some assistance. Some chop and clapotis, reverberating off the headland, give me something to digest, but not to the same extent as west coast helpings. Due to the lateness of the year and my new direction of travel, the morning sun shines directly into my eyes rendering the distant headland into a silhouette. I am kayaking on a shimmering expanse of golden tinfoil as I head east and then south.

I pass by The Gobbins, a four and a half kilometre galvanised walkway installed along the base of 100 foot high cliffs just south-east of Larne. Intended for walkers to view the volcanic coastline, it is a unique and impressive structure. Originally the idea of Berkeley Deane Wise, chief engineer of the Belfast and County Down railway, it opened in 1909 giving locals a chance for a Sunday stroll beyond compare. Unfortunately, the walkway fell into disrepair and closed in the 1950s but thankfully its latest iteration finally reopened in 2016. One section, boasting a 'hole' cut through the basalt rock, is referred to colloquially as 'Wise's Eye' after its creator. The Gobbins features steps, bridges, hewn paths, caves and even a 20 metre tunnel below sea level. I learned from a local that it ran way over budget, but in the end it created a unique tourist attraction.

After The Gobbins, I round Black Head and provide a shock for a father and son fishing from shore. They suddenly appear from behind a large rock and I stand on the brakes lest I get tangled in their lines. All three of us burst into nervous laughter, followed by an embarrassed exchange of apologies. I then wheel 90 degrees around the curved headland into Belfast Lough, as overhead Black Head lighthouse looks out, sentinel-like, above my passage.

I continue into the lough, now on a southwesterly track. I am bound for Whitehead along the coastal path linking the town with the lighthouse, another creation of the aforementioned engineer Berkeley Wise. I land and carefully lift my kayak onto the bone dry slipway that has been soaking up the sun's rays for hours. I continue to its promenade to tuck into some vittles. Whilst busy munching away I am interrupted by an ear-piercing shriek. Originating from behind the town's colourful promenade, I see a large plume of white smoke over the rooftops and realise a steam engine is heralding its presence in the town. I later learn that the recently opened Whitehead Railway Museum sits behind the town's impressive Victorian terrace. The steam engine trundles off on its short excursion, belching steam and smoke into the crisp afternoon air.

With air and sea temperatures dropping, open water crossings by kayak are becoming more serious undertakings. Belfast Lough is one

Leaving Larne at dawn

such animal today. Now that we are in mid-October, the 11 kilometre outer section of this lough is a tantalising challenge. Thanks to a fresh westerly breeze blowing out of a blue sky, the air is noticeably cooler, bringing a chill to my bones. Across the lough, Groomsport is my immediate goal. Once there, I will be in County Down, the last of my three Northern Ireland counties.

An uneventful crossing has me landing on Groomsport beach and ringing Will Brown, my contact in nearby Donaghadee. While continuing the last few kilometres I spot a blue sea kayak launching from shore up ahead. It turns out to be Will who has estimated my passage and is joining me for my day's final moments. Meeting him for the first time it seems appropriate that we shake hands 'offshore'. He is another paddler I cold called and within minutes an enthusiastic conversation ensued. The impressive Donaghadee Light passes abeam, and beyond it an assortment of three story harbourside buildings lie in its shadow.

An hour after landing I settle into Will's homemade sauna behind his house. The exquisite experience of soaking up the moist heat is intoxicating. What an antidote to an occasionally chilly trip from Larne. The only downside is the sprint back across the yard in my togs into

Passing the Donaghadee promenade

the warm and inviting house. I recall my seasick laden channel crossing from here to Scotland almost twenty years earlier and marvel at
how far I have travelled since those challenging times.

My dawn departure coincides with a blood red sky heralding what
hopefully is not a shepherd's warning. My route tracks south along the
outer flank of the Ard's panhandle towards the mouth of Strangford
Lough. I am aboard the south-bound conveyor again, my biggest
challenge being to avoid the underlying rocks lying across my path.
My destination is Ardglass, a healthy 50 kilometres away. This is my
fourth to last leg and bears down on my final 100 kilometres. My back
has begun acting up, constantly sapping my energy, but I know that I
am nearing the end of my run.

An hour south of Donaghadee I spot something moving in the water. About a kilometre ahead, it looks like a small boat with someone
aboard. At this stage I am in an area of low lying rocks, paddling along
an inner channel. Eventually, I realise the object ahead is another early
morning kayaker. An older guy wearing a broad-brimmed hat slowly
materialises, plodding north in a tired fibreglass touring kayak. His
paddles seem way too long, his short stroke like an old man's shuffle,

Company in Donaghadee

and his life vest, faded as if from another era, has me rubbing my eyes in wonder. The whole package is so intriguing I shunt across so our paths almost touch. I shout over a good morning, but strangely, he barely makes eye contact, not missing a stroke, and passes me in silence. Usually liaisons with fellow paddlers provide some distraction, but this particular wayfarer leaves me none the wiser. To this day the mystery of the ghost-like paddler remains.

A Presbyterian, muted influence is on display here in the homes and buildings lining the shore. Devoid of colour, they look functional, dour and tired. The only break from the humdrum are scores of shoe-box-shaped mobile homes lined up in neat rows like military barracks, only brighter. Villages I am unfamiliar with pass my starboard quarter. Millisle, Ballyhalbert, Ballywalter, Portavogie, Cloughey and Kearney are all bypassed, culminating in me reaching the southern extremity of the Ards peninsula, Ballyquintin Point. I take a few minutes basking here, absorbing the accumulated miles and the achievement thus far.

I am parked by the eastern mouth of the Narrows, a nine kilometre channel funnelling into Strangford Lough. The lough itself, not visible from here, covers an impressive 150 square kilometres and boasts over 70 islands. The Vikings, active in these parts during the Middle Ages, called the channel 'Strangr-fjörðr' or strong sea inlet after the robust flows that occur here. Reaching speeds of 14 kilometres an hour during spring tides, these potentially treacherous waters must be afforded the respect they deserve.

I aim at the opposite bank, a place called Millard Point, barely two kilometres away. Moving out across the glassy water I become aware of a strong flow that is shoving me sideways. I am being swept south by the giant lough emptying another tide in its allotted six hour time frame. Out to sea is an area of breaking waves, the result of the southerly breeze blowing against the outgoing tide. Imperceptibly I am shunted sideways and soon I am in among these breakers and, bizarrely, struggling to control *Murchú*. I snap completely awake and engage my brain into a surprise two kilometre rollercoaster. After six hours of easy paddling, this crossing has me searching for another gear. In the chill of mid-November, I definitely must keep *Murchú* topside up. If I become dislodged from my boat I will be syphoned out to sea at a good rate of knots, a scenario I dare not think about. I continue the battle, eventually running into calmer waters close to the far shore. My lapse into a false sense of security is blown wide open and an old lesson is relearned. Always be ready.

Relieved, I continue south inside Guns Island. At some stage, I pass over a submerged cable running from here to Peel in the Isle of Man. Forming part of the link between the newly created Northern Ireland and the mainland UK, it was laid in 1929 and made international phone calls possible via Rugby, near Birmingham. The Rugby transmitter spawned from the British Government's desire to connect to its sprawling empire after the First World War. It was referred to as the Imperial Wireless Chain. The hefty initial cost for a three minute call was £9.00 (or €400.00 in today's money). Incredibly, it remained in use until the early 2000s.

Barely a kilometre away, behind Ballyhornan's modest beach, lies Bishopscourt, a disused Royal Air Force base. It once boasted a radar facility for monitoring all air traffic crossing the North Atlantic, forming part of the UK's Military Air Traffic Operations. It was known as Ulster Radar, with Prestwick in Scotland taking over the service in 1978, a role that continues today and one I used as a commercial pilot.

Landing at Ardglass Harbour

Its present use as a racing circuit, glider base and driving school is an optimal choice for this once disused facility.

Bearing down on Ardglass, and nearing my 50 kilometre total for the day, I am puzzled by something unusual up ahead. A few kilometres away lies a large vessel, canted at an unusual angle. Its hull, a garish red, is heeled over partly revealing its underbelly. Some rocks are obstructing my view, so the picture is incomplete. As ever, my mind races to explain the scene which reveals itself as a grounding right outside the entrance to Ardglass Harbour. The *Dillon Owen*, a state of the art fishing trawler, struck rocks only five nights ago whilst attempting to land a catch in Ardglass and remains solidly stuck in position. Despite the best efforts of the RNLI, a helicopter had to be called to hoist its crew to safety. It was to sink a few days later after attempts to haul her afloat on the rising tide failed. It provides a reminder of the potential perils awaiting the unwary at sea, a useful lesson at the end of a tiring, but successful, day.

Trevor Fischer, a fellow adventurer, has kindly offered to ferry me to Newry train station, where my dearly beloved Angela will collect me later. Trevor runs the Tollymore Adventure Centre, and had originally hoped to accompany me for some of today's leg to Ardglass, but sadly that never happened. As a conciliation of sorts, he offers me a tour of the centre which houses a rolling pool I am curious to see. It is designed for kayakers learning their Eskimo roll, with the instructor remaining at ground level filming their efforts through a large underwater window. I make a mental note to book in to try it for myself in the near future.

We stop off for some well earned pizza in Newry before going our separate ways. I promise to be back up North very soon for my next two-day foray. This hopefully will have me deposited in Bettystown, only a short paddle from Skerries. The one-hour spin home with Angela reinforces how close I am to completion, and I know that soon my great adventure will be over.

My goal to propel *Murchú* from Ardglass to Greencastle at the mouth of Carlingford Lough is a respectable 46 kilometre paddle, and I am tasked with squeezing it into a short November day. Needs must though, as I am determined to finish the project before Christmas. With that in mind, a 6.00 a.m. alarm call in Trevor's home kicks me into action. Ardglass harbour is in darkness as we pull up under the glow of the sodium street lights. A chilly northerly airflow hastens my preparations which ends in us manhandling *Murchú* down towards the inky black water lapping at the base of the slipway. I manoeuver towards the pier end light and spot a silhouetted Trevor waving me on my way.

The 20 kilometre crossing of Dundrum Bay, which has been occupying my mind for the last few days, looms large as the day's biggest challenge. The northerly breeze is swinging towards west creating a small cross chop which spices up the first few kilometres. The majestic beauty of the wasp-coloured St. John's Point Lighthouse appears up ahead. This unique yellow and black banded sentinel makes for a fabulous waymark. It takes my breath away, especially since it stands at 40 metres, the tallest of Ireland's 65 mainland lights.

It has been witness to some famous events, not least of which occurred in 1846, only two years after going into service. The captain of the then largest vessel in the world, the 3,700 ton *SS Great Britain*, mistook it for the Calf Light on the Isle of Man and ran aground in Dundrum Bay. Built by world-renowned engineer Isambard Kingdom Brunel, it was the first ship to combine an iron hull with screw propellers serving the north Atlantic route between the UK and New

Approaching St John's Point Lighthouse, Ardglass, County Down

York. She remained grounded for over a year before being refloated, repaired and returned to service. She then ferried thousands of immigrants to Australia for decades, eventually being used for transporting bulk coal. After running aground again, this time in the Falklands, she returned to Bristol dry docks in the 1970s and remains there as a maritime museum.

Sixty-six years later, in 1912, another ill-fated vessel, and again the largest of its day, the *RMS Titanic*, underwent sea trials in the area. She used St John's Light for navigation whilst testing her top speed, turning circle and emergency stop distance before being transferred to Southampton for her final fit out. Interestingly, her emergency stop distance was under 800 metres, and one wonders whether her fate could have been different if this manoeuvre was executed instead of trying to avoid the iceberg by turning.

As I head further out into open water the northwesterly seems keen to meet me. This is a beam wind and my heartbeat rises anticipating a busy crossing. Slieve Donard, Ulster's highest peak lying ahead, is a most impressive target to aim for. Slowly I reel in this massif, landing beneath its lower flanks onto a tiny gravel patch between rocks.

The Mourne Mountains are a tonic as I paddle along this stretch of County Down. I continue down the low lying coastline, stopping off occasionally as I go. More caravan sites and fishing ports pepper my journey. I finally nose around a featureless promontory and pass into Carlingford Lough. My head feels heavy after nearly seven hours paddling, and for the first time in ages it throbs. Thankfully, my lodgings for the night, an enchanting old lighthouse keeper's cottage, are visible only a few kilometres away.

A car ferry from nearby Greenore links the Republic to Northern Ireland, the fifteen minute crossing saving commuters a road distance of 60 kilometres. A clutch of cars disgorge onto the landing ramp and scurry into the countryside. Distracted by these happenings it takes me a while before I notice Slieve Foye further up the Lough. I jolt back to myself and ponder my great pal and inspiration, Mark Murphy, who died there. Since it is my last layover of my trip, I am planning to savour every minute, with Mark in my thoughts more than ever.

Stage 30

ON MY LAST LEGS
AS SKERRIES BECKONS

What a lovely location Greencastle is for a layover. A string of older houses look across the channel to Greenore. A fleet of Pilot boats are moored just offshore, ready to assist ships manoeuvre into the port of Warrenpoint, 12 kilometres further inland. The small Carlingford Ferry, now in its third year of operation, obediently sticks to its schedule. The locals cleverly influenced the positioning of the slipway away from their shoreside houses, maintaining the quiet of their sleepy location.

I end up in Kilkeel's Kilmorey Arms Hotel for my dinner, thanks to my host Jackie, who insists on giving me a lift. I am served by a guy who once worked in The Black Raven in Skerries, so we engage in some friendly banter comparing notes on the place. My taxi back to base is driven, at speed, by an ex-fisherman who regales me with tales of fishing off Shetland, Norway and The Minches in Scotland. He also warns me of some bad weather due later tomorrow. Retired or not, these guys always seem to have an eye on the sea. Retiring for the night, Jackie has agreed to a 6.30 am breakfast to ensure an early start. I must beat that weather.

A 7.30 am start has me on my way across the languid estuary heading for the open sea. A large vessel, anchored offshore, waits to enter port on the rising tide. Today's mission is to make it to Laytown, leaving a short 17 kilometre final leg to close the loop at Skerries. Nicely spaced along my route are the two protruding headlands of Dunany Point and Clogher Head. These are stepping stones for today's travel,

305

Final overnight away in Greencastle, County Down

the first after a 15 kilometre trek across Dundalk Bay with the second an easier seven kilometres along Port Beach. The final 20 kilometres will be off the beaches of Louth and Meath, separated by the mouth of the River Boyne. By day's end I will have accumulated another marathon distance paddle.

Dundalk Bay is a large, square-shaped indentation in the coastline. Composing vast areas of shallow water potentially hazardous to shipping it will be my last significant open water crossing. Unfortunately, water inside my boat is becoming concerning. A stop at Templestown Beach to make some final adjustments has me notice some water lapping under my seat. I puzzle over its origins. I turn *Murchú* over, inspect the hull and fail to find any obvious breach, leaving me none the wiser. I reassure myself that the water is only getting into the cockpit as the other compartments are still dry. I decide to press on.

Landing at Dunany Point is a lacklustre affair. The low tide has uncovered a vast area of rocky seabed far from dry land, and I feel as though I am stopping at sea rather than on the shore. On exiting my boat I notice at least 10 centimetres of water has accumulated inside. This time I pump it out, inspecting the hull for what surely must be a

Approaching the mouth of the River Boyne

hole. When I find none, I am completely baffled. I reluctantly decide to press on, mostly because Ireland's east coast has miles of long sandy beaches for easy get-outs.

Clogher Head is stepping stone number two and at this stage the sun is out in its mid-November glow. This bustling fishing port has all manner of goings on, from walkers passing through to workers plying their trade. Gulls swoop as catches are landed and the rumble of trucks fills the air. After being alone all day it is heartening to bump into an old paddling friend, Brendan Devlin, who just happens to be passing by. A keen sailor and sea swimmer, we shared time in the Wild Water Kayak Club on the Liffey back in the 1980s. It gives me a buzz to tell him of my travels, especially since today is the second last of my trip.

My last few kilometres for the day includes landing to empty my boat for a fourth time and finding a felicitous location to leave my boat. An old kitesurfing buddy, Bill Connell, has offered to store my boat at Laytown. Luckily for me he lives by the beach, and his company, Advanced Composites, carries out composite repairs on anything from wind turbines to formula racing cars. I will be entrusting him to find the source of my recently arrived and stubborn leak.

I approach the long shingle beach near Bettystown in a moderately fatigued state and decide to empty *Murchú* so as to finish with little water inside. The promised southerly breeze has arrived and my progress has slowed. I manoeuvre *Murchú* to a landing directly opposite Bill's house, surf a small wave into the shallows, and ground *Murchú* onto the sand.

With today's significant distance in the bag, I declare that I have reached what will be the finale of my voyage. Only a short 17 kilometres spin for home is left undone. Out of the corner of my eye I see someone jumping around the place in unbridled joy at my arrival. It is my 19-year-old son Fionnán, a normally quiet guy acting somewhat out of character, which only shows what this means to him. Having excelled in Gaelic football in the last few years, he knows how commitment and discipline are needed to achieve anything of worth. He makes his way to me and we collide into a big hug, and I feel that I am on home turf. We share a special moment together out here in the middle of the flat sands of Laytown Beach on a blustery November evening on the eve of my penultimate landing.

I arrive home to another warm welcome from Angela and Hannah. I recall my recent adventures and take out a pen to scratch another three centimetre mark along the outline of my Ireland Map attached to one of our kitchen cabinets. This Tourism Ireland map has been here for the last three summers where a snaking line has slowly encircled the island. Only the smallest gap remains which will be bridged before the year is out.

Later that week, Bill sends me a strange photo of *Murchú* from his workshop. It shows two of his fingers protruding through the hull from inside my boat, showing where my heels have been rubbing since I started my journey. These strange circular sections have been allowing water into my boat when afloat. He pierced them quite easily with his fingers. I compliment Bill for his discovery and task him with the repair, reminding him of my intention to continue southward for Skerries soon. Thank goodness this never happened off the west coast.

The final section from Laytown to Skerries is a morning paddle with my kayaking pal Shane Holland travelling alongside. It's a fresh

Murchú in Bill's workshop

November morning with minimal breeze and clear skies. I notice the cold as we load up Shane's kayak and head north to collect *Murchú*. We have shared many kayaking trips, punctuating our Januarys with mid-winter overnight trips away, normally in one of the well maintained cabins run by the National Trust in Northern Ireland. After the madness of Christmas and New Year's, it provides a great opportunity to relax and plan for the year ahead.

We head to sea, soon passing across the sandy mouth of the River Nanny, and continue along the shingle strand towards Benn Head. The site of an Army rifle range, it is backed by Gormanstown Military Camp, set up by the Royal Flying Corps in 1917 as a British flight training school before being transformed into a military base for the nascent state in late 1922. Closed as an airfield since 2002, I remember while visiting my uncle's farm seeing aircraft leaping into the air over the hedges as novice flying cadets were put through their paces with the Irish Air Corps.

We hug the shore allowing us to easily monitor our progress by the passing countryside. We chat as we paddle, an experience still strange but a welcome distraction after spending so many days on my own. We cross the narrow Delvin River, pulling in for a cuppa on a

The final kilometre with Mick O'Meara as escort

grassy bank behind a small crescent beach. This river marks my final county crossing. We are now in County Dublin with the royal county behind us, heralding another closure to my mission. County Meath has the second shortest coastline, all 20 kilometres of which is a ribbon of beach running in an almost straight line between the majestic Boyne and its smaller watery cousin, the Delvin.

We crack open our flasks and enjoy some snacks while looking out over the sea. The rocks nearby, the fields and trees behind, create the impression of being on the western seaboard, not somewhere close to home. Coincidentally, whilst pondering this my phone rings. It is Mick O'Meara, my circumnavigation motivator *extraordinaire*. When I hear that he is about to get into his kayak in Skerries and head towards us, I am blown away. He had told me he would try to make it up but I was not sure that he could. We dally, eventually returning to the sea and heading onwards to Balbriggan, the penultimate town before Skerries. After what seems like minutes, a spear-shaped craft appears a few kilometres away. Powering towards us is Mick at full tilt in his latest speedy all-white sea kayak.

We meet and greet, and then strike out across open water towards Skerries as Ardgillan Castle majestically looks down at us. Shane and Mick respectfully drop back, allowing me to continue up front. We round the low Skerries headland and I spot some fellow Frostie sea

Celebrating with Shane and Mick O'Meara

swimmers taking the plunge from the Captains local bathing area. They spot me from a distance and begin waving frantically at our arrival. Some dive from their rocky platform and swim towards us. One of our crew, Suzanne, pretends to be giving me a warm embrace but is actually determined to upend me into the water. Fortunately, I stay dry, and Suzanne reluctantly returns to the water while slagging about me being a wuss and more besides.

We continue the final few hundred metres to the beach opposite my home. The tide is low and a scattering of people are crossing the open sands to my landing spot. Angela and our daughter Hannah are there, along with many friends, neighbours, and work colleagues. Legendary kayaking photographer Mick Feeney is there too, clicking away with his enormous lens. I just get lost in the celebrations of the moment, saying a few words and thanking everyone for their support. I am so swept away that I forget to thank my nearest and dearest, Angela, who has encouraged me every step of the way. Will I ever learn?

We retire to the grass strip in front of the house where I ceremoniously remove a small piece of plastic from my day hatch. On it is the Dublin's crest, the last county sticker to be attached to my kayak's long prow. As there are 17 coastal counties, eight are attached to either side of my foredeck, and a space remains for the final one across the ridge line. A huge cheer goes up from the gathering and I take another

The Big Homecoming

bow, slightly embarrassed by the attention but happy all the same. Behind me the house has large yellow Congratulations posters stuck to the windows as bunting flies in the easterly breeze.

Inside our bustling kitchen, Angela ceremoniously hands me a pen with the instruction to complete the loop around the outline of Ireland stuck to the wall. Another big cheer goes up, I say a few more words, and slowly people start leaking away from the house.

Murchú's storage rack, vacant now for three summers, is back on purpose. I am indebted to my trusty chariot, placing a hand on its flanks as it sits in its cradle. Someone mentions that I should commit to recording my experiences for all to hear. Someone else suggests I write a book. Somewhere, deep inside my mind, a little spark goes off. A tiny space, recently vacated, could be ready for just such a project. But that's for another day. In the meantime, now that my incredible dream has been realised, I can begin the long process of settling back into normal life, but now as a successful circumnavigator of my island home. The itch I had to scratch has finally been satisfied.